Dorian Williams has practised as a solicitor in private practice for over 22 years, acting almost exclusively for claimants in personal injury and clinical negligence claims. Initially he worked for clients referred from a major Trades Union, specialising in industrial disease and employers' liability claims. For the last 17 years, Dorian has received a broad spread of instructions whilst working in a general high street practice, Freeman Johnson. His caseload now mostly comprises clinical negligence cases which he has has been privileged to receive, and thanks all his clients for developing his experience.

When Dorian is not at work, he may be found climbing peaks in the Lake District, Peak District, Snowdonia or Majorca.

Arguments and Tactics for Personal Injury and Clinical Negligence Claims

Arguments and Tactics for Personal Injury and Clinical Negligence Claims

Dorian Williams,
BA, LLM, Solicitor

Law Brief Publishing

© Dorian Williams

All rights reserved. No part of this publication may be reproduced, stored in a retrieval system, or transmitted, in any form or by any means, electronic, mechanical, photocopying, recording or otherwise, without the prior permission of the publisher.

Excerpts from judgments and statutes are Crown copyright. Any Crown Copyright material is reproduced with the permission of the Controller of OPSI and the Queen's Printer for Scotland. Some quotations may be licensed under the terms of the Open Government Licence (http://www.nationalarchives.gov.uk/doc/open-government-licence/version/3).

Cover image © iStockphoto.com/gregobagel

The information in this book was believed to be correct at the time of writing. All content is for information purposes only and is not intended as legal advice. No liability is accepted by either the publisher or author for any errors or omissions (whether negligent or not) that it may contain. Professional advice should always be obtained before applying any information to particular circumstances.

Published 2017 by Law Brief Publishing, an imprint of Law Brief Publishing Ltd
30 The Parks
Minehead
Somerset
TA24 8BT

www.lawbriefpublishing.com

Paperback: 978-1-911035-24-4

PREFACE

The origin of this book arose from my wish to have a portable guide on advocacy covering legal principles and procedure. Inevitably compromises are necessary when it covers clinical negligence and the broad pastures of personal injury. So the compromise to be struck is general coverage at the expense of detail. There are bound to be omissions in a book this size but that is the price to be paid for brevity. Hopefully it may encourage those embarking on their career in legal practice or those seeking a 'how to' guide, if representing themselves, to read the book rather than be faced down by a weighty tome. If it provides some benefit to more experienced practitioners then even better.

It comes at a time of substantial change (plus ça change…) in the specialisms of personal injury and clinical negligence. The golden years (for claimants at any rate), was the availability of legal aid. Even with the advent of conditional fee agreements allowing for the recoverability of additional liabilities – success fees and after the event insurance premiums, claimants enjoyed relatively open access to bringing claims. Costs followed the event and everyone was happy and got paid a reasonable rate. Perhaps insurers were less than content but that will always be the case I suspect. Most importantly the injured (let's not forget they are the wronged party) was fully compensated.

Legal aid is long gone for virtually all claims. It remains for birth injury cases and those bringing abuse claims but for everyone else, unless a member of a Trades Union, then reliance will be on a conditional fee agreement or legal expenses' cover. It has always been a 'David v Goliath' struggle for claimants and always will be until some form of no fault compensation scheme arrives.

Fees are squeezed which places pressures on claimant lawyers to accept difficult cases. Now, there is the inevitability of fixed fees for clinical negligence following the publication of LJ Jackson's Review of Civil Litigation Costs. Also there will an increase in the small claims limit in personal injury claims, likely to increase to £5,000. Further belt tightening (as if any is needed) is necessary to make the system work in the face of this brave new world. The online court is a reality but do the parties get a fair hearing.

It is expected that more claimants will represent themselves. Those lawyers who do act for them will need to progress the case as efficiently as possible, perhaps without recourse to Counsel. Counsel for their part, offering direct access, with a background in traditional advocacy, will need to undertake the case management duties formerly the preserve of solicitors and legal executives. All will face the same challenges to ensure cases are resolved fairly and proportionately.

The original working title was 'a practical guide to advocacy' but thought to be too narrow and not representative of the contents. Advocacy is less about the spoken word and all about preparation and persuasion. So the book is intended as a toolkit for those bringing and responding to such injury claims. I can well remember my first trial when speaking with the defendant's solicitor who enquired whether I was all 'tooled up'. Naturally as a fan of the Sweeney, I was 'tooled up'. Hopefully you will be too.

My own background as a claimant solicitor may reveal my prejudices, but the intention of this guide is to reflect fair combat between the parties. Inevitably perhaps, there is more for claimants but that reflects the simple fact that they bring the claim. It is hoped that the book will also be of some use to defendants and their insurers.

Traditionally advocates learnt on their feet and experience was gained over time. The 'iron fist in the velvet glove' was the style to which many aspired but it's not necessary to win the day. Judges are less likely to be impressed by style (read charm or aggression), than substance, i.e. an advocate who knows the evidence required and how to present it. So some tips and tactics are provided along the way together with arguments to deploy to ensure the best chance of success. That needn't be at trial as by that stage the stakes are high and someone's got to lose. It all starts with case selection and risk assessment.

I encourage the reader to add their own notes and to update rules and cases as necessary for which space is left at the end of each chapter. Interchangeably I have referred to a section in the Civil Procedure Rules (CPR) as either a Rule or Part or just CPR. They all mean the same. The numbering of paragraphs or sub-paragraphs bear no relation to the CPR and are for convenience only. Needless to say, this book cannot replace the full text of the CPR, nor the possession of case law and Statutes. But it may ease the burden if passed a file at short notice on a Friday afternoon to do a colleague's application hearing.

I wish to extend my thanks to my publishers, Tim Kevan and Garry Wright at Law Brief Publishing for their patience and friendly persuasion to help bring this book to fruition. It has been enjoyable, illuminating and occasionally frustrating, when discovering errors made by me in my practice, during the course of research for this book. I have learned things that I never knew (who ever stops learning?) and grappled with the CPR in more detail than anyone should ever have to bear. Who knew that the CPR could be so engrossing?

Dorian Williams
Solicitor
Durham
July 2017

CONTENTS

Chapter One	The Basics of Advocacy	1
	Case Theory	1
	Preparation and Presentation	2
	Key Points	5
Chapter Two	Proving the Claim	7
	Clinical Negligence	8
	Breach of Duty	9
	Pre-Treatment Cases	10
	Pure Diagnostic Cases	12
	Causation	14
	Material Contribution	15
	Material Increase in Risk of Injury	18
	Burden of Proof	22
	Consent	23
	Road Traffic Accidents	32
	Liability	34
	Alleging Fraud	35
	Pedestrians and Contributory Negligence	37
	The RTA Protocol	38
	Employers' Liability Claims	41
	Pleading the Claim	47
	Statutory Duties	48
	Public Liability Claims	59
	Occupiers' Liability	60
	Occupiers' Liability Act 1957	61
	Occupiers' Liability Act 1984	66
	Highways Act	67
	The EL/PL Protocol	73
	Quantum	78
	Key Points	89
Chapter Three	Evidence	91
	Witness Statements	91
	Experts	103
	Hearsay Evidence	107
	Conference With Counsel	111
	Key Points	114

Chapter Four	Case and Costs Management	115
	The Directions Questionnaire	116
	The Case Management and Costs Conference	126
	Case Management	127
	Conducting the Hearing	128
	Costs Management	131
	Layout of a Costs Budget	133
	Key Points	135
Chapter Five	Alternative Dispute Resolution	137
	What is ADR	137
	Round Table Meeting	140
	Joint Settlement Meeting	140
	Mediation	141
	Arbitration	146
	Key Points	148
Chapter Six	Tactics	149
	Part 36 Offers	149
	Withdrawing or Changing Terms of Part 36	152
	Issues Based Part 36 offers	157
	Calderbank Offers	158
	Key Points	161
	Requests for Further Information, Admissions and Notices to Admit	163
	Requests for Further Information	163
	Admissions	167
	Notices to Admit	171
	Key Points	173
	Summary Judgment/Dismissal	174
	Key Points	178
	Interim Payments	179
	Key Points	185
	Exit From the Portal	186
	Key Points	192
	Know Your Limitation(s)	193
	Limitation Periods	194
	Date of Knowledge	195
	Section 33 Discretion to Disapply Limitation	199
	Case Law	202
	Accidents at Sea	205
	Accidents in the Air	207
	Problems to Look Out For	209

	Procedural Points	210
	Key Points	215
Chapter Seven	Interlocutory Applications	217
	Specific Disclosure	225
	Service of Claim Form	227
	Service of Particulars of Claim	230
	Variation of Case Management Timetable	235
	Relief From Sanctions	237
	Setting Aside Judgment	251
	Application for an Interim Payment	263
	Application for Summary Judgment	265
	Key Points	269
Chapter Eight	The Trial	271
	What Does the Judge Need to Know	271
	Common Approaches in All Cases	274
	Skeleton Argument	275
	Opening the Case	280
	Examination-in-Chief	289
	Cross-Examination	291
	Example of Cross-Examination of a Defendant's Witness	293
	Key Points	302
Chapter Nine	The Appeal	303
	Avenues of Appeal	304
	Appeals from Case Management Decisions	304
	Procedure for All Appeals	305
	The Test	309
	The Grounds	310
	Key Points	315
Chapter Ten	Case Law Tool Kit	317
	Clinical Negligence	317
	Personal Injury	325
	Relief from Sanctions	329
	Statute Law Tool Kit	331

Appendix I	Where Sanctions Apply	345
	Knowing your CPR	347
Appendix II	Hearsay Notice	351
	Mediation Agreement	351
	Model Directions in Clinical Negligence	354
	Model Directions in Personal Injury	360

CHAPTER ONE
THE BASICS OF ADVOCACY

1.1 Case Theory

1.1.1 The objective is to win the case fairly and at proportionate cost; that means ideally resolving before trial as the litigation risk of an adverse outcome is always present, although it can be limited. Much of this book will concentrate on efforts to avoid the trial process but if not, you must be prepared for that eventuality.

You should assume that the case may go to trial, so it must form part of a claimant's case theory when carrying out a risk assessment. Is the claim viable and can it be proved at trial. If injury is not foreseeable, for example, should you be taking the case on? Does the defendant owe a duty of care. Do you have the correct defendant or has the NHS Trust contracted its radiology function to a private provider. Is the actual defendant a medical practitioner sub-contracted by the private agency. If you cannot prove negligence, or breach of statutory duty or that a defective product caused injury, then why are you taking the case on. You don't want to find that Counsel (if so briefed) refuses to accept the brief because the risk of a loss is too great.

1.1.2 The danger is to suppose that with QUOCS (qualified one way cost shifting) applying, that there is no real costs risk to a claimant progressing a very weak claim to force a settlement. That could create a dangerous situation of lateral drift. Going through the motions, hoping that your Part 36 offer will be accepted or you receive a Part 36 offer ready to snap the other's hand off. But it won't happen because the opponent will have conducted their case assessment and will know of your weaknesses. By this stage you may be receiving offers to discontinue but your own work in progress will be substantial and you may be less inclined to throw in the towel.

The better way is to start off with confidence in your case and that means owning it or knowing how to prove the claim. If you think it can't be done, speak with a colleague or counsel for their opinion.

Therefore, knowing the legal issues at the outset is as important as getting the facts right. Of course in a clinical negligence claim, you cannot know at the outset whether the case has merit until you have a breach of duty report.

1.1.3 Analysing the merits of a case requires an assessment of evidence as the court will makes it assessment based on relevant and admissible evidence. It does not follow that your evidence will be preferred on the balance of probability to that of your opponent's evidence. Clearly anticipating your opponent's evidence at the outset of a case will be difficult. But it forms part of a risk assessment in determining whether it is viable to continue with the claim.

1.2 Preparation and presentation

1.2.1 The first interview- take an initial statement. Dictate in front of client. Let client tell his story in his own words. Set out facts in chronological order. Compartmentalise the statement with subheadings, e.g. introduction, employment duties, accident, aftermath, injuries, impact, HSE investigation etc.

Draw up a list of issues – those likely to be agreed, those in dispute. What legal principles apply. Think about submissions or what you would like to include in a skeleton argument and how to prove the case.

Research the law. Comply with case management directions. Know trial procedure. Know the facts of the case.

1.2.2 *Addressing the court*

District Judges- Sir/Ma'm

Circuit Judges- Your Honour

High Court judges- My Lord/Lady

      - Your Lordship/Ladyship

Addressing your opponent:

My friend (legal executive, solicitor)

My learned friend (counsel)

Or simply by name

1.2.3 *Style of presentation*

As advocate for your client, your job is to persuade the court to see things from your client's point of view and to make it as easy as possible for the judge to find in your favour. You are assisting the court to help them understand your case and to help the judge overcome any objections or weaknesses in your client's case. Indeed your first duty is to assist the court and not to mislead it, irrespective of any instructions given by your client.

You should aim to create a good first impression by being assured, organized and clear. Knowing your case by thorough preparation provides good reason to be confident, particularly if you have researched case law that will support your opponent's case and know how to distinguish them.

To ensure that the message is not lost, personal presentation should take account of the following:

1. Be COURTEOUS to the judge, your opponent and all officers of the court. Even if others are impolite to you, retain dignity and composure. If the judge interrupts, let him speak. If there are constant interruptions, be apologetic and advise the court that you wish to assist further by making your point another way. Try to anticipate and answer the judge's questions. Never lose your temper or be impolite.

2. Maintain CONTROL of the court and witnesses

3. Do NOT READ out your opening address or submissions. If nervous or have lost your line of thought, take a brief time to review the

headings of your skeleton to refresh the issues, before addressing the court further.

4. Be CONFIDENT or act as if you are. Breathe deeply and speak slowly in a low or measured tone. Smart dress and good posture helps build confidence. Humility and confidence are key, rather than arrogance.

5. Use SIMPLE language and SHORT sentences. Avoid pomposity or verbosity as it is rare for an advocate to carry this off with charm.

6. Use PAUSES and SILENCE as part of your address as it can create EMPHASIS to the point you are making. It also allows the judge sufficient time to note up your submissions.

7. Avoid REPETITION and do not waste time. Be guided by the judge. If he tells you to move on, move on.

8. Remain OBJECTIVE and avoid expressing personal opinions. I 'suggest', 'contend', 'submit' rather than I believe, assert or it is the case that. The court is not interested in your opinion on the facts or whether you consider the law is good or bad.

9. EVIDENCE must be truthful, reliable and cogent.

10. Be TRUSTWORTHY; that means putting forward correct propositions in law and making appropriate concessions where there are any weaknesses in your case.

Key points

- Perform a risk assessment at the outset – especially pertinent for claimants; can this case be won profitably. Is their evidence to support the case.

- Get the medical records and carefully review to check consistent with client's account.

- Assemble evidence. Consider other forums of enquiry – HSE investigations, police reports, root cause analysis investigation reports and inquests.

- Prepare an early skeleton argument identifying the issues, the facts and the law. Amend as the case progresses.

- Know the civil procedure rules and the court process and etiquette.

CHAPTER TWO
PROVING THE CLAIM

The aim of this chapter is to provide a brief overview of the constituent elements necessary to prove a claim. Clearly the requirements vary dependent on the type of claim.

The following types of case are considered, before rounding off with a discussion on quantum.

2.1 Clinical negligence

2.2 Road Traffic Accident (RTA)

2.3 RTA protocol

2.4 Employers' liability claim (EL)

2.5 Public liability claim (PL)

2.6 EL/PL protocol

2.7 Quantum

2.01 All claims have one thing in common and that is the necessity of the claimant to prove **negligence.** There are some limited alternative causes of action such as a medical claim in **contract** for patients receiving private treatment. This in all likelihood will be brought alongside a negligence suit. Product liability claims for patients receiving a dangerous product, e.g. a prosthetic metal-on-metal hip have various potential causes of action. They may bring a claim in negligence for an unreasonably unsafe product; a claim in contract for breach of warranty; or under the Consumer protection Act 1987 for a defective product. They may plead all or some of these claims dependent on the circumstances.

2.02 The common law of negligence takes on greater significance for workplace accidents following the **Enterprise and Regulatory Reform Act 2013** (in force from 1.10.2013) as that repeals strict liability for breach of health and safety regulations (the 'six pack' regulations). For claims prior to October 2013, a claimant would seek to prove breach of statutory duty in EL and PL claims. The Workplace Regulations still apply and should still be pleaded as the court will consider the extent of any breach in construing the standard of care to be applied

2.1 Clinical Negligence

2.1.1 For most clinical negligence actions, the principal claim will be for negligence. That requires the claimant to establish a **duty owed** by the doctors or the NHS Trust. This is not usually disputed. Occasionally, defendant trusts may seek to argue that the diagnostic element has been outsourced to a private agency thus alleviating them of a duty. That is almost certainly wrong in law as previous authorities confirm that whether or not a visiting doctor is an employee or independent contractor, the Trust retains its duty to its patients and cannot discharge that duty by delegating the performance to someone else (see *Gold v Essex CC* (1942 2KB 293), *Wilsher v Essex AHA* (1987 QB 730) and *M v Calderdale & Kirklees HA* (1988 Lloyds Law Reports MED 157).

There has been an attempt to extend the duty to hospital receptionists arising out of inaccurate information given to a patient about waiting times whilst he was waiting to be seen. As a result the patient walked out without telling staff. The Court of Appeal in *Darnley v Croydon Health Services NHS Trust* [2017] EWCA Civ 151 found that it was not the function of a receptionist to give wider advice and people must accept responsibility for their own actions.

Another difficult duty situation concerns victims in nervous shock claims. This is outside the scope of this book as being a relatively unusual claim so for the sake of brevity will not be discussed.

2.1.2 Once duty has been established, the claimant must prove that there has been a **breach of duty** by failing to exercise the care and skill of a reasonable professional. How is that standard assessed? By reference to accepted medical opinion as 'proper', often known as the *Bolam* test.

There has been some slippage away from the standard assessed by the medical profession to that determined by the trial judge.

Situations that arise to found a claim for breach of duty include a failure to diagnose or to treat, or to advise sufficiently or by providing poor quality treatment.

2.1.3 The third element is **causation.** The claimant must show that the breach was the factual cause of the damage – or the 'but-for-test'. **Factual (or medical) causation** is modified in cases of *material contribution* and where a *hypothetical* situation arises as to whether the claimant would have been treated in the same negligent way. He is able to rely upon an irrebuttable presumption that competent care would have been provided.

2.1.4 **Legal causation** or **remoteness** must be established to determine the extent of the damage suffered by the claimant that is attributable to the defendant. For how much of the damage is the defendant responsible. Was the injury foreseeable or too remote? Such cases arise where there is an intervening act as this will break the chain of causation. An example could be a delayed referral for appropriate treatment by a GP and also delay occasioned by a hospital specialist.

2.1.5 <u>**Breach of duty**</u>

This is the legal standard of care to be determined by the courts, rather than by the doctors, although medical practices and guidelines laid down by Governing/ Regulatory bodies (such as The National Institute for Health and Care Excellence (NICE)) will be highly relevant.

Put simply, examination of the standard of care may be divided between those cases involving an exercise in clinical judgment in providing treatment (the 'pure treatment' cases) and those requiring a diagnosis where the issue is the interpretation of data (the 'pure diagnostic' cases).

Bolam

2.1.6 Pure treatment cases – Bolam

The classic test in determining the legal standard of care in a clinical negligence claim is derived from *Bolam v Friern Hospital Management Committee* [1957] 2 All ER. Provided that the doctor acts in accordance with the practice of competent respected professional opinion, then he or she is not negligent. This standard is to be assessed at the time of treatment, applying the state of knowledge at that time.

In this case, there were conflicting views from experts on how treatment should have been applied in administering electro-convulsive therapy to the claimant. As there were doctors who would have acted in the same way, the treating doctor had acted in accordance with a competent body of medical opinion and therefore was not negligent.

McNair J stated:

> '*A doctor is not guilty of negligence if he has acted in accordance with a practice accepted as proper by a responsible body of medical men skilled in that particular art… Putting it the other way round, a doctor is not negligent, if he is acting in accordance with such a practice, merely because there is a body of opinion which takes a contrary view.*'

Bolam should not be interpreted as implying that provided the defendant is able to obtain an opinion that gainsays the claimant's expert then the claim must fail.

What the court must do is examine the evidence and evaluate the experts, and the weight of their evidence. If at the end of that evaluation, the defendant's actions conform with the practice of a *responsible* body of opinion, the courts will not find negligence (per Lord Scarman in *Maynard v West Midlands Regional Health Authority* [1984] 1 WLR 634).

Inherent in the *Bolam* test is the requirement that the specialist achieves the standard of care of the reasonably competent specialist practising in that field. This was recognised by Lord Bridge in *Sidaway v Governors of the Bethlem Royal Hospital* [1984] QB 493 when he said:

> '*The language of the Bolam test clearly requires a different degree of skill from a specialist in his own special field that from a general practitioner. In the field of neurosurgery it would be necessary to substitute for the ….phrase "no doctor of ordinary skill", the phrase "no neurosurgeon of ordinary skill". All this is elementary, and … firmly established law."*

Bolam has been considered as too protectionist, with doctors setting their own standards. This paternalistic view has been rolled back considerably following the more recent cases of *Bolitho* and *Montgomery* (see below).

Bolitho

2.1.7 The *Bolam* test was refined by the House of Lords in *Bolitho v City and Hackney Health Authority* [1997] 4 All ER 771. Lord Browne Wilkinson stated that the court is not bound to hold that a defendant doctor escapes liability for negligent treatment or diagnosis just because he leads evidence from a number of medical experts who are genuinely of opinion that the defendant's treatment or diagnosis accorded with sound medical practice. *Bolam* was applicable to the issue of causation as well as liability.

In *Bolitho,* the defendant admitted breach of duty in failing to attend the child but contended that even if the doctor had attended she would not have arranged for the child to be intubated, so that the breach of duty gave rise to no injury or damage. The defendant's expert evidence was to the effect that intubation would not have been appropriate. Therefore, a decision not to intubate was consistent with a body of responsible opinion and therefore not *Bolam* negligent.

Whilst the standard in *Bolam* was referred variously as *responsible, reasonable* and *respectable*, the body of opinion must have a <u>logical basis</u>. The court must be satisfied that the experts have considered the question of *comparative risks and benefits and have reached a defensible conclusion on the matter.* In *Bolitho* the House held that if the defendant's expert opinion was not capable of withstanding logical analysis, then the court would be entitled to hold that the body of opinion was not reasonable or responsible.

So one could say that the question to be asked of an expert is whether the decision was <u>properly considered, rational and reasonable.</u>

Reasonable skill and care does not amount to best practice. The doctor is to be judged by the standards of the ordinary competent practitioner in the relevant speciality.

Bolitho is also an important authority on causation (see below).

The court may prefer one party's expert to another by holding that the expert does not represent a responsible body of opinion, either because the expert is partisan and dogmatic, has failed to consider a particular issue or is disbelieved when they claim to support the treating doctor's decision. Importantly the court must weigh up and evaluate the expert evidence and explain why one expert is preferred to the other. This will entail consideration of the qualifications, experience and credibility of the experts

2.1.8 Pure Diagnostic cases – **Penney**

Bolam will not apply to cases where there is a dispute of fact when the judge will need to decide on balance of probabilities which of the two expert explanations is to be preferred. In deciding how an injury was caused where there are differing views, the determination is a factual one. The range of possible outcomes from a course of treatment is also a matter of fact.

It may be that the issues in a clinical negligence claim will concern competing expert theories as to what occurred and the explanations for what went wrong. These will be matters of fact for the judge rather than application of the *Bolam* test.

The factual test is exemplified in the interpretation of data – diagnosis.

Such cases frequently arise in the interpretation of radiology or histopathological samples on a microscope slide, or the diagnosis of an external lesion (turning out to be cancer).

The case of *Penney* reviewed the legal tests for different types of clinical negligence claims at opposite ends of the spectrum:

> (1) <u>Pure diagnosis</u> case. Where the patient's condition is unknown and the allegation of negligence concerns diagnosis. The diagnosis is either right or wrong. If wrong, it may be negligent or not.

> (2) <u>Pure treatment</u> case. The patient's condition is known and the alleged negligence is the decision to treat (or advise treatment of) a condition in a particular manner. This is application of the *Bolam* principle.

Penney concerned examination of slides of cervical smears which were pronounced negative. The claimant went on to develop cervical cancer. This was a pre-diagnostic test. There was no weighing of risks against benefits and no decision to treat or not to treat; just a diagnostic decision of misreporting which was either negligent or not negligent.

Penney is authority permitting the court to choose between competing expert opinion on the issue the court has to decide; whether the act or omission fell below a reasonable standard.

2.1.9 The analysis in *Penney* was applied in the case of <u>Muller v King's College Hospitals NHS Foundation Trust</u> [2017] EWHC 128. An histopathologist misdiagnosed a foot ulcer as non-malignant when it was a malignant melanoma. The defendant argued *Bolam* applied; that when diagnosing an ulcer, the doctor acted in accordance with respected professional opinion, relying on <u>C v North Cumbria University Hospitals NHS Trust</u> [2014] EWHC 61 (QB). In that case *Bolam* applied as it concerned the exercise of clinical judgment in administering a particular form of treatment. The claimant successfully argued that *Bolam* did not apply, rather the case of *Penney* was relevant as the issue was one of interpreting data wrongly. It was therefore a pure diagnostic case. Kerr J observed that in deciding which expert to prefer must be viewed through the prism of the *Bolitho* exception, rather than holding *Bolam* does not apply where no 'Bolam-appropriate' issue arises.

2.1.10 Causation

In drafting instructions to an expert, the claimant must prove that injuries or damage were caused by the negligence. If the negligence made no difference to the outcome, then there is no claim. The medical expert evidence is therefore critical to the success of the claim.

In clinical negligence, the instructions in say a cerebral palsy claim may ask a Paediatric Neurologist or Neonatologist to prepare a report solely on causation. In most personal injury cases (possibly with the exception of some industrial disease cases), the issue of causation will be covered in the report on condition & prognosis as it will be fairly evident that the accident caused the injuries. The question will be whether the claimant had any relevant pre-existing condition or underlying illness such that the accident caused an exacerbation of that condition.

Causation is often the most difficult area to determine in clinical negligence claims yet not well understood by claimants who can readily appreciate the existence of a breach of duty but not the concept of causation of their injuries, as they will be very real to them.

2.1.11 Factual causation

Or better known as the 'but for' test. If harm to the claimant would not have occurred 'but for' the defendant's breach of duty, then the defendant is liable in negligence. The harm may be injury, delayed recovery, death or financial loss.

In establishing liability, the court will assess the factual and expert evidence on a balance of probability test. The mere possibility of avoidance of injury is not enough.

It is necessary to show that the breach of duty <u>could</u> cause the injury as a medical fact and also that it <u>did</u> actually cause the injury or was an inevitable consequence of the claimant's illness, injury or disease.

The first criterion is exemplified in the case of <u>Loveday v Renton</u> [1990] 1 Med LR 117. The claimant alleged that brain damage was caused by the administration of whooping cough vaccine. The court held that the scientific evidence did not establish a link, so the alleged breach could not cause injury.

The more likely scenario is the second situation shown in the case of <u>Barnett v Chelsea and Kensington Hospital Management Committee</u> [1969] 1 All ER 1068 (QBD) which was a failure to treat case where the claimant died of arsenic poisoning. Even if he had received proper care, he would have died anyway, so his death was not caused by negligence. This was a clear-cut decision as the evidence created a straight choice – negligence was either the cause or not at all.

However, there may be a number of competing causes – cumulative or alternative, that result in the disease or injury. In cumulative causes, the defendant's actions or omissions may not be the sole cause of injury, but may be a contributory cause, ie he may have 'materially contributed' to it. This is really an exception to the 'but for' principle as both causes could be responsible for the injury. It may be that the state of scientific knowledge may be insufficient to say to what extent negligence contributed to the injury.

2.1.12 Material contribution

Where the defendant's actions were not the sole cause of the accident, and their contribution to the injury is more than minimal, then the claim may be pursued on the basis of <u>material contribution or loss of a chance.</u>

This is based on policy considerations rather than principle because it does not follow the logical *'but-for'* factual analysis. So in certain prescribed circumstances where the state of scientific knowledge and medicine is limited such that the cause and extent of injury are not known, the claimant may still recover damages.

The *'but-for'* test cannot be applied in cases involving material contribution. Indeed 'material contribution' is a less stringent test to be considered where the *'but-for'* test cannot be satisfied.

The first authoritative case on multiple causes was <u>Bonington Castings Ltd v Wardlaw</u> [1956] AC 613.

In *Bonington* it was held that in a claim for industrial disease namely asbestosis resulting in death, in order to succeed, the claimant only had to prove that the extent and exposure to asbestos had constituted a material increase in the risk of contracting mesothelioma. No measurement of the duration was necessary.

Where *'material contribution'* causation is found at the liability stage, can the claimant recover in full or should damages be apportioned to allow for the chance or fact that he may or would develop the injury anyway, notwithstanding material contribution.

In <u>Hotson v East Berkshire Area Health Authority</u> [1987] AC 750, HL, Lord Bridge said that the claimant had to prove that the delay in treatment was 'at least a material contributory cause' of his injury. Once it is established that on a balance of probabilities that the damage was caused by the negligence, then the claimant recovers in full even if he would not have made a full recovery but for the negligence.

The facts in *Hotson* were that a boy injured his thigh but the surgeons delayed by 4 days in performing surgery. The issue was whether the injuries of bone death would have arisen in any event even if there had not been a breach of duty. On appeal the claimant lost his claim on damages as the lost chance of avoiding bone death were less than 50%.

Hotson is really a 'loss of a chance' case because the claimant started out as injured and the claim was that the defendant failed to make him better or produce a complete recovery.

For those types of situation where the claimant starts out healthy and the claim is that the defendant injured him, the courts tend to describe the test as 'materially increasing the risk'.

Both descriptions are really one and the same as 'materially increasing the risk of injury is equivalent to the loss of a chance of avoiding an injury.

But consider the situation where there are a number of possible causes of the claimant's injuries. *Wilsher* is such an example.

In *Wilsher v Essex Area Health Authority* [1988] AC 1074 the House of Lords approved the corollary of the argument in *Hotson* so that if the claimant had received proper treatment thus reducing his chances of avoiding injuries to less than 50%, then there is no cause of action because those chances were reduced to nil by negligence. In *Wilsher* the administration of excessive oxygen to a neonate was one of the possible causes of loss of sight that did not preclude the court from attributing the injury to that cause. The House of Lords ordered a retrial as the trial judge as failed to make any finding that the excess oxygen was the actual cause, the effective cause or even the most likely cause.

Wilsher was also important for reaffirming the appropriate standard of care. A junior doctor in training is to be judged by the same standards as a more experienced colleague. So inexperience is no defence.

It is also an important authority to rely upon for a claimant where there is evidential uncertainty; where the defendant may not be the cause of the claimant's injury but may be a *contributory* cause. The defendant 'materially contributes' to the injury if it could not have occurred without their negligence.

However *'material contribution'* is not proven where there are two independent causes (one of which was a negligent cause) and each could have brought about the injury.

2.1.13 Material increase in risk of injury

Where the claimant has sustained injury from one or more various sources but the actual tortfeasor cannot be identified, then the courts have created a fiction of recovery for an increased risk of injury. It only applies in exceptional cases.

Typically the situation may arise in an industrial disease claim where the claimant has had various employers all of whom have exposed him to noxious substances, some of which are tortious whilst others are not but injury results. However, the limitations of medical knowledge are such that the employer who was responsible for causing the injury cannot be identified.

The principal authority is *Fairchild v Glenhaven Funeral Services Limited* [2003] 1 AC 32. The House of Lords decided that a claimant who had contracted mesothelioma after wrongful exposure to asbestos at different times by more than one negligent employer, could sue any of them even though he could not prove which exposure had caused the disease. This arises because all had materially contributed to the disease by increasing the risk.

This case exceptionally followed the previous decision of *McGhee v National Coal Board* [1973] 1 WLR which was considered to be wrongly decided in the light of *Wilsher*. However, the Lords stated that *McGhee* had modified the nature of the burden of proof of causation, but only in those cases where the damage was caused by one substance, exposed by various tortfeasors. It was distinguished from *Wilsher* as in that case there were a number of possible causes for the injury.

Fairchild has not been applied to clinical negligence cases for loss of a chance following *Gregg v Scott* [2005] 1 AC 176. Here, the claimant could not establish that the negligent delay in the diagnosis of cancer had caused any measurable reduction in life expectancy. So he sought to recover damages for the chance that life expectancy may be affected. He was not successful as the House of Lords established that diminution caused by negligent delay had to be proved (which was not) on the balance of probabilities.

2.1.14 A summary of the analysis of factual causation is:

1. The burden of proving causation is on the claimant.

2. Causation is a question of past fact, to be decided on a balance of probabilities (see *Mallett v McMonagle* [1970] AC 166).

3. If the claimant proves negligence was the sole cause, or a substantial cause, or that it materially contributed to the damage, he will succeed in full (see *Bonnington Castings* and also *McGhee*).

4. If the claimant fails to cross this threshold then he fails to recover any damages (see *Barnett*).

In recovering damages, the claimant must establish one of the following:

5. 'But for' the negligence he would not have suffered any injury; or

6. 'But for' the negligence he would not have suffered an *identifiable part* or *particular aggravation* of the injuries, in which case he recovers damages limited for the injury related to the breach of duty; or

7. That the negligence *materially contributed* to the whole injury or an identifiable part or particular aggravation of the injuries. This will apply where the defendant's negligence is only one of a number of cumulatively operative factors that affect the injury, rather than being the sole cause (see *Bonnington Castings*).

2.1.15 A helpful first instance decision analysing the breach of duty and causation tests in a clinical negligence case is that of *John v Central Manchester & Manchester Children's University Hospitals NHS Foundation Trust* [2016] EWHC 407 QB.

The claimant lost his footing and fell sustaining a brain injury. He alleged breach of duty in the delay before a CT brain scan was carried out. On causation he alleged that if there had been an earlier CT scan then he would have been transferred earlier to a specialist centre at Hope Hospital resulting in earlier surgery. The defendant denied both aspects of negligence. It argued initially that only if the damaging intra-cranial pressure caused by negligence was the cause of neuropsychological deficits (the '*but-for*' test) could the claimant recover. Subsequently the defendant changed its position on causation to that of the '*material contribution*' test. It suggested that the claimant should not be able to recover for the entirety of the injuries as there were 3 different agents operating by a different mechanism to cause damage. If liability was established then an apportionment of damages was appropriate.

The judge reviewed the authorities:

Bolam on breach of duty, supported by *Sidaway*, *Maynard* and *Bolitho*.

He found there was delay in carrying out the CT scan and on transfer to Hope Hospital.

On factual causation, the judge stated that he had to consider what would have happened on the balance of probabilities had there not been negligence. He found that there would have been earlier surgery which would have avoided the damaging effects of raised intra-cranial pressure.

On medical causation, the judge stated that he must determine whether the injury in a legal sense was attributable to the defendant's breach of duty.

In reviewing the legal principles, he noted that the claimant relied on *Bailey* and *Williams* whilst the defendant initially relied on the *Wilsher* '*but-for*' test of causation but changed its position to '*material contribution*' applying the *Holtby* approach to quantification.

The judge held that as a matter of law, the '*material contribution*' approach was appropriate in a multi-agency case and *Bonington* was not authority for confining '*material contribution* only to single agency cases. He also accepted the claimant's submission that *Wilsher* did not preclude full recovery of damages notwithstanding there were other non-negligent factors which caused or had materially contributed to the claimant's condition.

In supporting the appropriateness of the '*material contribution*' test, the judge referred to the Court of Appeal judgment in <u>Heneghan v Manchester Dry Docks Ltd</u> [2016] EWCA Civ 86. There are 3 ways of establishing causation in disease cases:

(1) But-for the defendant's negligence, the claimant would not have suffered the disease.

(2) Where the disease is caused by the cumulative effect of an agency part of which is attributable to breach of duty on the part of the defendant and part of which involves no breach of duty, the defendant will not be liable on the ground that his breach of duty made a 'material contribution' to the disease: *Bonington Castings.*

(3) Where causation cannot be proved in either of these ways, for example the disease is indivisible, causation may be established if it is proved that the defendant materially increased the risk of the victim contracting the disease: the *Fairchild* exception. Mesothelioma is an indivisible disease.

The final consideration was whether the court should engage in an apportionment exercise as in *Holtby* which was rejected by the judge. Where it was not possible to attribute particular damage to a specific cause, the claimant was entitled to recover in respect of the entirety of the loss. Apportionment was not appropriate where it was impossible to allot a particular loss to a particular cause. (*Bailey* and *Williams*). *Holtby* was a case where it was merely difficult to work out what damage had been caused by particular factors. *Heneghan* did not suggest that damages should have been apportioned had the claimant established there was a material contribution to cancer caused by breach of duty.

The conclusion from the authorities and summarised by Picken J in this case was that:

> '*in 'material contribution to damage cases (as opposed to 'material contribution' to risk cases) the claimant is able to recover in relation to the entirety of his or her injury without apportionment…*'

2.1.16 Burden of proof

It is trite to say that the burden of proof rests on the claimant. It is true that breach of duty and causation must be satisfied on the balance of probabilities but there are occasions when the burden is displaced.

Consider the maxim *res ipsa loquitur*, literally 'the thing speaks for itself'. This applies when an incident that should not have happened whilst under the defendant's control raises a prima facie presumption of negligence which calls for an explanation. It will be a rare event in a clinical negligence claim but there are cases where it has been successfully relied upon as in *Cassidy v Ministry of Health* [1951] 2 KB 343. A patient went into hospital with two stiff fingers and came out with four stiff fingers. Lord Denning stated that this should not have happened and asked of the hospital to 'explain it, if you can'.

The reality is that the parties will be reliant on expert evidence which will mean that there will be few occasions when the court will be invited to make inferences of fact. If it is invited to do so, then the claimant must still show that the cause of the damage occurred whilst in hospital, is unknown, but would normally not occur without negligence. It would be expected that defendants would raise causation arguments which would then require expert evidence.

Difficulties arise where the expert evidence is not capable of being deciphered by a court so as to accept one opinion to the other. In that situation the court must fall back on the burden of proof resting on the claimant. This is what happened in *Barnett v Medway NHS Foundation Trust* where the trial judge dismissed the claim on the basis that the claimant had not discharged the burden of proof. The judge heard expert evidence from two microbiologists. The judge was not satisfied that blood cultures would have revealed an infection or antibiotics would have prevented the paraplegia so the claimant had not proved his case. This was affirmed by the court of appeal which considered the case of *Stephens v Cannon* [2005] EWCA Civ 222. The court should strive to make a finding of fact but may rely on the burden of proof as a last resort.

2.1.17 Consent – disclosure of risks

Patients must be in a position through medical education to give their informed consent to the proposed procedure. This means that the treating doctor must explain the potential risks as well as benefits and alternative treatments if the patient is to gain sufficient understanding. If they have not given their consent then any procedure is likely to constitute a battery and/or be actionable in negligence for breach of duty.

For valid consent the patient must have capacity, so where a patient is under 18 then it will generally be a parent having parental responsibility. A child over 16 may be mature for their years and show greater understanding or insight into their condition. Such 'Gillick' competent children may give valid consent, though it would be wise that such decisions are taken in conjunction with a parent, provided of course that the child is agreeable.

An incompetent adult – one being incapable of making a treatment decision -must be treated by doctors in their best interests as set out in **section 1(5) MCA 2005.**

That involves a determination not simply of age, appearance or behaviour, but a consideration of whether they are likely to regain capacity in the future. So far as reasonably practicable, the patient should be encouraged to participate in decisions affecting them. Where ascertainable, past and present wishes and feelings as well as beliefs and values should be taken into account.

Decisions on withdrawal of life-saving treatment and Advance Decisions/Directives are outside the scope of this book and will not be reviewed.

In bringing a claim for breach of duty in for lack of consent requires the claimant to prove:

1. That there is a duty to disclose.

2. Sufficient information concerning the risks and alternative procedures was not provided.

3. Causation.

We shall review three of the principal cases to demonstrate the necessary disclosure of risks in order that the patient is adequately consented and then consider the guidance provided by the Department of Health and the GMC.

Montgomery

2.1.18 The most significant recent case on consent and which has considerably extended the requirements of doctors to explain not only **material risks** but also **alternative or variant treatments** is that of *Montgomery v Lanarkshire Health Board* [2015] UKSC 11. The decision represented a move away from medical paternalism by placing the doctor/patient relationship on a level footing where the patient could be expected to appreciate that treatment might not necessarily achieve the desired outcome and may involve risks for which they would wish to accept responsibility. But this involved a discussion of the alternative treatments available and the risks involved in those alternatives. Dialogue between doctor and patient was crucial so that the patient received necessary and comprehensible information (but not technical information that could not be grasped). The Supreme Court held:

"...An adult person of sound mind is entitled to decide which, if any, of the available forms of treatment to undergo, and her consent must be obtained before treatment interfering with her bodily integrity is undertaken. The doctor is therefore under a duty to take reasonable care to ensure that the patient is aware of any material risks involved in any recommended treatment, and of any reasonable alternative or variant treatments. The test of materiality is whether, in the circumstances of the particular case, a reasonable person in the patient's position would be likely to attach significance to the risk, or the doctor is or should reasonably be aware that the particular patient would be likely to attach significance to it."

The court also found that the assessment of whether a risk is material will reflect a variety of factors, for example the nature of the risk, the importance to the patient of the benefits to be achieved, the alternatives available and the risks involved.

The doctor must ensure that she has taken reasonable care to ensure that the patient is aware of the potential risks and possible alternatives.

The doctor's duty to advise before consent is obtained is not determined by the *Bolam* test of a responsible body of medical opinion (as was applied in *Sidaway*). This is because not only medical issues are relevant but also the patient's own values in assessing comparative merits.

2.1.19 Before *Montgomery*, the two other notable cases were <u>*Sidaway v Board of Governors of the Bethlem Royal Hospital*</u> and <u>*Chester v Afshar* [2005] 1 AC 134.</u>

Sidaway went to the House of Lords who supported the Court of Appeal and the trial judge, finding that the patient had not been told of all the material risks so as to give her informed consent. But as the surgeon had acted in accordance with standard practice as supported by a responsible body of medical opinion as per *Bolam*, the claimant's case failed. This was so despite the fact that the surgeon failed to warn of the risk to the spinal cord in an operation to the cervical vertebrae, resulting in paralysis. That risk was assessed at 1% yet the higher risk of 2% for damage to a nerve root was mentioned even though damage would be far less serious.

It was recognised in *Sidaway* that *Bolitho* might apply where the failure to warn of a particular risk may be negligent even where a body of doctors would not warn. The practice must be reasonable and responsible, so even where no expert is critical of the failure to disclose, it will be down to the judge to ascertain whether the risk was so obviously necessary for the patient to make an informed choice.

The court is the final arbiter of what constitutes informed consent (rather than to hand over the question of the scope of duty to the doctors) so held the Law Lords in *Chester*. Here the surgeon neglected to warn of the risk of cauda equina syndrome that developed. The case was also significant in considering causation by finding that the 'but-for' test did not apply in a failure to warn case. Where there was a negligent failure to warn and the patient was unable to state that she would have declined the operation at all, the court held that the claim should succeed.

Examples of consent cases

• Change of operating surgeon after consent form signed. Nerve damage ensued. The court referred to DOH guidance. Claimant successful. (*Jones v Royal Devon & Exeter NHS Foundation Trust* CC 22/09/2015).

• Change in treatment plan from conservative (non-operative) treatment to premature surgery. Despite the patient not questioning why the operation was brought forward, defendant held liable for causative breach of duty. *Chester* did not need to be considered. The court was not persuaded that necessarily the outcome of future surgery would be the same (*Crossman v St George's Healthcare NHS Trust* [2016] EWHC 2878 (QB).

• Failure to discuss in detail the increased risks of delaying labour, when had such been given as required by *Montgomery*, such as contrary arguments in favour of non-intervention, the claimant would still have wanted early delivery thus avoiding brain injury. Breach of duty and causation proven (*Webster v Burton Hospitals NHS Foundation Trust [2017] EWCA Civ 62).*

2.1.20 Professional Guidelines

Department of Health Guidelines

The DOH provides guidance in a document available at:

www.gov.uk/government/publications/reference-guide-to-consent-for-examination-or-treatment-second-edition-Referenceguidetoconsent-forexaminationortreatment

Since 2001 the DOH guidance on consent has required NHS Trusts to adopt a model consent policy, model forms and information. These guidelines were published in July 2009.

GMC Guidelines

These guidelines are said to provide a framework for good practice that covers various situations that doctors face. They came into effect on 2 June 2008 and are accessible on www.gmc-uk.org/guidance

It sets out information that should be given to patients, namely:

"*1. Diagnosis or prognosis*

2. Any uncertainties about the diagnosis or prognosis including options for further investigations.

3. Options for treating or managing the condition, including the option not to treat.

4. The purpose of any proposed investigation or treatment and what it will involve.

5. The potential benefits, risks and burdens, and the likelihood of success, for each option; this should include information, if available, about whether the benefits or risks are affected by which organization or doctor is chosen to provide care.

6. Whether a proposed investigation or treatment is part of a research programme or is an innovative treatment designed specifically for their benefit.

7. The people who will be mainly responsible for and involved in their care, what their roles are, and to what extent statements may be involved.

8. Their rights to refuse to take part in teaching or research.

9. Their right to seek a second opinion.

10. Any bills they will have to pay.

11. Any conflicts of interest that you, or your organization, may have.

12. Any treatments that you believe have greater potential benefit for the patient than those you or your organisation can offer."

Discussion of side effects, complications and other risks

In addition to the above, doctors must identify adverse outcomes that may result from proposed options. This includes the potential outcome of taking no action. Risks can take a number of forms, usually:

- side effects
- complications
- failure of an interaction to achieve the desired aim

The patient's views:

"You must do your best to understand the patient's views and preferences about any proposed investigation or treatment and the adverse outcomes they are most concerned about. You must not make assumptions about a patient's understanding of risk or the importance they attach to different outcomes. You should discuss these issues with your patient."

"You must tell patients if an investigation or treatment might resort in a serious adverse outcome, even if the likelihood is very small. You should also tell patients about less serious side effects or complications if they occur frequently, and explain what the patient should do if they experience any of them.

You must give information about risk in a balanced way. You should avoid bias, and you should explain the expected benefits as well as the potential burdens and risks of any proposed investigation or treatment."

2.1.21 Royal College of Surgeons' Guidelines on consent

These are available online at the site www.rcseng.ac.uk and were revised on 28.10.2016 following the decision of *Montgomery*, reflecting the retreat of medical paternalism. The RCS recognised that the duty of doctors was to be more receptive to the specific needs of the patient to acquire more information on risks and benefits.

The guidelines are set out in the document entitled: *Consent: Supported Decision-making a guide to good practice**

In relation to elective treatment for competent adults, the key principles are:

"• *The aim of the discussion about consent is to give the patient the information they need to make a decision about what treatment or procedure (if any) they want.*

- *The discussion has to be tailored to the individual patient. This requires time to get to know the patient well enough to understand their views and values.*

- *All reasonable treatment options, along with their implications, should be explained to the patient.*

- *Material risks for each option should be discussed with the patient. The test of materiality is twofold: whether, in the circumstances of the particular case, a reasonable person in the patient's position would be likely to attach significance to the risk, or the doctor is or should reasonably be aware that the particular patient would likely attach significance to it.*

- *Consent should be written and recorded. If the patient has made a decision, the consent form should be signed at the end of the discussion. The signed form is part of the evidence that the discussion has taken place, but provides no meaningful information about the quality of the discussion.*

- *In addition to the consent form, a record of the discussion (including contemporaneous documentation of the key points of the discussion, hard copies or web links of any further information provided to the patient, and the patient's decision) should be included in the patient's case notes. This is important even if the patient chooses not to undergo treatment."*

The process suggested by the RCS is similar to the information set out in the GMC Guidelines with the emphasis on ascertaining the patient's wishes, needs, views and expectations.

Whilst it is helpful to appreciate the recommendations made by the professional bodies, they are disciplinary in nature and have no wider legal import. So a failure to comply with the professional guidelines will not alone be sufficient to prove negligence of a failure to warn about risks. Nevertheless, such an omission may be persuasive evidence as to what constitutes a reasonable standard of care. One might expect that following *Sidaway* and *Bolitho*, the guidelines should represent the minimum criteria to be followed.

2.1.22 Contract

A claim in contract could be considered where private treatment has been provided, for example aesthetic surgery at a cosmetic clinic. If the NHS contracted treatment out to a private hospital, then the claim will be against the NHS Trust rather than the clinician or clinic that provided the treatment.

The standard of care provided by a private clinic is expected to be the same as under the NHS, so the test for proving a breach of contract will be still on the *Bolam* standard. There may be circumstances when the contractual standard is higher than the *Bolam* standard. Then, it would be necessary to establish that there was an express provision in the contract or in advertising materials that the quality of the outcome would be better than provided elsewhere, i.e. to exceed the reasonable standard that is required under *Bolam*. A claimant might be reliant on a brochure showing what appearance might be expected or achieved which created a reasonable expectation of the outcome.

For claims in contract that are likely to include cosmetic cases or claims against care or nursing homes, there is the possibility of being able to claim damages for distress and inconvenience based on the principle of loss of enjoyment. This stems from the holiday cases dating back to *Jackson v Horizon Holidays Ltd* [1975]. According to the dicta in *Farley v Skinner* [2001] UKHL 49, where the object of the contract is to provide pleasure, relaxation, peace of mind or freedom from molestation, then damages would be recoverable. Clearly the purpose of the medical procedure would be relevant as one might struggle to show that removal of a gallbladder was intended to provide a pleasurable experience. The extent of the pleasure principle has been held to apply to the outcome of an inquest in *Shaw v Leigh Day (a firm)* [2017] EWHC 825 QB where the contractual duty does extend to solicitors to take reasonable care to make a proper investigation.

There will be difficulties in proving a breach of contract on the basis of an expected clinical outcome. In *Thake v Maurice* [1986] 1 All ER 497 the Court of Appeal noted that reasonable people know that medical operations are not always successful. In that case the contractual action for damages failed where the costs of bringing up a child following a failed vasectomy were claimed. The clinic stated that the operation was 'irreversible' did not amount to a guarantee that it would work as there was no binding promise. It is suspected that in today's climate that a close examination of the consenting process would be examined to discern what was discussed as almost certainly the possibility of failure would be documented.

2.2 Road Traffic Accidents

2.2.1 These types of case were once considered routine for personal injury practitioners starting their career when the claimant suffered soft tissue whiplash type injuries. They provided an early opportunity to draft the Particulars of Claim or Defence without too much complexity as the facts and allegations of negligence tended to be straightforward. Indeed the government in its Prisons and Courts Bill in February 2017 in seeking to reform whiplash claims states that 90% of RTA personal injury claims are neck, back or whiplash claims. The small claims limit is expected to increase to £5,000 for RTA-related personal injury claims, with a new threshold of £2,000 for all other personal injury claims. This Bill is likely to become law by 1 October 2018.

The current proposals in the Bill are for a tariff for general damages in RTA-related whiplash claims. There are mooted 7 categories, from 0-3 months (£225) to 19-24 months (£3,275). This is based upon a 'prognosis approach'. At the time of writing, the definition of 'whiplash' is not clear, but it may be expected not to include all soft tissue injuries and is unlikely to include the same class of injuries falling within the existing Pre-Action Protocol for low value claims in RTAs.

The scope of the entire scheme may involve some changes to the low value pi protocol. As claims are submitted onto the pi portal for all claims, whether RTA, EL or PL valued at under £25,000.00, the forthcoming changes are not anticipated to make much difference to pleading points or establishing proof of liability. Traditional pleadings will continue to apply to fast-track or multi-track claims above £25,000.00. However, the allegations one would raise, albeit in less detail still apply for drafting the Claim Notification Form ('CNF'). There may be more significant changes with a greater reliance on alternative dispute resolution ('ADR').

Establishing liability in a vehicle collision is not particularly troublesome. If the police attend the scene and prepare a report incorporating witness statements, photographs and plans then this will assist, Where a driver is prosecuted and convicted of careless or dangerous driving, then this conviction may be pleaded in the Particulars of Claim.

The police do not attend every incident so obtaining evidence in a contested case has become more important.

Around the time of the introduction of the pre-action protocol for low value personal injury claims, motor insurers for the defendant driver started alleging that claimants were fraudulently bringing claims and were therefore fundamentally dishonest. Undoubtedly there were fictitious claims brought out of deliberate or staged crashes. Insurers have become suspicious about cases, particularly rear end shunts and may allege fraud, inviting discontinuance on pain of seeking costs if the case is stuck out. Added to allegations of fraud, insurers may allege that some claimants deliberately exaggerate their claims or accuse them of malingering. It may be coincidental that fraud allegations have increased substantially around the same time that one way qualified costs shifting (QUOCS) was introduced on 1 April 2013 following the **Legal Aid, Sentencing and Punishment of Offenders Act 2012.** Essentially genuine claimants who lost their claim were protected from paying the defendant's legal costs. The issue being that if the claimant was not genuine because he had brought a fraudulent claim then he would pay for it if he was found to be fundamentally dishonest - and QUOCS would not apply (see **Part 44.16**).

2.2.2 Grounds for establishing liability

There is little Statute to know about in this chapter and much of that will not generally be required reading. However, they are: **Road Traffic Act 1988, The Road Vehicles (Construction and Use)(Amendment) (No.4) Regulations 2003** and the **Law Reform Contributory Negligence) Act 1945**. Relevant extracts are contained within Appendix I.

In addition, consider **The Official Highway Code** as this is helpful for pleading and evidential points, although not binding on a civil court. Also consider advice to motorists set out in **The Official DVSA Guide to Driving – the essential skills**.

The general principles of negligence hold good as for other personal injury and clinical negligence claims, namely the requirement to prove duty, breach of duty and foreseeability of loss.

Clearly the facts of the case determine how the claim is pleaded. Typically in a collision between vehicles or between a vehicle and a pedestrian, then allegations of negligence are likely to contain some or all of the following:

- Driving too fast
- Failing to keep any proper look out
- Failing to have any or any sufficient regard for (other traffic/pedestrians) that was using the road
- Failing to see the claimant's car
- Failing to stop, slow down, to swerve or so control the vehicle so as to avoid a collision
- Proceeding into collision with the claimant/claimant's vehicle
- Failing to heed the weather conditions at the time and to take all appropriate care in the circumstances
- Driving a vehicle with defective brakes
- Failing to accord precedence to the claimant who had right of way

- The claimant will rely upon the conviction of the defendant at the Oxton Magistrates' Court on [date] for the offence of driving without due care and attention. The conviction is relevant to the issue of negligence and the claimant intends to rely on it as evidence in this action, under the provisions of s.11 of the Civil Evidence Act 1968.

PD 16, para 4 sets out what must be included in the particulars of claim, namely the claimant's date of birth and brief details of the claimant's personal injuries. A medical report and schedule of loss must be attached. In a soft tissue injury claim, the claimant may not proceed unless the medical report is a fixed cost medical report from an accredited medical expert selected via the MedCo Portal.

Fatal accident claims require additional information under para 5: that the claim is brought under the Fatal Accidents Act 1976; the dependants on whose behalf the claim is made; the date of birth of each dependant; and details of the nature of the dependency claim.

2.2.3 Alleging fraud

Defendants may seek to put the claimant to proof in its defence, possibly intimating fraud by alleging a lack of good faith by the claimant. Such a defence is not in breach of the CPR surprisingly. **Part 16.5** sets out what must be included in the defence. A defendant is permitted to deny, admit or require a claimant to prove an allegation, including the sustaining of any injury.

A defendant intimating fraud does not need to plead it provided there is compliance with **Part 16.5**. There is a tension on the one hand between a claimant not making out their claim and the defendant arguing the claim was fabricated. Defendants are reluctant to plead fraud but they may set out facts from which the court would be invited to draw the inference that the claimant has not suffered the injuries or damage.

This was considered in the case of _Francis v Wells_ [2007] EWCA Civ 1350 where the defendant's insurer alleged an invented accident. The Court of Appeal reaffirmed that the claimant has the burden to prove that the collision occurred by the negligence of the defendant and that the claimant suffered damage. The evidential burden shifts to the defendant where they allege fraud. Lloyd J stated that just because the defendant had not made out its claim of an invented accident, does not mean that the claimant had proved its claim on the balance of probability.

There may be instances of multiple claimants such as a driver and passengers in a car where one of the claimants gives weak oral evidence. Perhaps they are evasive under cross-examination or fail to reveal a relevant previous medical history recorded in their medical records. That could lead to dismissal of their claim for fundamental dishonesty, whilst other claimants in the same action succeed on the claim.

As a result, claimant's advisors must be alive to the (rare) possibility of claimants who either deliberately or otherwise fail to disclose information in their witness statements that might undermine their claim on liability or on quantum. It cannot be assumed that inconsistencies in the GP or hospital records will be picked up by a medical expert. So police reports, medical records and any road traffic reconstruction expert report must be carefully reviewed by the legal representative before the claimant's statement is exchanged with the defendant. A failure to prepare sufficiently may cause problems with credibility later on.

Claimants must also realise that insurers may carry out video surveillance of their activities and rely upon any incriminating evidence in an application to strike out the claim or at trial.

The question of what constitutes 'fundamental dishonesty' was considered in the case of _Gosling v (1) Hailo (2) Screwfix Direct_ (2014) CC (Cambridge). The claimant injured himself whilst using a ladder. After disclosure of surveillance video evidence, the claimant discontinued his claim. The defendant applied for recovery of its costs under **CPR 44.16**. The judge found that a claimant should not be exposed to costs liability merely because he was dishonest as to some collateral matter or some minor, self-contained head of damage. But if the dishonesty went to the root of the claim or a substantial part of it, then that would be fundamentally dishonest. In this case, the claimant alleged permanent loss of function which represented about half of the total quantum claim of £80,000. The court held that dishonesty relating to a substantial part of the claim was 'fundamental'. Such was the glaring dishonesty that the claimant did not need to be cross-examined and he was ordered to pay costs.

2.2.4 Pedestrians and Contributory negligence

Contributory negligence is a partial defence applicable when the claimant's conduct has caused or contributed to his own injuries. The relevant statute is the *Law Reform (Contributory Negligence) Act 1945*. This provides that the claimant's damages shall be reduced to such an extent as the court thinks just and equitable having regard to the claimant's share in the responsibility for the damage.

Drivers of cars owe a high standard of care to pedestrians, especially to children and the infirm. Foolish or unpredictable pedestrian claimants may still succeed in a claim but with substantial findings of contributory negligence. So in *Watson v Skuse* [2001] All ER (D) 208, a claimant pedestrian's 'folly' was his failure to wait for a green light at a pedestrian crossing. His evidence was that he felt it was unnecessary to look at pedestrian lights at the age of 49. The defendant driver of a lorry failed to see the pedestrian as he had failed to look to his left before starting off. There was an apportionment of liability, the court holding that the claimant had been principally responsible for the accident with the driver being held 20% contributorily negligent.

Pedestrians must observe the Green Cross Code when crossing a road. Rule 7 of the Official Highway Code as we all know stipulates that if traffic is coming, let it pass and when safe to do so, go straight across the road. Those pedestrians who stop or pause in the centre of the road to allow traffic to pass are likely to be subject to a finding of contributory negligence of between 20% to 30%, though all cases are fact sensitive of course.

Contributory negligence requires the defendant to prove that the claimant failed to take 'ordinary care for himself', i.e. such care as a reasonable person would take for their own safety, and, second, that such failure was a contributory cause of the accident (*Lewis v Denye* [1939] 1 KB 540).

As a defence, contributory negligence does not require the defendant to admit a duty owed to the claimant. All the defendant need do is establish that the claimant did not take reasonable care of himself and contributed either wholly or partly to that injury. The defendant's objective is to secure a percentage reduction against the full liability valuation of damages.

Classic examples where contributory negligence applies are a failure to wear a seat belt provided it contributed to the damage. In *Froom v Butcher* [1976] QB 286 (CA), the claimant was a passenger involved in an RTA. The Court of Appeal determined a sliding scale of reductions for contributory negligence for failing to wear a seat belt: 25% where injuries would have been avoided altogether; 15% where injuries would have been less severe; and no reduction if the injuries would have been the same even if a seatbelt had been worn. The *Froom* guidelines have been applied to cases involving motorcycles and bicycles.

Another situation where a claimant's damages are reduced for contributory negligence apply where he deliberately places himself in a position of danger, such as a passenger in a car where the driver has been drinking alcohol and is over the drink drive limit – *Owens v Brimmell* [1977] QB 859 where damages were reduced by 20%.

2.3 The RTA Protocol

2.3.1 The protocol was introduced in 2010 and extended in July 2013 to all road traffic accidents with an anticipated net value of between **£1,000 and £25,000** (after any deductions for contributory negligence). It is intended to avoid the issue of proceedings by notifying the defendant's insurers of a claim through an online portal. There are three stages and only after the third stage is exhausted may proceedings be issued under **Part 8.** There are limited circumstances when **Part 7** proceedings would be appropriate.

The protocol applies where the claimant's injury has been '...*caused by....a motor vehicle on a road or other public place in England and Wales*' (RTA Protocol, para 1.1(16)).

There may be some unusual circumstances where the protocol does not apply, nor does the EL or PL protocol. This happened in *Prescott (A child) v Trustees of the Pencarrow 2012 Maintenance Fund*, Plymouth CC 12 June 2016 but DJ Richards held that the claimant was still only entitled to fixed costs where he was injured in a car caused by a fallen tree owned by D. The protocol did not apply as the accident was not caused by a motor vehicle.

2.3.2 Excluded cases

The RTA Protocol does not apply to claims:

(a) Where there is an untraced driver and the claim is to the MIB.

(b) Where C or D is deceased.

(c) Where C or D is a protected party.

(d) Where C is bankrupt.

(e) Where D's vehicle is registered outside the UK.

2.3.3 **Stage 1 – submission of claim**

Claimant sends Claim Notification Form (CNF) to defendant's insurer. D sends electronic acknowledgment the next day. D has **15 business days to respond** on liability via the 'Insurer Response' (CNF response). A 'Defendant Only CNF' is sent to the defendant at the same time. If there is no insurer, the Motor Insurers' Bureau deals with the claim and they have 30 days to respond. If an admission is made, D pays Stage 1 fixed costs within 10 days after sending CNF response.

2.3.4 Stage 2 – submission of Settlement Pack

• Claimant obtains a medical report. Where the claim is less than £10,000, it is expected that the medical expert will not need to see the medical records (para 7.5). Updating reports may be justified where C is receiving continuing treatment or has not recovered as expected from the original prognosis. Further experts may be necessary where the injuries cover different disciplines.

• The <u>stage 2 settlement pack (form RTA 5) is submitted</u> with the medical report, any other expert report, witness statements (not normally required), evidence of financial losses and evidence of disbursements. C makes an offer in full settlement, allowing for any offered reduction for contributory negligence, if alleged by D. Claims for vehicle related damage are not usually included in the settlement pack unless C has already paid for it.

• D has **15 business days** <u>to consider the settlement pack</u> and then either to accept the offer or make a counter offer on the same form. Any counter offer must stipulate a value for each head of damage and any CRU deductible benefits.

• There is an <u>additional **20 days** – the 'negotiation period'</u> for the parties to negotiate. If settlement is achieved, then D pays agreed damages, Stage 1 and 2 costs and disbursements within 10 days (para 7.47).

• If one party withdraws an offer made in the Stage 2 Settlement pack after the 35 days' consideration period has elapsed, the claim exits the protocol and C may start proceedings under **Part 7** (para 7.46). <u>Claims which no longer continue under the Protocol cannot subsequently re-enter the process</u> (para 5.11).

• If there is no agreement, C sends D the <u>court proceedings pack</u> (forms RTA 6 and RTA 7) containing in Part A the schedule of losses and D's response plus supporting evidence from both parties. Part B contains C's final offer and D's counter-offer. No new evidence or claim may be served on D not already contained within the Stage 2 settlement pack.

D has 5 days to comment or nominate a legal representative for service. D has **15 days** from receipt of the pack to pay C its (ie D's) final offer of damages, any unpaid Stage 1 and 2 costs and agreed disbursements.

2.3.5 Stage 3 – issuing a Part 8 claim

- This is for determination of damages by the court either on paper or at a hearing. Under **PD 8B** para 6.1, C must file and serve on D the claim form and previous evidence – medical report, schedule of loss, evidence of disbursements and the court proceedings pack (Part B containing C's and D's final offers is in a sealed envelope as the offers are treated as Part 36 offers).

- D files and serves an acknowledgement of service (form N210B) within 14 days of service of claim form. If D opposes the claim because C has not followed the RTA Protocol or has relied upon new evidence that had not been provided under the protocol, the court will dismiss the claim leaving C to start **Part 7** proceedings (para 9.1).

- After receipt of the acknowledgment of service, the court will decide whether the assessment of damages will be based on the papers or at a hearing. It will be a hearing if requested by C on the claim form or by D in the acknowledgement of service. If the court considers that further evidence is required then it will be converted to a **Part 7** claim.

- The court has power to order a **Part 7** claim as if governed by the stage 3 procedure in **PD 8B** and conversely may order a **Part 8** claim to proceed as if it were a **Part 7** claim.

2.4 Employers' Liability Claims

2.4.1 Employers owe a duty of care and statutory duty to their employees, but also to workers. This is their primary liability. They may also be vicariously liable for the actions or omissions committed by their employees/workers whilst acting in the course of their employment.

We will review claims for negligence and breach of statutory duty, and then consider the procedure for bringing a portal claim, although there is considerable overlap with the RTA protocol.

EL claims or accidents at work require a consideration of negligence at common law and under statute or Regulations.

2.4.2 **Negligence**

Under the common law, the employer is under a duty to take all reasonable steps to avoid risk to his employees, by providing and maintaining proper plant and machinery; selecting properly skilled persons to manage and supervise the business; and to provide a proper system of working (_Wilsons and Clyde Coal Company Ltd v English_ [1938] AC 57 (HL).

The case established 4 duties which has been applied in subsequent cases and in the legislation:

- A safe place of work
- Safe plant and equipment
- Safe system of work and working practices
- Competent employees

In accordance with the general principles of negligence, it is the duty of the employer to take reasonable care, balancing the magnitude of risk of injury if the risk materialised against the cost of taking precautions to avoid the risk. In other words, is the precaution **reasonably practicable.** This underpins much of the health and safety legislation especially with regards to statutory duties but as mentioned below, their importance has diminished because they do not impose civil liability.

This balancing exercise was considered back in 1949 in the case of _Edwards v National Coal Board_ [1949] 1 KB 704, CA when Asquith LJ stated:

' "*Reasonably practicable*" *is a narrower term than "physically possible", and seems to me to imply that a computation must be made by the owner in which the quantum of risk is placed on one scale and the sacrifice involved in the measures necessary for averting the risk (whether in money, time or trouble) is placed in the other, and that, if it be shown that there is a gross disproportion between them – the risk being insignificant in relation to the sacrifice – the defendants discharge the onus on them.*'

Reasonable practicability requires a precaution to be taken unless the time, effort and expense of taking it as compared to the avoidance of risk, is grossly disproportionate (as affirmed by the House of Lords in *Marshall v Gotham Co Ltd* [1954] AC 360).

As in other areas of negligence, the claimant must prove the existence of a duty of care; breach of that duty; damage caused by the breach (causation); and damage which is not too remote.

2.4.3 Duty of care

This will be dealt with briefly because in the employer/employee context in most cases a duty will be established as there is a special relationship between the parties in accordance with the neighbour principle. The most recent formulation of this principle was considered in *Caparo Industries plc v Dickman* [1990] 2 AC 605 (HL) which established 3 criteria to establish a duty of care:

- Reasonable foresight of harm
- Sufficient proximity of relationship
- That it is fair, just and reasonable to impose a duty.

A situation where imposing a duty may be controversial is when an activity arranged by the employer takes place outside of work premises. This is illustrated in the case of *Grant v Fife Council* Court of Session (Outer House) [2013] CSOH 11. The defendant argued that the claimant whilst injured in a team building event outside of work premises on an army assault course was not acting in the course of his employment and thus no duty was owed. The court found against the defendant and disagreed with their submission that it was not 'fair, just and reasonable' to imply a duty of care to make a risk assessment at common law.

2.4.4 Breach of duty

Once a duty of care has been established, the next step is for the claimant to prove a breach of duty such that the defendant has not met the standard of care of a reasonable employer. All circumstances are taken into account, including:

• The likelihood of injury, i.e. foreseeability. This comes down to a risk assessment. The greater the risk of damage, the greater the standard of care that applies.

• Proportionality of precautions, i.e. the costs and practicability (time and effort) to the employer of reducing risk. The court will consider what measures the defendant could have taken to reduce the risk, the cost of doing so and how easily the measures could have been implemented. In this regard the common law test is **reasonable practicality**. Here the burden of proof is on the defendant not claimant. This should be contrasted with the **reasonable practicability** test in proving breach of statutory duty.

• The magnitude of the risk of injury. This is determined by the likelihood of injury occurring and the seriousness of the potential injury. If potential injuries are serious then the chance of the risk of injury developing may still be considered low for a breach to be established. If a defendant knows that a specific employee is at a higher risk of suffering more serious injury, then a higher standard of care may be required.

• Size of employer. The standard of care is not reduced simply because an employer has limited resources. A defendant cannot argue (successfully) that the costs of precautions are too expensive to excuse a breach of duty.

2.4.5 Causation

Causation of injuries arising from negligence or breach of statutory duty is the same test and must be proved on the balance of probabilities. It is determined on a factual basis rather than foreseeability. The 'but for' test applies, as discussed earlier in the clinical negligence section. But for the defendant's breach of duty, would the damage have occurred. Causation is unlikely to be too much of a problem in EL cases although industrial disease cases may be problematic. This is exemplified in the case of _Rothwell v Chemical & Insulating Co Ltd: Re Pleural Plaques_ [2007] 3 WLR 876 (HL) which underlines the need to prove damage. The claimants were exposed to asbestos and developed pleural plaques and were at risk of developing asbestos-related disease. The House of Lords held that symptomless plaques were not compensatable damage and that the risk of future illness did not create a cause of action.

The courts however may infer that increased exposure to risk has contributed to, and hence caused, the accident, e.g. the absence of a guard rail on a scaffold.

Causation will be more difficult to establish in cases with multiple causes of damage (see *Bonnington* and *Wilsher,* earlier), a material contribution (see *McGhee* earlier) or loss of a chance (see *Hotson* and *Gregg,* earlier).

But where the injury would have occurred anyway even without breach of duty then causation is not established (see *Barnett,* earlier).

2.4.6 Remoteness

This is otherwise known as legal causation or foreseeability. The claimant must establish that it was foreseeable that there would be injury to the claimant of the kind which he or she suffers as a consequence of the breach, and that the damage suffered is of the sort for which the law permits recovery. The principal case setting out the test is colloquially known as _The Wagon Mound (No 1)_ [1961] AC 388. If the injury is foreseeable, but the severity of injury is not, due to some pre-existing condition of the claimant, then the defendant is liable for all damage (the 'eggshell skull' principle). As Lord Parker CJ said in that case, 'the tortfeasor takes his victim as he finds him'.

2.4.7 The impact of the *Enterprise and Regulatory Reform Act 2013*

Prior to October 2013, a claim could be advanced by pleading a breach of duty of care under common law negligence or as a breach of statutory duty. Typically a claimant would plead both. But now, in order to succeed in a claim, a claimant must prove negligence, as following the introduction of the **Enterprise and Regulatory Reform Act 2013 (ERRA)**, no absolute or strict liability attaches to most breaches of statutory duty. Section 69 of the Act amended section 47 of the *Health and Safety at Work Act 1974* to provide that:

> '*a breach of duty imposed by a statutory instrument containing health and safety regulations shall not be actionable except to the extent that regulations under this section so provide*'.

So, unless a regulation explicitly states a cause of action, then a breach imports no automatic finding of liability.

Nevertheless, a failure by an employer to comply with statutory duty via regulations, the six pack regulations or internal method statements will represent good evidence of the standard of conduct expected. A recognised standard of conduct is found in official guidance. Useful information on risk assessments is found at www.hse.gov.uk. This should assist in drafting the particulars of claim and witness statements. If acting for the claimant, the statement should cover how the defendant should have avoided the accident and why this fell below the standard to be expected of a reasonable employer. Reference to internal memos or risk assessments or training or a lack thereof should be referred to in the statement.

2.4.8 *Exceptions*

Certain older statutes are not affected by the ERRA. For example, strict liability applies in: the *Employer's Liability (Defective Equipment) Act*

1969, the Defective Premises Act 1972 and *The Consumer Protection Act 1987.*

Also, ERRA has no retrospective effect, so any cause of action preceding October 2013, such as an industrial disease claim where there was latent injury may still rely upon breach of statutory duty.

There is a significant disparity between claims made against private employers and those claims against public bodies. The ERRA may only be effective in removing civil liability against private employers because the six pack regulations are derived from European Directives which remain directly actionable against *'emanations of the state'*. So claims against local authorities, government departments, police authorities and public health bodies for example, may arguably still rely upon strict or absolute liability where it applies.

The result is that in a claim against a public body, it may be necessary to plead not only the Regulation but the relevant Directive as it may not be fully incorporated into the UK Regulations. A claim against a private employer will be reliant on proving negligence.

Despite the impact of section 69 ERRA, all is not necessarily lost as the claimant may still rely upon a defendant's failure to take the steps required under the relevant statutory duty by pleading, for example:

Pleading

2.4.9 *Negligently requesting the claimant to lift a weight of 50kg without mechanical assistance.*

The claimant will rely upon Regulation 4(1) of the Manual Handling Operations Regulations which provide that:

> *So far as is reasonably practicable, avoid the need for his employees to undertake any manual handling operations at work which involve a risk of their being injured*

And further failing contrary to Art 6.2 of the Council Directive 90/269 EEC, to ensure that the claimant received proper training on how to handle loads correctly and the risks to which he might be open if manual handling was not performed correctly contrary to the duty to provide such information pursuant to reg 10 of the Management of Health and Safety at Work Regulations 1999.

The claimant has to plead all the facts necessary so as to come within the statute and refer to the particular provision relied upon. In the above example, reference to the EU Directive has been made which may be relevant if the claim is being made against a public body.

Even if an employer shows compliance with a statutory duty, it does not inevitably relieve an employer from liability in negligence (see *Franklin v Gramophone Co Ltd* [1948] 1 KB 542.

A detailed considered of the health and safety legislation is outside the ambit of this book but it is useful to consider the main regulations.

2.4.10 **Statutory Duties**

The principal safety legislation is contained within **the Health and Safety at Work Act 1974** (HSW) which delegates power to make Regulations to Subordinate legislation in the *Management of Health and Safety at Work Regulations 1992 (*subsequently updated in 1999). This Act incorporates the European Directives into English law as the 'six pack' regulations. They have not taken the wording from the Directives explicitly so they are worth checking. The regulations are:

- *the Management of Health & Safety at Work Regulations 1999 (MHSWR)*
- *the Workplace (Health, Safety and Welfare) Regulations 1992 (WHSWR)*
- *the Provision and Use of Work Equipment Regulations 1998 (PUWER)*
- *the Personal Protective Equipment at Work Regulations 1998 (PPE)*
- *the Manual Handling Operations Regulations 1992 (MHOR)*

- *the Health and Safety (Display Screen Equipment) Regulations 1992 (amended 2002) (HSDSER)*

Excerpts are set out in the toolkit in Chapter 10.

The six pack and other health and safety statutes set out obligations on an employer to institute an appropriate assessment of workplace risk, monitoring of workplace health and safety, and providing information and training as to risks and risk avoidance. Statutory duties represent evidence of good practice that a reasonable employer should adopt

Other important statutory duties include:

- *the Control of Substances Hazardous to Health Regulations 1999 (COSHH)*
- *the Control of Asbestos at Work Regulations 2012 (CAWR)*
- *the Lifting Operations and Lifting Equipment Regulations 1998 (LOLER)*
- *the Work at Height Regulations 2005 (WHR)*
- *Employer's Liability (Defective Equipment) Act 1969*

It is important to recognise that the six pack and other regulations mentioned here (save HSW) do not apply to accidents prior to 1 January 1993. This has particular force to historical claims involving latent injury where the cause of action predated 1993. In these cases regard must be had to an historical Act or regulation such as the *Factories Act 1937 or 1961* or in the case of asbestos exposure as far back as the *Asbestos Industry Regulations 1931*. Since the period between exposure to asbestos and development of asbestosis or mesothelioma may be 20-30 years, then there is every likelihood that earlier legislation will apply and need to be pleaded. In the case of asbestos claims, there have been various incarnations of Act passed to control asbestos, the most recent being the *Control of Asbestos at Work Regulations* in 2012. Prior to that Act, previous statutes were passed in 1998, 1997, 1969 and 1931.

Extracts from some of these regulations appear in the toolkit in Chapter 10.

A brief resumé of some of the six pack regulations are set out here:

2.4.11 MHSWR

The Regulations are accompanied by a guide found on the HSE website, 'Managing for Health and Safety'. The advice may be useful as evidence of good employer practice and whether a risk should have been known and what steps should have been taken to reduce it (per *Franklin*). Even before the ERRA, Reg 22(1) states that 'breach of a duty imposed by these Regulations shall not confer a right of action in any civil proceedings'. Therefore one cannot infer from a cause of action predating 1993 that strict liability automatically applies because it doesn't under MHSWR.

The main part of the Regulations is the need for an <u>employer to carry out a suitable and sufficient risk assessment</u> to the health and safety of employees whilst at work (reg 3). There should be consultation with employees. A useful area for disclosure may be minutes of meetings between employee reps and management to ascertain what recommendations may have been made and what action was taken in response. An employer may have taken advice from outside consultants about particular risks.

Reg 4 states that where an employer implements any preventative and protective measures, then the 'principles of prevention' in art 6(2) of the Directive apply. These concern themselves with avoiding risks, evaluating them, instructing employees appropriately and developing a prevention policy covering organisation of work, working conditions and use of technology. Significantly there is a duty to warn and tailor advice to individual employees based on their level of understanding, knowledge and experience. So a 'one size fits all' training system may not be sufficient for all employees across the board.

2.4.11 WHSWR

These regulations concern themselves with the structure and layout of a building and provision of services. So they cover sufficiency of lighting, layout of traffic routes, seating and rest facilities by way of examples. Claims for tripping or slipping on floors because of the presence of debris or liquid, or an obstruction or injuries caused by a fork lift truck where there was an inadequate pedestrian route would come within this Act.

The Regulations impose a duty on employers but also on those in control of a workplace not only to employees but also to visitors or self-employed workers.

Reg 5 requires the workplace to be maintained in an efficient state, in efficient working order and in good repair.

Reg 12 covers floor and traffic routes. This covers pedestrian or vehicular routes, including stairs, ladders, doorways and loading bays. There must be no unevenness or slipperiness. *Reg 12(3)* uses the phrase '*reasonably practicable*' such that floors are kept free of obstructions, articles and substances likely to cause someone to slip, trip or fall.

Reg13 concerns prevention of falls. There must be 'suitable and effective' measures so far as 'reasonably practicable' to guard against falling a distance or being struck by a falling object.

Reg 17 deals with the layout of traffic routes. Pedestrians and vehicles must circulate safely, so ensuring a clear demarcation between them.

2.4.12 PUWER

These Regulations govern machinery and equipment at work so that it is safe and well maintained. It includes appliances, tools or installation or almost any equipment for use at work. The Regulations are supplemented by Guidance and Approved Code of Practice (ACOP) found on www.hse.gov.uk . ACOP's are not law but under section 16 of the *Health and Safety at Work Act* they have a special status so have evidential value, if not imposing strict liability. The introduction to the PUWER ACOP states:

'Following the guidance is not compulsory and you are free to take other action. But if you do follow the guidance you will normally be doing enough to comply with the law. Health and safety inspectors seek to secure compliance with the law and may refer to this guidance as illustrating good practice'.

PUWER applies not only to employers but also the self-employed and those 'in control to any extent' of non-domestic work premises and to factory occupiers.

In some respects there is overlap with the *Employers' Liability (Defective Equipment) Act 1969 (ELA)* in that both include the requirement to provide safe equipment in the course of an employer's business. Significantly the 1969 Act imposes *strict liability* for a defect attributable to the fault of a third party to negligence of the employer.

It therefore appears that the higher standard on the employer is imposed by the ELA rather than PUWER. But with the ELA it is necessary to prove *fault*. 'Fault' is defined in section 1(3) of the Act as meaning *'negligence , breach of statutory duty or other act or omission which gives rise to liability in tort in England and Wales or which is wrongful and gives rise to liability in damages in Scotland'.*

A situation might present where equipment fails but where the employer has a good system of maintenance which reasonably could not have detected the problem. Therefore the defendant could avoid liability at common law and if no third party can be pursued then the claim would fail under that Act. In that instance, a claim under PUWER would have succeeded.

So claimants will need to give careful consideration as to whether both PUWER and ELA are pleaded, as well as negligence. The temptation is to include all of them.

Reg 4 requires the work equipment is so constructed or adapted so as to be suitable for the purpose for which it is used or provided. 'Suitable' means that it is reasonably foreseeable that it will affect the health or safety of any person. Reg 4(2) requires risk assessments to be made in selection of work equipment, having regard to the working conditions and risks posed by the premises. Reg 4(3) imposes the obligation that work equipment shall only be used for *suitable operations and under suitable conditions.*

*Reg 5 (*and *Reg 22)* addresses maintenance. Reg 5(1) requires every employer to ensure that work equipment is maintained *in an efficient state, in efficient working order and in good repair.*

Reg 6 requires employers to carry out inspections of machinery in specified circumstances. Reg 6(3) imposes an obligation to keep records.

Reg 8 employees (or others) using work equipment must be given adequate health and safety information, and, where appropriate, written instructions on its use.

Reg 9 requires adequate training for those using work equipment including: methods of use, risks of use, and precautions to be taken.

Reg 11 requires provision of guards or devices to prevent access to danger areas, or to stop moving dangerous parts.

2.4.13 PPE

This is essentially protective clothing or equipment such as safety helmets, gloves, eye protection, high-visibility clothing, safety footwear and safety harnesses. It also includes respiratory protective equipment.

Where an employer is under a specific duty to supply protective equipment under a different regulation such as *COSSH* or the *Noise at Work Regulations 1989* for example, then those Regulations apply and not PPE.

Reg 4 addresses what constitutes *suitable* PPE for the level of risk and for the particular worker involved. 'Suitable' does not mean 'perfect' but equipment must be current in accordance with developments in safety.

Reg 6 requires the employer to make a risk assessment comparing the ideal equipment with the actual equipment. If an inadequate assessment is made, then this may be relied upon in proceedings as evidence of why PPE was not suitable.

Reg 7 imposes on the employer a duty to ensure that PPE is maintained in *efficient working order and good repair*.

Reg 9 concerns the need to provide employees with adequate information, instruction and training on the risks that the PPE is to guard against. Employees must be warned of the risks of injury if they do not use PPE.

2.4.14 MHOR

This is an important regulation as many EL claims involve injuries caused by manual handling. A manual handling operation is defined in Regulation 2 as:

> "'*Manual handling operations' means any transporting or supporting of a load (including the lifting, putting down, pushing, pulling, carrying or moving thereof) by hand or bodily force.*"

A 'load' is referred in the Guidance Notes as a 'discrete moveable object'. It includes any person or animal. Whilst lifting might be the most obvious situation giving rise to a claim, the regulations also cover pushing objects, dropping or throwing them.

The European Directive contains a broader definition of manual handling and does not qualify the duties by reference to *reasonable practicability*. So if the claim is against a State employer, then the claimant may wish to plead the Directive additionally as the defendant cannot then rely upon the defence of *reasonable practicability* - see the pleading extract above.

Reg 4(1) sets out the duties of an employer:

'(a) *so far as is reasonably practicable, avoid the need for his employees to undertake any manual handling operations at work which involve a risk of their being injured'; or*

(b) *where it is not reasonably practicable to avoid the need for his employees to undertake any manual handling operations at work which involve a risk of their being injured -*

(i) Make a suitable and sufficient assessment of all such manual handling operations to be undertaken by them, having regard to the factors which are specified in column 1 of Schedule 1 to these Regulations and considering the questions which are specified in the corresponding entry in column 2 of that Schedule,

(Schedule 1 addresses the nature of the task (e.g. twisting, stooping, reaching upwards, excessive carrying distances, insufficient rest periods etc); the weight of the load and how easy it is to grasp; the working environment (space, condition of floor, lighting etc); capability of person doing the moving; and other factors such as any restrictions on movement or posture by protective clothing, for example).

(ii) take appropriate steps to reduce the risk of injury to those employees arising out of their undertaking any such manual handling operations to the lowest level reasonably practicable, and

(iii) take appropriate steps to provide any of those employees who are undertaking any such manual handling operations with general indications and, where it is reasonably practicable to do so, precise information on –
(aa) the weight of each load, and
(bb) the heaviest side of any load whose centre of gravity is not positioned centrally.

According to the HSE Guidance, the risk assessment should involve consultation with employees and professional advisors if necessary. Employers are entitled to make a realistic assessment and need not look at every possible risk, however unlikely.

A failure of an employer to carry out a risk assessment of itself will not be sufficient to establish liability, unless the failure is of causal significance to the injury. It would certainly assist a claimant in proving negligence as one of the factors to be relied upon in showing an employer's lack of care.

2.4.15 Burden of proof/Evidence

An employee must demonstrate that an employer's standard of care fell below that of a reasonable and prudent employer. There must be evidence of <u>how the accident occurred</u>. This is usually provided by the claimant and any eye-witness. Many larger organisations have CCTV so this is worth checking. A court is entitled to draw inferences of how an accident is likely to have happened if there are sufficient facts or circumstantial evidence.

Evidence is needed to point to the standard of care. This may be based on general and approved practice or contained within regulations. An expert consulting engineer may be required in a case of some complexity requiring an assessment of the facts of the accident and the adequacy of the systems in place. An expert who simply gives an opinion on an interpretation of the applicability of the regulations and any breach will be subject to criticism by a judge. They should not give their opinion on whether the task involved a risk of injury either as these are matters for the court. In a portal claim, the cost of an expert may not necessarily be recoverable or the fees may be disproportionate. If the claim is defended, then it will drop out of the portal and proceedings issued. Thereafter permission of the court should be obtained before obtaining a report, the costs of which may not be recoverable. Where proportionality is a significant issue, the court may order a single joint expert.

Previous 2013 cases have placed significant reliance on risk assessments, e g *Sherlock v Chester City Council* [2014] EWCA Civ 210 where the Court of Appeal heard experts for both parties stating that a risk assessment should have been carried out, even if it did not need to be as formal as that envisaged by reg 3 of the *Management of Health and Safety at Work Regulations 1999*.

2.4.16 Pre-action disclosure is important and should include some or all of the following:

- Manual handling policy documents
- Risk assessments
- Risk assessment reviews
- Training records
- Safety committee minutes and records
- Accident report
- Health and Safety Executive reports and documents
- Occupational medical records
- HR records

Many of the six pack regulations refer to '**reasonable practicability**' which a defendant will rely upon by requiring the claimant to prove negligence. The claimant must then show that the steps required by the regulation resulted in injury. So for example under the MHR, regulation 4(1)(b) stipulates that each employer shall -

(a) so far as is reasonably practicable, avoid the need for his employees to undertake any manual handling operations at work which involve a risk of their being injured.

The statute goes on to say that where it is not reasonably practicable to avoid the need for employees to undertake manual handling operations at work that involves a risk of injury, then the employer must make a suitable and sufficient assessment; reduce the risk of injury to the lowest level reasonable practicable; and give employees general or precise indications (where reasonably practicable) of the weight of a load.

The claimant will wish to rely on these recommendations but will need to show what measures could have been taken that were 'reasonably practicable'. It will be dangerous simply to allow a court to make inferences so expert evidence is much more likely now than before ERRA.

If a defendant pleads that the measures taken were 'reasonably practicable' then they must set out the particulars upon which they intend to rely (*Larner v British Steel plc* [1993] ICR 551). A failure to set out sufficient detail may persuade a claimant to apply for Further information under **Part 18**.

2.4.17 Reversal of burden

In establishing the burden of proof for breach of statutory duty, the courts will take a similar approach to the test for common law duty. This is likely to entail shifting burdens of proof. Take the slipping case of *Ward v Tesco Stores Ltd* [1976] 1 WLR 810 (CA). The claimant was a customer and slipped on some yogurt on the supermarket floor that had not been immediately cleaned up. Normally such an accident should not happen which required some explanation from the defendant. Certainly the claimant could not prove definitely who caused the spillage or how long it had been present. At first instance and in the Court of Appeal, it was held that the defendant bore the burden of showing that even if there was a proper system of inspection and cleaning the claimant would still have slipped. The defendant's traditional argument on causation was that it was for the claimant to establish for how long the spillage had been present in order to prove breach of duty. This was rejected by Lawton J who stated that if an accident happens because the floors are covered with spillage, then some explanation should be forthcoming from the defendants to show that the accident did not arise from any want of care on their part and in the absence of an explanation, then judgment would be given for the claimant.

Another useful case to know about is *Hall v Holker Estate Co Ltd* [2008] EWCA Civ 1422 where the claimant was injured by collapsing goal posts. At first instance the claimant lost because he could not establish when the defect occurred in the face of the defendant's argument that they had a regular system of inspection. On appeal, it was held that once the claimant has established a prima facie case of lack of care, the evidential burden was then on the defendant to show that the accident would have occurred even if adequate care had been taken.

Both these cases illustrate the shifting burden in occupiers cases (and by extension to workplace claims) for the defendant to prove that they had a system in place to reduce the risk of injury and that it was working well. This emphasises even where the 'reasonable practicability' defence is not mentioned in some of the statutes, that defendants will need to prove that they took all reasonable steps to avoid the accident occurring and of injury being sustained. This is perhaps more pertinent now following the abolition of civil liability after 1 October 2013.

2.5 Public Liability Claims

2.5.1 Claims for injuries against a third party that occur on public land, whether it be at an amusement park, on the highway, in a supermarket or in a rented property are all collectively known as public liability (PL) cases. There are many other types of scenarios but these are probably the most common. Cases relating to incidents on another's land fall within the umbrella of PL cases and are referred to as Occupiers' liability (OL) cases.

This chapter will consider the most common types of claim and the legal tests to establish liability.

As well as the common law of negligence, a working knowledge of the relevant statutes will be needed in order to prove a claim. Most PL cases will fall within the following statutes: the *Occupiers Liability Act 1957/1984;* the *Highways Act 1980;* the *Defective Premises Act 1972;* or the *Landlord and Tenant Act 1985.*

The same principles for proving negligence hold good as in EL claims so this will not be considered further for PL claims.

2.5.2 *OL claims*

A visitor to premises owned or under the control of another – the 'occupier' is entitled to expect that the premises are safe and not dangerous. The occupier has a duty of care towards those who come onto the premises.

An occupier has been defined by Lord Denning in *Wheat v E.Lacon & Co Ltd* [1966] AC 552 (HL) as someone who has an element of control over premises.

A visitor is one who has express permission to enter the premises and acts in accordance with any permission granted. So inviting someone into your house to use the staircase, does not entitle them to slide down the bannisters (*The Calgarth* [1927] P 93 (CA)).

2.5.3 Occupiers' Liability Act 1957

The occupier's obligation for *lawful visitors* is enshrined in the *Occupiers' Liability Act 1957.*

Section 1(1) sets out the duty owed by an occupier to a visitor:

'in respect of dangers due to the state of the premises or to things done or omitted to be done on them.'

Premises include any *'fixed or moveable structure, including any vessel, vehicle or aircraft'* (section 1(3)(a)).

2.5.4 Scope of duty

The scope of the duty imposed on the occupier does not alter the common law position.

Section 2(1) states:

An occupier of premises owes the same duty, the 'common duty of care' to all his visitors, except insofar as he is free to and does extend, restrict, modify or exclude his duty to any visitor or visitors by agreement or otherwise.'

Sections 2(2) defines the common duty of care as one which is *reasonable* in all the circumstances for the purposes for which the visitor is invited or permitted to be there.

The relevant circumstances are set out in section 2(3) and include the degree of care and want of care. So an occupier must recognise that their duty will be circumscribed by the type of visitor. Children will be less careful than adults. Nevertheless, visitors must be expected to take some care for their own safety and guard against any special risks.

2.5.5 Children/vulnerable visitors

The type of visitor is therefore significant and whether they have any special expertise (section 2(3)(b)).

Courts have held that parents have a responsibility for the safety and control of their children provided the risks are known and obvious. So in *Bourne Leisure v Marsdon* [2009] EWCA Civ 671, the Court of Appeal held that there was no breach of duty by the occupiers of a holiday park when a child drowned in a pond as the danger would have been obvious to adults and the child should have been supervised by an adult.

The degree of control exercised by the occupier was examined in *Bailey v Armes* [1999] W.L. 250126. This involved a child who fell from the flat roof of a supermarket where his friend's parents (the defendants) lived in a flat above. The court found as a fact that the child had probably climbed onto the roof from the wall below. The Court of Appeal upheld the finding at first instance that the defendants did not have sufficient control over who used the flat roof to make them occupiers. The occupation of the flat gave no right to occupy the roof of the supermarket. So the defendants did not owe any duty under the 1957 Act, nor under the 1984 Act which concerns trespassers. The 1984 Act gives a lesser duty to trespassers under section 1(3) – see below. In any event the court found that the claimant could not be regarded as a visitor as there was no indication that he had been on the roof before, or that the defendants were aware that he had been on the roof, so there was no acquiescence or permission for being on the roof.

The position of vulnerable adult visitors is less clear than with children when establishing a duty of care. It depends on the extent of the vulnerability. So where a blind guest at the defendant's home fell out of a bedroom window, not knowing that it was open or even its location, the court imposed a liability. The reason being that the defendant knew that the claimant was blind and that the window was open so a greater standard of care applies than to an able bodied person (see *Pollock v Cahill & Anor* [2015] EWHC 2260 (QB)).

2.5.6 Skilled visitors

Occupiers still owe a duty to skilled visitors but this may be limited by the nature of the expertise and awareness of the risk of the visitor.

Occupancy and activity

The extent of duty must relate to '*occupancy*' duties, which are covered by the Act, whilst '*activity duties*' are not covered (see *Fairchild v Glenhaven Funeral Services Ltd* [2002] 1 WLR 1052). This means that the extent of the duty owed relates to the premises and not things done on them. LJ Brooke stated:

> "...the phrase 'care.....to see that the visitor will be reasonably safe in using the premises for the [invited or permitted] purposes' is a fairly strong indication that Parliament intended the Act to be concerned with what used to be described as 'occupancy liability'".

Consider the case of *Geary v JD Weatherspoon Plc* [2011] EWHC 1506. The claimant had been drinking in a pub owned by the defendant and decided to slide down a sweeping bannister. In so doing she fell backwards landing on the floor and was rendered tetraplegic. Post accident, the defendant carried out alterations by winding a thick rope over the tops of the banisters to prevent someone sliding down them. This was therefore a foreseeable risk of injury and foreseen by the defendant. Claims were brought alleging breach of the Occupiers' Liability Acts 1957 and 1984. There were two issues before the court:

(1) Whether there was a voluntary assumption of an obvious and inherent risk by the claimant to negate liability of the defendant;

(2) Was there an assumption of responsibility by the defendant to the claimant.

Both sections 2(5) of the Occupiers' Liability Act 1957 and section 1(6) of the Occupiers' Liability Act 1984 stipulate that no duty is owed by an occupier to a visitor or trespasser in respect of risks '*willingly accepted as his*'. This is the same as the common law – *volenti fit injuria*. The court found there was some pre-planning by the claimant and that she was the author of her own misfortune for which the defendant owed no duty to protect from such an obvious and inherent risk. Furthermore, there was *no assumption of responsibility* by the defendant. It was the activity of sliding and not the banister itself that was unsafe. The fact that there was a foreseeable risk of injury did not of itself create a duty of care.

There is a clear distinction between occupancy and activity or as Brooke LJ said in *Tomlinson v Congleton* BC [2004] 1 AC 46 '*things done or omitted to be done means activities or the lack of precautions which cause risk, like allowing speedboats among swimmers*'. So a claimant injured whilst performing activity does not come within the duty of the 1957 Act whilst a person injured whilst using an unsafe system of work is caught by the Act.

However, where the unsafe activity is carried out on the occupier's premises by a third party and causes damage to the claimant then this is an '*occupancy*' type of liability which is actionable (*Lear v Hickstead Ltd* [2016] EWHC 528 (QB).

2.5.7 Warning signs

Section 2(4)(a) of the Act provides that where the visitor has been warned by the occupier, the warning is not to be treated without more as absolving the occupier from liability, unless in all the circumstances it was enough to enable the visitor to be reasonably safe.

- Danger

There are various factors that will be considered, such as whether the danger was obvious. A hidden danger requires the occupier to make a greater effort to warn the visitor.

That there is no duty to warn of obvious dangers is illustrated in *Edwards v London Borough of Sutton* [2016] EWCA Civ 1005 where the claimant whilst pushing a bicycle over an ornamental footbridge, inexplicably lost his balance and fell over the side of the bridge into the water below. The Court of Appeal held that the first instance judge had erred in failing to recognise that under the 1957 Act it was necessary to identify the relevant danger before considering whether the occupier is required to do something about it. Whilst the bridge had a low parapet wall, there was not a serious risk of an accident occurring as it was remote, with no previous accidents occurring. Secondly, pursuant to *Staples v West Dorset District Council* [1995] 93 LGR 536 (CA), there was no duty to warn of obvious risks. The court held that a risk assessment would have made no difference.

- Other safety measures

These may constitute fences or barriers, for example, but the type of visitor must be considered and their vulnerabilities. In the case of *English Heritage v Taylor* [2016] EWCA Civ 448 the claimant was visiting a castle and following the designated walk but there was an informal pathway to the side of which there was a slope leading to a dry moat. The claimant fell landing in the moat. It was argued that nobody would have been aware of the sheer drop. He was successful at first instance with a finding of 50% contributory negligence. At appeal, the issues were causation and signage. Would a sign have altered the claimant's behaviour. In considering section 2, regard was had to how obvious the danger was, whether aesthetic views were relevant, steps needed to take reasonable measures to reduce or eliminate danger. The Court of Appeal dismissed the defendant's appeal, holding that the 12 foot drop was not an obvious danger and there should have been signage.

2.5.8 Independent contractors

A person is entitled to delegate work to another and not be liable if that other person is negligent. The position of occupiers delegating work /duty is limited under the Act.

Section 2(4)(b) addresses the liability of occupiers for independent contractors:

> '*Where damage is caused to a visitor by a danger due to the faulty execution of any work of **construction, maintenance or repair** by an independent contractor employed by the occupier, the occupier is not to be treated without more as answerable for the danger if in all the circumstances he had acted reasonably in entrusting the work to an independent contractor and had taken such steps (if any) as he reasonably ought in order to satisfy himself that the contractor was competent and that the work had been properly done.*'

So an occupier will be potentially liable if it was work that he could have carried out himself and failed to ensure that the contractor was competent and that the work done was carried out to an appropriate standard.

In _Bottomley v Todmorden Cricket Club_ [2004] P.I.Q.R P18 the claimant was injured whilst assisting a stunt team (independent contractors) in carrying out a pyrotechnic display at the defendant's premises. The defendant was vicariously liable for the negligence of the stunt team because it had failed to take reasonable care to select a reasonably competent stunt operator, and had failed to take any adequate steps to ascertain whether there was adequate insurance for the display.

2.5.9 Occupiers' Liability Act 1984

This Act extends protection to occupiers who are:

- Trespassers
- Exercising private rights of way lawfully
- Visitors to land covered by section 60 *National Parks and Access to the Countryside Act 1949* and the 'right to roam' legislation.

Most claims will concern themselves with trespassers. They enter land without the owner's express or implied permission.

The scope of protection under the 1984 Act is narrower than the 1957 Act as it only covers liability for injuries and not damage to property.

Section 1(1) in relation to trespassers states:

(a) he is aware of the danger or has reasonable grounds to believe that it exists;

(b) he knows or has reasonable grounds to believe that the other is in the vicinity of the danger concerned or that he may come into the vicinity of the danger…

(c) the risk is one against which, in all the circumstances of the case, he may reasonably be expected to offer the other some protection.

The standard of care is the same as under the 1957 Act, namely

"take such care as is reasonable in all the circumstances of the case…"

The reference to independent contractors is not mentioned in the 1984 Act.

But aside from the fact that one occupier is lawful, (1957 Act) and the other is a trespasser (1984 Act) (bar some limited other occupiers), both impose the same duties with the same standard of care.

2.5.10 Highways Act claims

Commonly these concern 'slips and trips' on pavements, with claimants bringing claims alleging breach of statutory duty and negligence for a failure to maintain them, resulting in a dangerous defect.

The principal statutory duty is the *Highways Act 1980 (as amended)* which provides under **Section 41(1)** that:

The authority who are for the time being the highway authority for a highway maintainable at the public expense are under a duty....to maintain the highway.

However, the absolute duty to maintain pursuant to section 41 was accompanied by a qualified duty under section 41 (1A):

To ensure, so far as is reasonably practicable, that safe passage along a highway is not endangered by snow or ice.

An important case encapsulating the liability position and defence open to the highway authority is that of *Burnside v Emerson* [1968] 1 W.L.R 1490, CA where Lord Denning said that there were three issues:

(a) The claimant must show that the road is in such a condition as to be dangerous for traffic.

(b) The claimant must then prove that the dangerous condition was due to a failure to maintain.

*(c) If there is a failure to maintain, the highway authority is **prima facie** liable for any damage resulting therefrom. It can only escape liability if it proves that it took such care as was reasonable in all the circumstances.*

Clearly this was a case on the road involving traffic but it can equally apply to defects on pavements involving pedestrians.

Who is the highway authority?

For a highway maintainable at public expense, it is usually the County Council or metropolitan district council. In London, borough councils or the Common council of the City of London would be relevant. District councils, parish or community councils may in some cases be responsible if they have undertaken the duty. The Secretary of State for Transport, or in Wales, the Secretary of State for Wales is the responsible authority for trunk roads or any road constructed by them (unless the local highway authority is designated as the highway authority for the road).

If a dangerous defect has been created by an independent contractor, the claim will still be against the highway authority if the work being done was part of the essential works undertaken as part of the statutory duty. If the defect was incidental to the repair or maintenance work, e.g. a tool left by the contractor on the highway caused the claimant to trip, then that contractor will be liable.

2.5.11 Private roads

Roads that are not adopted and therefore not maintained by a highway authority at public expense are referred to as unadopted roads. An individual, developer or management company cannot become liable in the same way as a highway authority, but may be liable through tenure, prescription or by statute. In the first two instances where a person or body (or predecessors in title) has repaired a road for time immemorial then they may be liable. Some consideration must have been given for the repair otherwise an action will fail. It will also not succeed if the road or its usage originated within legal memory.

It could be argued that a private road does not come within the definition of section 329(1) as to whether it constitutes a carriageway highway. The public would not have a right of way for vehicles so if a claimant injured themselves whilst driving a vehicle along such a private road then no cause of action is likely under the Highways Act. If they were injured as a pedestrian then it would need to be determined whether there was a public right of way on foot to classify the road as a non-carriageway highway.

If there is no public right of way by foot or vehicle then the road will not come within the definition of the Highways Act.

The reality is that a claim for damages occurring on a private road is more likely to be pursued alleging a breach of the Occupiers' Liability Act 1957.

2.5.12 Proving a claim

The claimant must prove on the balance of probabilities that the highway where the incident occurred was <u>not reasonably safe</u> and that the accident was caused by the <u>dangerous condition of the highway.</u>

The test is *reasonable foreseeability of danger* so each case turns on its own facts.

Courts should not infer that the defect was dangerous nor impose unreasonably high standards [with respect to the state of repair] where a compromise has to be reached between private and public interest (as per Steyn LJ in <u>Mills v Barnsley Metropolitan Borough Council</u> [1992] PIQR 291. The Court of Appeal found a hole 2 inches wide by 1 ¼ inch deep caused by a missing corner of a brick, was a minor defect). This is especially pertinent where there are increasingly financial constraints placed on local authorities.

If there is a difference in levels, then case law has found that for an actionable defect, it must be at least 1 inch.

The first step is to obtain photographs of the defect and surrounding area. Is the defect obvious from photographs taken from a few metres away. Google maps may be helpful in establishing for how long the defect may have existed and may counter arguments from the council that it was a recent defect or only recently became dangerous.

Pre-action disclosure under the protocol is important, especially to obtain inspection records. Local authorities should try to follow the guidance in 'Well-managed highway infrastructure' published on 28 October 2016. This is not yet mandatory as authorities have until October 2018 to adopt a risk based approach. Until then, they should be adopting the previous code of practice, 'Well-maintained Highways' published first in 2005 and last published on 17th January 2014. This may be accessed on the website of the UK Roads Board at www.ukroadsliaisongroup.org. It should be recognised that the code is not a statutory document but does provide guidance which courts will consider in deciding whether some of the recommendations were implemented by the authority (see for example its reference in *Wilkinson v City of York Council* [2011] EWCA Civ 2017).

The claimant does not need to prove that the authority did not take sufficient care, nor does he have to show that the lack of reasonable care was the cause of the injury. The authority for this is *Griffiths v Liverpool Corporation* [1967] 1 QB where Diplock LJ stated:

> *It was an absolute duty to maintain, not merely a duty to take reasonable care to maintain…*

The claimant must prove that there was a breach of duty to maintain *not* a negligent breach of duty to maintain (see *Wilkinson*, earlier).

2.5.13 Maintenance and repair

Maintenance includes repair (section 329(1) HA) but according to *Haydon v Kent County Council* [1978] QB 343, it involves more than repair to ensure pedestrian and vehicular passage. The Court of Appeal held that it included removing snow and ice but the claimant failed in that case as the authority had acted promptly by sending a workman to grit the area but the claimant fell in the interim.

But the case of *Goodes v East Sussex County Council* [2000] 1 WLR, the House of Lords held that the highway authority's duty to repair does not include the removal of ice. They had an absolute duty under s.41(1) HA to keep the fabric of the highway in a good state of repair so as to render it safe for ordinary traffic at all seasons of the year. The ratio in that case was applied by the court of Appeal in *Valentine v Transport for London* [2010] EWCA Civ 1358 when a motorcyclist skidded on loose gravel. The claim was struck out as the highway authority's duty did not extend to the removal of materials lying on its surface.

The absence of previous accidents does not evidence sufficient maintenance or repair – see *Maguire v Lancashire County Council* 11/11/2004

2.5.14 The section 58 statutory defence

Section 58(1) of the *Highways Act 1980* states:

In an action against a highway authority in respect of damage resulting from their failure to maintain a highway maintainable at the public expense it is a defence (without prejudice to any other defence or the application of the law relating to contributory negligence) to prove that the authority had taken such care as in all the circumstances was reasonably required to secure that the part of the highway to which the action relates was not dangerous for traffic.

The claimant must firstly establish that the highway was not reasonably safe and that this caused his injuries before the defendant need rely upon section 58. The burden of proof then shifts to the defendant to prove their reliance on section 58. The highway authority must demonstrate that they operated a *suitable system of inspection* and that they responded to complaints about the state of the highway in a timely manner.

The court must have regard to the criteria set out in **section 58(2)**:

(a) The character of the highway and the traffic which was reasonably to be expected to use it.

(b) The standard of maintenance appropriate for a highway of that character and used by such traffic.

(c) The state of repair in which a reasonable person would have expected to find the highway.

(d) Whether the highway authority knew, or could reasonably have been expected to know, that the condition of the part of the highway to which the action relates was likely to cause danger to users of the highway.

(e) Where the highway authority could not reasonably have been expected to repair that part of the highway before the cause of action arose, what warning notices of its condition had been displayed.

The final part deals with independent contractors:

(f) ... for the purposes of (the statutory) defence it is not relevant to prove that the highway authority had arranged for a competent person to carry out or supervise the maintenance of the part of the highway to which the action relates unless it is also proved that the authority had given him proper instructions with regard to the maintenance of the highway and that he had carried out the instructions.

In examining the maintenance regime, how regular should it be for a defendant to avail itself of s.58(2)(b). In *Wilkinson,* referred to above, it was submitted by the claimant and accepted by the first instance judge and the Court of Appeal that an inspection regime every 3 months, and not the defendant's actual inspection every 12 months was appropriate. The three-monthly inspection was that recommended by the National Code. The defendant placed great emphasis on financial constraints and this found favour with the circuit judge at the first appeal. However, the Court of Appeal held that manpower resources do not feature as part of a section 58 defence. Toulson LJ said:

S. 41

The obligation to maintain highways in a structural condition which makes them free from foreseeable danger to traffic using the road in the ordinary way is an unqualified obligation of highway authorities of long standing. If Parliament had wanted to weaken that fundamental obligation, now contained in s 41, it would have done so.

In relation to section 58, he continued:

S.58

Section 58 was designed simply to afford a defence to a claim for damages brought against a highway authority which was able to demonstrate that it had done all that was reasonably necessary to make the road safe for users, not an authority which decided that it was preferable to allocate its resources in other directions because other needs were more pressing than doing what was reasonably required to make the roads safe.

As mentioned above with respect to the case of *Griffiths,* it is not for the claimant to establish a lack of reasonable care on the part of the highway authority. Rather, the highway authority may plead that it has taken reasonable care as a defence and the burden is on them to prove that.

2.6 The EL/PL Protocol

2.6.1 The pre-action protocol for low value EL and PL covers claims for damages arising out of an accident or disease. It applies to claims up to a value of **£25,000** where the accident occurred on or after 31 July 2013 or to a disease where no letter of claim was sent before that date. If the claim is settled in the portal, then fixed costs are payable.

2.6.2 Exceptions where the portal does not apply

Section 4.3 sets out the cases that do not come within the protocol. The main exceptions are:

- C or D is the personal representative for an estate.
- C or D is a protected party.
- D is an individual in a PL claim. If sued in their business capacity or as an office holder then the protocol applies.

- More than 1 defendant in a disease claim.
- A claim for harm, abuse or neglect of or by children or vulnerable adults.
- A claim for mesothelioma

The 3 stages follow the same procedure as in the RTA protocol but the time limits are more generous, as are the costs.

2.6.3 Stage 1 – submission of claim

The Claim Notification Form (CNF) is sent to the defendant's insurer with the defendant only CNF sent to the defendant.

If the insurer is not known in an EL case, the claimant must carry out a database search of the Employers' Liability Tracing Office.

WARNING!

If the claimant fails to provide mandatory information in the CNF and the defendant considers that it is inadequate, the claim will then exit the portal. If the claimant starts **Part 7** proceedings then there is a risk that the court may find that the claimant acted unreasonably by discontinuing the process and allow only recovery of fixed costs (**Part 45.24**).

To ensure that there is no risk of inadequate particulars, the claimant should ensure detailed accident circumstances are set out in the CNF.

2.6.4 D reply to CNF

The defendant acknowledges receipt electronically the day after receipt and sends the CNF response to the claimant within **30 days** in an **EL** claim and **40 days** in a **PL** claim.

Exit points from Portal

The claim exits the portal where:

- D alleges contributory negligence
- D does not send the CNF response
- D denies liability
- Notifies C that inadequate mandatory information in CNF
- Suitable for small claims track

2.6.5 Stage 2 – submission of settlement pack

• A Stage 2 settlement pack is submitted with a medical report and any other expert evidence. A consulting engineer's report or from an ergonomist may be required to prove the claim. The same documentary evidence applies as with the RTA protocol, so evidence of disbursements and any witness statements are uploaded.

• The defendant should then pay Stage 1 fixed costs within 10 days after receiving the settlement pack. If D fails to do so, then under **section 6.17** the claimant may give written notice within **10 days** of expiry of the period for making payment, i.e. within 20 days from submitting the pack, that the claim will exit the portal. If the claimant does not give notice then it continues under the protocol.

• The defendant has **15 days** (the 'initial consideration period') to consider the Settlement pack containing the claimant's offer and either accept or make a counter offer. The remaining **20 days** is to allow the parties to negotiate should this may be necessary. The total consideration period of 35 days may be extended by the parties.

• If the parties fail to reach an agreement on the damages to be paid, then the claimant must send to the defendant the *Court Proceedings Pack* (Part A and Part B). These forms contain in Part A the final schedule of the claimant's losses and the defendant's responses, whilst Part B contains the final offer and counter offer.

2.6.6 Further exit points

This is considered in more detail in chapter 6 on tactics. However, one of the most likely reasons for exit from the portal is where the defendant fails to respond within the initial consideration period. It will also exit where the claimant give written notice in a situation where the defendant does not agree/pay Stage 1 and 2 costs and disbursements.

If the claimant needs to obtain expert engineering evidence and considers on receipt that the claim is too complex to proceed under the protocol and is more appropriately a multi-track claim then under **section 7.59** the claimant may give notice to the defendant and the claim will then exit the process. However, if the court considers that the claimant acted unreasonably in giving such notice, then the claimant will only receive fixed costs in **rule 45.18.**

2.6.7 Costs

The court has discretion to award costs exceeding fixed recoverable costs in 'exceptional circumstances'. This would generally apply in a complex claim involving non-medical expert evidence with complex points of law, or a multi-party claim or where there are disputed allegations of fraud. Under **rule 45.13** the court may summarily assess costs or order detailed assessment. It does not follow that simply because the claimant makes the application that she will be successful in which case only the usual fixed costs would be recoverable.

2.6.8 Stage 3 – issuing a Part 8 claim

This is set out in **PD 8B** and applies equally to RTA's and EL/PL claims where damages will need to be assessed by the court. This occurs when the stage 2 settlement pack is not agreed or where the court must approve a settlement for a child or protected party.

The court makes an assessment based on the contents of the Court Proceedings Pack. No new evidence may be contained in the Pack.

The procedure is a modified Part 8 procedure in which the claimant drafts a claim form N208 stating:

- that the protocol has been followed
- the date that the Court Proceedings Pack was sent to the defendant
- whether the claimant wants the claim determined on the papers or at a Stage 3 hearing
- the value of the claim

If the litigation friend acts for a **child** then the settlement hearing must be heard at court. The child may need to attend dependent on age and state of recovery. In addition to the Court proceedings Pack and accompanying documents, the following enclosures must be filed at court and served on the defendant:

- draft consent order
- counsel's opinion (or from a solicitor/legal representative)
- witness statement from litigation friend advising on the child's condition and prognosis from the perspective of recovery.

2.6.9 Defendant's acknowledgment of service

The defendant must file its acknowledgment of service in Form N210B within **14 days** after service of the claim form, stating whether the amount of damages are contested, whether they object to an order for damages being made, or object to use of the Stage 3 procedure. The final ground for objection is the court's jurisdiction which might apply if the limitation period had expired or the case was one that should in their view be classified as a small claim.

The defendant may rely on a witness statement adducing evidence of the claimant's non-compliance with the protocol.

Should the defendant not be able to file a witness statement within 14 days, then an application to the court should be made seeking an extension or by reaching agreement with the claimant. If the deadline is missed the court may proceed without the defendant's evidence. Relief from sanction is not guaranteed.

The claimant has the right of reply by filing evidence within **14 days.**

If the defendant opposes the claim because the claimant has not followed the procedure in the protocol or filed new evidence with the claim form that had not been provided previously then the court will dismiss the claim under **section 9.1**. There may be costs consequences under **rule 45.24** as the claimant may only recover fixed costs if they are found not to have complied with the protocol.

Following a dismissal of Part 8 proceedings, the claimant may elect to start **Part** 7 proceedings. He will have no choice unless he decides to accept the defendant's previous offer or can persuade them to increase despite exiting from the portal.

2.7 Quantum

2.7.1 This is such an expansive topic that it is not possible, nor is it the intention to cover the entire law on recoverability of damages.

In assessing the value of a claim, principles on assessment have been gleaned from cases such as *Roberts v Johnstone* [1989] QB 878 (how to value a claim for cost of alterations); *Hunt v Severs* [1994] 2 AC 350 (entitlement to recover damages for gratuitous care); *Wells v Wells* [1999] 1 AC 345 (use of multipliers for calculation of future loss); and *Smith v Manchester Corporation* (1974) 17 KIR 1 ('Smith v Manchester' award for handicap on the labour market) to name just some seminal cases.

Statute that is relevant to quantum is likely to be confined to consideration of the *Damages Act 1996* (regarding periodical payments and the discount rate applied to a multiplier for future losses. The discount rate is currently -0.75%); *The Law Reform (Miscellaneous Provisions) Act 1934* (damages recoverable on behalf of the deceased's estate including general and special damages and funeral expenses); and the *Fatal Acci-*

dents Act 1976 (an award for bereavement damages, currently £12,890 and a dependency claim for financial losses suffered by dependents).

2.7.2 The intention of the courts is to recompense the injured party or the estate of the deceased, for actual and anticipated losses incurred exclusively as a result of injuries sustained ('**special damages**'), and to award compensation, for the pain, suffering and loss of amenity ('PSLA'), as well as handicap on the labour market, loss of enjoyment & leisure time and loss of congenial employment ('**general damages**') sustained through injury. '

The objective is to return the claimant to the same financial position had s/he not been injured, otherwise known as the 'full compensation principle'. The payment of damages may be via a lump sum or in cases of high value (exceeding at least £100,000), periodical payments (PP's) may be considered.

2.7.3 *Valuation of general damages*

The starting point should be the *'Judicial College Guidelines for the assessment of general damages in personal injury cases'* ('JC guidelines'). This sets out an informal tariff prepared by a working party of judges using settlements awarded in previous cases. Every case is different of course and everyone's experience and reaction to injury varies, so the guidelines are just that and not intended to fetter the discretion of a judge, or practitioners for that matter.

In addition, lawyers will have access to *'Kemp & Kemp'* and other databases of previous decided cases when trying to draw parallels with the injuries sustained by the claimant. Insurance companies representing defendants may use their own computer software programmes to produce valuations, although these records would not be disclosable and a court would not place any reliance on such material. However, for the most part the parties will refer to the JC guidelines whilst cross-referencing with the medical reports obtained on the claimant.

For low value soft tissue injury claims, also known as 'whiplash' claims, it is anticipated that a tariff for fixed damages will be introduced by the

Ministry of Justice. It is proposed that the tariff will apply to cases where the claimant makes a full recovery from injuries within a period of up to 24 months. Dependent on how the scheme works, there may still be debate on the valuation of the claim and the interpretation of medical evidence as to whether there are ongoing symptoms.

Clinical negligence cases are especially difficult to value because often the claimant will have some underlying illness or disease. Therefore the assessment may need to focus on the exacerbation of injury. It will be based on the claimant's condition had they received non-negligent care and treatment.

Where the claim is brought on behalf of the estate, PSLA is recoverable for the period that the deceased suffered as a consequence of negligence. It may be only hours or a few days but it's still compensatable. If death is instantaneous or minutes following the negligent act then PSLA is unlikely to be recovered for that head of claim (*Hicks v Chief Constable of South Yorkshire* [1992] 1 All ER 690).

Elements of general damages:

- PSLA
- Loss of congenial employment (*Hearnshaw v English Steel Corporation Ltd* (1971) 11 K.I.R. 306 (CA).
- Handicap on the open labour market, e.g. loss of mobility (*Smith v Manchester*).
- Loss of amenity – effect on lifestyle, e.g. inability to pursue leisure pursuit, loss of driving ability, spoilt holiday, effect on sexual relations etc.

Virtually all claims require an assessment of both general and special damages. Frequently the area of contention is the calculation of special damages in a schedule of loss as that represents the significant value of the claim. Specials are composed of past losses already incurred and anticipated future losses.

2.7.4 Heads of loss of special damages

Heads of loss for special damages may include some of the following:

- net loss of earnings
- loss of pension
- car hire
- care and assistance (professional or gratuitous)
- costs of child care
- costs of medical treatment or therapy
- aids and appliances
- alternative or replacement accommodation
- travel expenses
- costs of medication

There are two elements in drafting a schedule of loss – knowing what to claim and how to prove it.

2.7.4.1 *loss of earnings*

If acting for a claimant, it is worthwhile suggesting that they keep a diary of expenditure and a folder of receipts. This will assist in formulating past losses. One of the largest elements of specials will be loss of earnings, so pay slips for an employed person will be required. Firstly, an average weekly income is calculated based on income earned pre-injury. This is used to ascertain what income should have been earned during the period whilst absent from work. The difference between the amount of projected earnings and that received whilst incapacitated represents the loss. It may be that the claimant returns to employment on a phased basis so suffers an ongoing partial loss. Also consider loss of overtime or bonuses that may be lost because of unavailability or because of incapacity to work longer hours post injury. Perhaps a promotion has been lost or deferred in which case allowance will need to be made for that dependent on whether it was speculative or certain. It may form part of a future loss of earnings claim or loss of a career opportunity. If the prospects are small then the court may apply a percentage to a lump sum representing the lost opportunity (*Miles v Steele* 3 March 1989, QBD).

Loss of earnings is calculated on a net basis as that is the loss to the claimant. Clearly for those who are employed, that presents no difficulty because the pay slips state the amount received by the claimant net of income tax and national insurance. Pay slips are usually requested for a period of 13 weeks pre-injury to establish an average weekly wage. If pay slips are not available then request a P60 End of Year certificate or draft an authority for the claimant to sign, consenting to disclosure from their employer.

Unless the claimant receives their full pay whilst off sick, they will receive statutory sick pay (SSP) as an employee for up to 28 weeks. Credit will need to be given for receipt set against the full loss of earnings.

In the case of someone who has been absent from work for a long period of time or has lost their job because of incapacity, then it will be necessary to obtain the wage details of a comparable employee or comparator. Preferably they will have been on a similar income to the claimant at the time of injury and their career was at a similar level. A comparator's wage details will be anonymised so it may be difficult to establish a true reflection. If the legitimacy of the comparator is questioned, then a statement may be required from the payroll department of the employer confirming the comparator's length of service, seniority etc.

Ascertaining the lost income of a self-employed claimant is more difficult as business records or accounts will need to be obtained. Tax paid to HMRC is recorded in SA302 tax certificates and may be obtained from the Gov.uk website. In cases where lost profit is claimed, an expert report from a forensic accountant may be necessary. In determining the loss, a claimant may have decided to employ a locum to carry out his duties, in which case he may elect to claim for the salary and any lost profits. He could argue that he attempted to mitigate his losses by such actions.

The loss of earnings is calculated for the duration of the loss or where such is ongoing up to the date of trial. Losses beyond the actual or notional date of trial then become future losses.

If the period of loss extends beyond the date that an employer gives pay rises, then the schedule should reflect losses from the date of first loss, usually the date of the injury, up to the annual pay review date. The next year's losses may then incorporate the weekly salary with the percentage pay rise factored in.

Where pay rises are too uncertain, the alternative is to apply an increase using the Retail Price Index as the factor.

2.7.4.2 *Future loss of earnings*

A claim for future losses will be made where incapacity is ongoing that impinges on the claimant earning a salary in the future, and in serious injury claims, perhaps up to the date of retirement. If it is such that the claimant's working life is likely to be reduced because of the negligence or perhaps is not expected to live up to retirement age, this does not affect the claim for loss of future earnings up to the date of retirement. Thus the claimant is entitled to claim for those lost years. This is on the supposition that pre-accident, the claimant would have been expected to work up to normal retirement age. If there were reasons why working life was likely to be curtailed not related to the negligence, then whatever the anticipated working life would be represents the cut-off date for calculating loss of earnings.

There are two payment methods for future losses, either by way of a **lump sum** or **periodical payments**. The lump sum is payable immediately on settlement of the case for the claimant to use as they wish.

Periodical payments are indicated in high value claims where the claimant's prognosis is uncertain or where there is a risk of deterioration in the future. The *Damages Act* 1996 came into force on 1 April 2005 and enables a court to order payments of future losses by instalments. These are generally now via periodical payments which are assessed on the claimant's annual needs.

The first step in calculating future losses is to establish the annual net salary, otherwise called the '<u>multiplicand</u>' which was payable before the injury occurred. A <u>multiplier</u> is then applied to the capital sum (or multiplicand) for the number of years representing future losses. The multiplier is not actually the number of lost years because that would over compensate the claimant as they could invest the capital sum which they would otherwise not have. Also it ignores the impact of inflation which would increase future costs and therefore eat away at the lump sum.

So, in <u>Wells v Wells</u> a discount was introduced to reflect immediate payment of money now. This is known as the 'discount rate' and is currently set at −0.75% since 27th March 2017 based on the average yield of Index-linked Government stock, reflecting the rate of inflation. The theory is that claimants could invest a lump sum in this stock to increase their return. Whilst traditionally (when the discount rate was 2.5% before 27th March 2017), a defendant might prefer to settle a claim on a lump sum basis with a high discount rate, now that it is low, the impact may be that defendants will look to offer PP's. PP's have been the preferred option for settlements provided by the NHS. Conversely, claimants may prefer to receive their settlement as a lump sum. Obviously each case is fact specific so generalisations are not always helpful.

In high value cases in times of economic uncertainty, a claimant would be best advised to take advice from a financial advisor prior to deciding the most appropriate form of settlement. It may be that a defendant will be reluctant to offer a decent lump sum and other than going to trial, a PP might be a better option for an out of court settlement.

Multipliers are obtained from using the **Ogden tables** which use figures produced by the Government Actuary's department. They reflect contingencies such as gender, whether employed or not, whether disabled or not, educational attainment and mortality. They are used not just for calculating future loss of earnings but other future loss heads of damage such as care and in dependency claims arising from a fatality. The supplementary tables to the 7th edition are set out on the gov.uk website reflecting the change in the discount rate to -0.75%.

There are 28 tables in total so for example if one were wishing to calculate loss of earnings on the multiplier/multiplicand basis for a male to pension age 65, then table 9 needs to be consulted. Applying the discount rate for a claim for loss of earnings from the date of trial at age 50 gives a multiplier of 15.29. A result that may seem surprising as there is no discount, until one considers that the investment opportunities are limited and the award in real terms will reduce with the cost of living. Contrast that with the multiplier when the rate was until recently 2.5% giving a multiplier of 12.11.

2.7.4.2 *Pension loss*

Calculations of lost pension entitlements are complex and are outside the scope of this text. However, it is crucial to obtain details of the pension scheme from the employer. Calculating losses incurred in a final salary pension will be more complex than defined benefit schemes. They will also comprise larger sums so it may justify instructing an actuary to make the calculation. If the pension loss is expected to be relatively modest, the cost of obtaining an actuarial report may not be proportionate.

2.7.4.3 *Gratuitous care*

This is a head of loss that frequently is not appreciated by claimants as an entitlement to claim. If, as is usually the case, the care and assistance has been provided by a family member gratuitously, some claimants are reluctant to claim as no payment was made to the carer. But they may claim for services provided such as domestic assistance and care according to the authority of *Donnelly v Joyce* [1974] QB 454. The issue was revisited by the House of Lords in *Hunt v Severs* [1994] 2 AC 350 which affirmed the earlier decision but stated that damages were to be held on trust for the voluntary carer. Where the carer was the tortfeasor, then no such claim was recoverable in negligence. It is suggested that where the tortfeasor is a close relative who intends to provide care and assistance, that a contract is entered into so that there is a contractual obligation to provide that care. Then the damages for that element of care should be recoverable.

Damages should be assessed for all the extra work going over and above the relative's usual domestic duties. If care is provided by a partner and they usually split domestic chores equally, then the claim is for the extra services over and above their half share.

A legitimate head of claim is also for loss of housekeeping ability which may be distinct from the care claim.

2.7.4.4 Professional care

If a domiciliary carer has been engaged then the costs should be recoverable. A care expert is indicated in substantial cases where future care is anticipated. The extent of care will be quantified by estimating the number of hours involved and applying the commercial hourly rate.

There has been debate on the issue of recoverability of residential care on a private basis or whether local authority provision is sufficient. Various challenges have been made by defendants to the provisions in section 2(4) of the *Law Reform (Personal Injury) Act 1948* which entitles a claimant to decline care provided by the NHS. It was examined in the case of *Sowden v Lodge* [2005] 1 WLR 2129 where the court held that whilst it was for the claimant to assert his or her reasonable needs, it is for the defendant to assert that local authority residential care meets the claimant's reasonable needs. *Crofton v NHSLA* [2007] EWCA Civ 71 concerned direct payments from the council to the claimant towards his care costs and whether personal injury damages should be reduced to reflect those payments. The Court of Appeal held that the claimant was entitled to withdraw her application for funding through council care and rely exclusively on private funding for her care.

The final case is that of *Peters v East Midlands SHA and Nottingham City Council* [2009] EWCA Civ 145 which also examined the recoverability of damages for private care as opposed to local authority funding and care. The Court of Appeal held that a claimant was entitled to recover damages for private care rather than rely on care and accommodation at public expense. So where a defendant seeks a care and welfare assessment for a child pursuant to section 47 *Children Act 1989* and arguing that credit be given for local authority funding, the claimant is entitled to oppose that argument by seeking damages from the defendant for private funding. Regard must be had to avoiding double recovery as a court will want to be satisfied that the claimant will not recover care costs from the defendant and also claim public funding of care as well.

2.7.4.5 *Medical treatment*

It is not obligatory to receive remedial treatment from the NHS. Under section 2(4) of the *Law Reform (Personal Injury) Act 1948*, a claimant may recover the costs of private medical treatment, even if available on the NHS. So, if for example, a scar revision is necessary, then a report from a Plastic surgeon should be obtained identifying the costs for performing the operation privately, including the costs of inpatient care. All items for rehabilitation should be considered and guidance will be obtained in expert reports as to what future treatment is necessary or beneficial. Consider which therapists are needed – speech therapist, occupational therapist, physiotherapy, hydrotherapist etc.

2.7.4.6 *Costs of accommodation*

In the case of a catastrophically injured claimant, adaptations may be required to their existing property. If unsuitable and an alternative property is needed, the additional costs should be claimed. The full capital cost is not recoverable but the costs associated with the loss of use of capital tied up in the property, such as lost income and investment may be claimed. This was the ratio in the decision of *Roberts v Johnstone* where damages reflecting the increased annual expense incurred in meeting accommodation needs were awarded at a rate of 2.5% based on borrowing costs. In that case the claimant had purchased the property out of capital from an interim payment. Her loss was the loss of investment return/income that otherwise would have been earned on the capital. The claimant could not recover the full value of the property as that would result in a windfall to the claimant or her estate.

Roberts v Johnstone was revisited in *JR v Sheffield Teaching Hospitals NHS Foundation Trust* [2017] EWHC 1245 (QB). The claimant needed alternative accommodation but the judge awarded nothing for this element of the claim, finding that there was no loss. He applied the discount rate of -0.75%. The rate using the multiplier produced a capital sum exceeding 100%. At the time of *Roberts* the discount rate was 2.5% so there was a shortfall in the capital.

In *JR* no alternative evidence was put forward to argue that the loss would reflect the current cost of borrowing such as in an interest only mortgage. That might still lead to a finding of no loss but expert financial advice would be required. Could an argument be advanced that a rate of 2% (or an actual or notional cost of borrowing) should be applied similar to that awarded on PSLA. Applying the discount rate is artificial in the current economic climate. There can be no doubt that the loss of use of capital does represent a positive rather than a nil loss.

The changes to the discount rate (which may change again in the foreseeable future) have brought about considerable disquiet to claimant's legal advisors as to how a fair remedy may apply in the situation when replacement accommodation is necessary. Options are an interest free loan or the defendant having a reversionary interest in the property.

Perhaps that hackneyed expression of 'swings and roundabouts' applies. The discount rate of -0.75% substantially increases other awards for future losses, so in the round the loss of accommodation head of loss may be tolerable provided an alternative structure is found for costing replacement accommodation. This is a complex area and requires expert advice.

2.7.4.7 *Costs of equipment*

This may include a specially adapted wheel chair, bath/shower, stair lift and furniture. Perhaps a garage needs to be converted into a downstairs bedroom. These are unlikely to be one off items as over the course of the claimant's life, replacements will be required due to wear and tear.

Evidence will be necessary from a care expert or occupational therapist.

2.7.4.8 *Costs of a case manager*

The costs of a case manager are recoverable. They are particularly important where the claimant's substantial injuries are such that many different medical and allied health disciplines are involved. The case manager may be jointly instructed by both parties or individually. Their role is draw up a plan to evaluate the services required for the claimant to meet his/her health and wellbeing. This may often address education, social and occupational needs. Often the case manager will have close contact with he claimant or their litigation friend and report to the instructing parties.

2.7.4.9 *Miscellaneous expenses*

These may include travel expenses, the costs of employing a gardener or a handyman, reliance on a family member for shopping assistance or driving the claimant to medical appointments or other engagements. As a result of remaining at home whilst incapacitated and being generally unwell, heating costs will be increased.

---

* Copyright The Royal College of Surgeons of England. Reproduced with permission.

Key points

- Clinical negligence – know the Bolam and Bolitho tests on breach of duty and the distinction with the Penney pure diagnosis tests. Consider Montgomery consent issues on a failure to advise on risks and alternative treatments. Cases turn on expert evidence so selection of expert is crucial.

- Personal injury claims – reliance on proving negligence, instead of breach of statutory duty, especially six pack and other regs, e.g. COSHH and WHR (save for some statutes which retain strict liability). Still plead relevant regs to set the standard of a reasonable employer. Courts may be willing to view breach of health and safety regs as prima facie evidence of negligence.

- Consider where no fault liability still exists. Certain old statutes still retain strict/absolute liability. Is the employer a public body, then plead breach of EU Directives which may be more extensive.

- Claimants should seek earlier and more detailed disclosure of H&S documentation, risk assessments etc. Greater reliance on expert evidence as to best practice.

- Look out for problems in proving medical causation – multiple causes of damage; 'lost chance' of recovery/avoiding injury; multiple consecutive causes of damage.

- In portal cases, vigilance is needed to ensure compliance with the process, and especially on whether Part 7 proceedings are justified – to avoid the possibility of non-recovery of costs or even adverse costs orders.

- Draft an early schedule of loss to focus on quantum and client's needs; will help with identifying quantum evidence. Revisions will need to be made as further expert evidence is obtained.

CHAPTER THREE
EVIDENCE

Rules of evidence

Governed by **CPR Parts 32, 33 & 35** and the **Civil Evidence Act 1995**

In this Chapter, witness statements of fact and expert witnesses are considered as well as the rules of evidence, before mentioning the importance of a conference with counsel to review the evidence.

3.1 Lay witness statements

3.1.1 Oral evidence is heard at the trial. Witness statements are taken as read and so most evidence is heard in response to cross-examination of the witness.

Evidence at an interim hearing is by way of witness statements.

The witness statement is therefore a crucial piece of evidence. It will be a factual statement given by a claimant or defendant supported by other witnesses who have something relevant to say concerning the cause of action forming the subject matter of the claim.

As well as factual witnesses, there will be at least one expert witness testifying to the nature of the claimant's injuries, any relevant history, their current condition and prognosis. In a catastrophic claim, as well as medical experts, there will be quantum experts dealing with care and perhaps an architect to address accommodation. A clinical case manager, whilst not classified as an expert performs a vital role in ascertaining the particular care package required for the claimant and is therefore instructive in determining the likely experts that will be required.

3.1.2 Requirements for a good witness statement

Must be truthful, reliable and cogent.

It must be relevant and admissible if the court is to receive it or place any weight on it.

Admissibility is usually a question of law and is unlikely to be a problem in an injury claim unless it has not been served in accordance with directions or where permission has not been granted or where it is hearsay evidence where the requisite notice has not been filed and served. These problems are addressed in relief from sanctions in chapter 6.

Evidence is either oral evidence of the witness statement- this is likely to be taken as read, or exceptionally a hearsay statement or documentary evidence where the contents of a document are admitted. In the latter situation, this might be medical records or a photograph or video recording. A person's demeanor or credibility affects their witness evidence but it also allows the judge to form an overall impression and to draw inferences. It will be expected that demeanor will play a small part as a nervous witness may not give of their best but this should not be held against them.

Part 32.2 Any fact to be proved at trial is by oral evidence given in public, or at any other hearing by evidence in writing.

The court may limit the number of lay or expert witnesses or the issues contained within the statements. The overriding objective will be in the court's mind to conduct cases justly and at proportionate expense. The court is unlikely to review the contents of a statement unless the party seeks to call many witnesses. At a Case Management Conference, the court may decide to limit the number of witnesses and therefore question the relevance of a witness' evidence.

The court 's permission to rely upon expert evidence in a particular specialism is required. Permission to call the witnesses to give oral evidence is likely to be deferred beyond the Case Management Conference but if necessary, then application must be made in good time and before the listing questionnaire is sent out.

3.1.3 Burden and Standard of proof

3.1.3.1 The legal burden

The claimant has the onus of proving negligence or breach of statutory duty on the balance of probabilities - or more likely than not. The obligation on a party to prove (or sometimes to disprove) a fact in issue is known as the legal burden of proof.

At the heart of this is persuading the court.

Have you discharged the burden of proof? Avoid the trap of adducing evidence that refers to 'possibility' or speculation. It must be probable not possible.

With expert witnesses, this can be difficult to determine. Often the court will express their judgment in terms of preferring the evidence of one expert to the other but must analyse the evidence. In simple terms, is one expert more experienced in the procedure than the other or more measured or does he rely upon peer-reviewed literature supportive of the procedure.

This leads on to the weight and cogency of the evidence. It is not always easy to determine whether a piece of evidence is persuasive at the time of obtaining it, although it may turn out to be significant at trial. A good guide is whether the judge is asking questions about a particular issue. It may be because it supports the claim or weakens it. It needs to be addressed in your closing argument if not covered in the skeleton argument.

In exceptional cases, a judge may find it difficult to make a finding one way or another on a disputed issue of fact, and therefore may decide the issue on the legal burden.

The leading authority on how the court will apply the legal burden of proof is the case of *Stephens v Cannon* [2005] EWCA Civ 222. The court underlined that it would be an exceptional situation to rely upon the burden of proof when it has striven to make a finding in relation to a disputed issue and can understand the reasons why it has concluded that it cannot do so. The parties must be able to discern the court's 'endeavour' and to understand its reasons in order to be able to perceive why they have won and lost (see para 46).

This case was also cited in *Verlander v Devon Waste Management* [2007] EWCA Civ 835 in which the court expanded on the exceptional occasions when the burden of proof would be applied. Only where the available evidence conflicted and/or was uncertain and/or falling short of proof would the court conclude that the claimant had not proved his case.

A more recent case in which an issue of fact was resolved by applying the burden of proof approach was the clinical negligence case of *Barnett v Medway NHS Foundation Trust* [2017] EWCA Civ 235. The claimant relied upon the evidence of a microbiologist to establish causation that blood cultures would have revealed an infection or that further antibiotics and monitoring would have prevented paraplegia following on from a spinal abscess. At first instance, the judge concluded that there was no evidential basis to the required standard and the claimant lost. On appeal, the claimant's microbiologist stated that there was a 59-80% of detecting infection from blood cultures, with the defendant's expert demurring. The claimant relied upon *Stephens* and *Barnett*. The Court of Appeal concluded that whilst the trial judge was too brief in his reasons, he was justified in looking at the evidence as a whole and holding that it fell short of establishing probability. They therefore dismissed the appeal.

3.1.3.2 The evidential burden

This requires sufficient evidence of a fact to go before the court. The burden is discharged when there is sufficient evidence to justify as a possibility of a favourable finding by the judge. In civil claims, where a statement contains relevant evidence, then it will be admissible before the judge. It does not mean that where a judge does not accept the witness' evidence that the witness has failed to satisfy the evidential burden.

The most likely scenario in a trial when the evidential burden arises will be the operation of a rebuttable presumption. So where one party adduces sufficient evidence of the primary facts, the opponent has the evidential burden to adduce some evidence in rebuttal of the presumed fact. If they fail to do so, there is every possibility that the court will accept the evidence of the party adducing the evidence as they will have satisfied the evidential presumption.

An example of a rebuttable presumption is the presumption of res ipsa loquitur ('it speaks for itself'). Where an accident occurs which was unexpected had proper care been taken, and it was established that the defendant was responsible, then it must be presumed that in the absence of sufficient evidence to the contrary, that the accident was caused by the negligence of the defendant. This may be viewed as an evidential presumption but has also been described as a presumption of fact, so that proof of the basic facts gives rise to an inference of negligence, which in the absence of evidence to the contrary may (but need not) be drawn.

In a clinical negligence claim where the neurosurgeon accidently dropped a retractor onto the spinal cord causing injury, this raises a prima facie case, and the evidential burden (though not the legal burden) shifts to the defence (see *Harris v Johnston* [2016] EWHC 3193 (QB).

3.1.4 Capacity

It is important to determine whether a person has capacity to conduct litigation, otherwise another person – a litigation friend (usually a parent or close relative) will need to do so. This has implications as to who will prepare a witness statement on behalf of the claimant or defendant if they lack capacity.

A child, being under 18 will lack capacity whilst someone suffering from a mental disorder, a learning disability or from brain damage may lack capacity as defined in the *Mental Capacity Act 2005 (MCA).*

Section 2(1):

A person lacks capacity in relation to a matter if at the material time he is unable to make a decision for himself in relation to the matter because of an impairment of, or a disturbance in the functioning of, the mind or brain.

This is a two-stage test, because firstly it must be established that there is an impairment or disturbance in the functioning of the person's mind or brain (the diagnostic test), and secondly that the person as a result is unable to make the decision required.

Section 3(1) provides that a person is unable to make a decision if unable to:

- Understand the information relevant to the decision;

- Retain that information;

- Use and weigh that information as part of the process of making the decision; or

- Communicate his decision (whether by talking, using sign language or any other means).

Expert medical evidence will be required, usually from a psychiatrist if it is suspected that an adult lacks capacity. If that person is the claimant (perhaps suffering from a severe head injury), then this may already have been explored at an earlier stage, possibly shortly after receiving instructions from a close relative.

But capacity can fluctuate and so it should not be assumed that if a person is competent at the beginning of the claim that they will remain so throughout.

Once it has been determined that the claimant or defendant is a protected party (or is a child), then it must be determined whether they are competent to give a statement. Of course it may not be desirable for them to do so for any number of reasons, such as because they are scared or because the litigation friend is opposed or on the advice of their legal representative.

A child may give evidence under **Section 96 Children Act 1989** provided he understands that he must speak the truth and has sufficient understanding. There is no fixed age at which a child should be treated as competent and below which he should not be examined in court. In *R v Hayes* [1977] 1 WLR 234, which remains good law, competence of children was examined. The youngest age was said to be between 8 to 10. Much will depend on the maturity of the particular child.

Those adults who lack capacity are unlikely to give a statement. But in the case of *R v Hayes* in deciding whether someone was competent to give the oath, the proposed witness must have a sufficient appreciation of the seriousness of the occasion and the added responsibility to tell the truth on giving an oath, over and above the normal social responsibility.

So being a child or protected party does not prevent them from giving a statement and it being admissible - perhaps setting out their recall of the incident that befell them or how the injuries have had an impact on their life. Small details can be more telling, and for a child, giving examples will be easier.

3.1.5 Contents of the statement

3.1.5.1 Before starting on the contents, ensure that the layout of the statement complies with the Practice Direction and is clear to the reader, especially the judge.

PD 32 sets out how evidence is to be given and facts are to be proved. Statements, as affidavits have required for some time, require in short form the following details in the top right hand corner on the first page:

Claimant/Defendant
Witness name
Number of statement
Exhibits (number)
Date

The heading contains details of the court, case number and names of the parties (and litigation friend as appropriate). Initially the proceedings will have been commenced in the County Court Money Claims Centre. Subsequent statements will refer to the court to which the case is transferred, e.g. the County Court at Darlington.

The statement should be in numbered paragraphs, preferably with double line spacing on single pages of A4. At the end of the statement it must be verified with a statement of truth signed by the witness. All exhibits should remain separate from the statement and also contain a statement of truth.

Clearly the statement will be written in the first person and in the style of the witness telling a story, albeit succinct and to the point. The opening paragraph should state the witness' full name, their home address (or if made in a business capacity, the address at which they work, their position and name of employer). They should state their occupation or if none, their description and also confirm whether they are the claimant or defendant and that the statement is given for the purposes of litigation. The statement must indicate whether a particular fact stated is within their own knowledge or based on their belief and from where they have learned that information.

3.1.5.2 A draft statement should have been taken close to the first interview. The heading may state something like 'In the proposed action'. The statement will be refined as further information comes to light and the case develops. It is helpful to obtain a timeline at the outset. Some lawyers send out a questionnaire at the outset for completion but others will prefer to get the initial details by seeing the client during the first interview.

At the heart of the statement is to address the issues that the judge will require answering. Effectively the witness is telling the judge a story of facts based on their own recollection and knowledge of past events.

Use headings to define the issues, thus background; a chronology of the hospital appointments and the treatment received; what went wrong; and remedial treatment. If they are aware of the other side's response, then the witness, so far as they are able to respond, should address the allegations. If they are not helpful to the case, then they should be omitted from the statement and covered in a note not to be disclosed to the other side. Such a record would be beneficial later in the case such as at a conference with counsel (if so instructed). Details of losses should be proved so if there is a claim for care provided by family and friends then this should be confirmed with details of the assistance given and why it was necessary. If there is a loss of earnings claim, then details about the claimant's employment history may be relevant, particularly if there is an anticipated claim for future loss of earnings. The claimant will need to establish that they had secure employment that would have continued into the near future. If that is likely to be speculative because of redundancies being made, then it will inform you as to alternative claims that could be made such as a Blamire award dealing with such exigencies on a 'broad brush' lump sum basis.

3.1.5.3 Be aware of the legal test to establish liability. Whilst the claimant's witness statement obviously does not address the law, always bear in mind what facts need to be elicited and proven. Those facts must be relevant to the issues that must be determined. The statement should be drafted by the lawyer who is preparing the case, or an assistant involved in it. A draft statement prepared by the client will be helpful but inevitably will require some amendments. Invariably witnesses will include material that may seem important to them – and often go into much detail - but does not take the case any further. Only include information that the court needs to know about and no more.

3.1.5.4 The danger of failing to review the statement (consider running it past counsel) is that it will be taken as read at trial and additions or revisions to the statement will be rarely allowed. A court is unlikely to give leave to the advocate to adduce new evidence not contained within the statement. At best, with permission of the court, a witness giving oral evidence may amplify his statement and give evidence in relation to new matters which have arisen since the statement was served (see **rule 32.5(3)**). This should not be considered a licence to omit important facts from a statement and hope to rely on the court's indulgence. Any party seeking to adduce new evidence may be faced with an adverse costs order or perhaps wasted costs if an adjournment were necessary (and is unlikely given the overriding objective).

The court has the discretion to exclude irrelevant evidence under **rule 32.1(2)** and to exclude the number of witnesses to be called, and any evidence thought to be superfluous. So, the numbers game of seeking to call as many witnesses as possible to bolster the claim or defence will be challenged by the court at the case management conference. It is crucial to ensure that you call the most important witnesses who can give the most compelling evidence.

3.1.5.5 Probably two statements will be needed from the claimant, firstly addressing liability and secondly on quantum - when further evidence is obtained from experts that will help to refine the schedule of loss.

In considering the liability aspect, for example in a work place accident, you will be considering the system of work, the sufficiency of training, previous similar mishaps or 'near-misses' and compliance with the six-pack regulations. In a clinical negligence claim, it is necessary to prove breach of duty, causation and loss. The first two elements are often bundled up as liability but need to be considered separately, even with respect to the claimant's statement. Causation is often the troublesome area for claimant lawyers. But during the initial proof of the witness, it is unlikely that you will have expert reports on liability. So in broad terms the claimant can identify where the damage occurred and the injuries or outcome flowing from that damage, rather than some pre-existing cause.

3.1.5.6 The claimant should set out the injuries they have sustained, their symptoms and physical problems; fatigue and insomnia; how they struggle with daily activities and the reliance on family and friends. It is important to address if they were keen on sports and hobbies and how the injuries have curtailed that. Often claimants keep a diary and this may be a useful source of information.

Cover the basics first. So establish the type of injury sustained. How was this caused. If by medical negligence, what treatment or procedure resulted in the injury. Is it a product liability claim caused by a drug, hip implant or some other medical device. It is important to establish who is the likely tortfeasor as the client may not appreciate the distinction between different potential defendants and how the claim will need to be proved. Set out a detailed history of what happened, including any relevant history. It is helpful if the statement follows a chronological format with the symptoms suffered and the medical attendances.

3.1.5.7 Wherever possible the client should recall the advice given during each relevant consultation and the diagnosis made. What treatment was received and what was the response to that treatment. Often the witness cannot recall specific consultations where there have been many visits. This is why a detailed review of the medical records is necessary. Questions can be put to the client and their answers may provide a structure for the contents of the statement. Sometimes the claimant has a relevant medical history which they have not disclosed but could have an impact on the viability of the case.

Dates of treatment may be incorrectly stated or there could be confusion about the actual treatment received. The claimant may be correct and there could be errors in the records. If there was a suggestion of missing records or alterations to the records (this should be written up in retrospect), then the original records may need to be inspected. This should be forthcoming otherwise an application may be necessary.

3.1.5.8 Having read the records, the complexion of the case may change, for example if there is no injury (beyond which the claimant had already complained of before treatment). Is there a need to review the limitation period, perhaps relating to the date of knowledge. If there is a discrepancy between the client's account and in the clinical notes, the client's statement may need re-drafting.

Are there incomplete records, such as a missing internal investigation report. The duty of candour and transparency would require the report to be disclosed to the claimant but perhaps there was an oversight. If in doubt seek a statement from the trust's clinical director confirming all the records have been disclosed and exhibiting an index of those documents that were disclosed.

3.1.5.9 Brain injuries require especial attention from the relatively minor disability resulting in lack of concentration, memory and short temper to those injuries affecting speech and communication.

Physical & psychological problems may include:

- Hemiplegia
- Swallowing/eating disorders
- Gait/mobility
- Epilepsy
- Tremors/numbness/proprioception
- Dizziness/hearing/balance
- Cognitive issues – information processing, verbal or visual memory, attention span, decision making, ability to manage everyday issues, lack of insight, depression, anxiety, irritability.
- Problems at work – time off, loss of earnings, disciplinary issues
- Family relationship difficulties/breakdown
- Educational set backs – relationship with peers and teachers. Any unauthorised time off from school. Low attainment.

In a serious injury claim, be guided by the contents of the medical reports. It is unlikely that the claimant will have sufficient insight into all their problems or may not even recognize the extent of them.

3.2 Experts

Part 35

3.2.1 Getting the right expert evidence on breach of duty and causation is absolutely critical to the success (or defeat) of a clinical negligence claim, depending on your perspective. In personal injury cases expert evidence is particularly important in industrial disease and product liability claims when it comes to considerations of material contribution causation.

The most significant cases on establishing liability are set out in the toolkit in Chapter 10. A brief resume is included here for consideration of the legal tests when instructing an expert in a clinical negligence claim.

There are two requirements to be determined by the claimant in establishing **breach of duty**. Firstly, to ascertain the appropriate standard of care, and secondly that the conduct fell below that standard.

Once breach of duty has been proven, the claimant must prove that the conduct complained of caused harm or loss. This is known as **causation**.

It is important to know the principles underlying the tests because the instructions to the expert should ideally contain a synopsis of the legal principles. Knowing the relevant case law will also help you identify how the case may be proved (or disproved). For example, many cases may focus on the treatment decisions but others may focus exclusively on diagnosis. The tests are different.

3.2.2 Court's permission for expert evidence

Permission will only be given for experts which are 'reasonably required' to resolve matters [**Rule 35.1**].

Experts are there to assist the court [Rule **35.3**] and not act as a hired gun. However the experience of many practitioners is that claimants and defendants do rely upon experts whom they have instructed previously and found them sympathetic to their client's cause.

3.2.3 Selecting the expert

The objective is to instruct an expert who commands the respect of the court and has the required expertise and experience. And is objective. He must be fair and balanced and be able to understand and respond to the other side's expert opinion. He must therefore accept that there may be other views but can argue convincingly why his view should be preferred.

So how do you vet your expert? Examining their CV is the starting point. It may detail their research interests and any published articles. Are they still practising as a clinician or recently retired? This may be important in a clinical negligence case to ensure that they are up to date with current developments. It is less important in a personal injury case.

Are they experienced in the procedure performed? Do they appreciate that there may be different approaches to performing the procedure and may be Bolam reasonable. If the case concerns management of labour and the report is to address breach of duty, does the Obstetrician understand what is required of him. Undoubtedly the expert will have undertaken medico-legal reports before but it should not be assumed that he will understand the legal issues that need addressing. This must be distinguished from the expert going beyond his expertise and believing that he has to prove the case. That is the role of the lawyer.

There is a tendency for some experts to provide reports exclusively for claimants or defendants. We all know when a named expert crops up that a firm predominantly instructs in the belief that he will be sympathetic. That is a dangerous practice for he may be cross examined on the extent of his medico-legal practice as in the case of *John v Central Manchester Trust* (2016) EWHC 407 (QB).

What you need are the reasons given for the opinion that is held and why the reasons set out in the opponent's report is fallacious or should bot be accepted, such as because it is not current medical practice. If the reasons stand up, the opinion does, if not, not (taken from the dicta of Justice Jacob in *Routestone v Minories Finance* [1997] BCC 180).

Reports should concentrate on analysis and opinion rather than the history and factual narrative.

It will be difficult to interview your prospective expert with a view to assessing how she will perform in court. An expert may be prepared to share their initial thoughts after receiving a letter of enquiry from you. If you don't like their response, then don't instruct them. Even if you think you have identified a 'strong' expert, could he be too dogmatic, maintaining his opinion until the joint experts' meeting and then condescending to the opposing expert's views – or worse still – 'turning turtle' in the witness box. This may be avoided if your expert is objective. The expert who disregards the other's viewpoint is probably one to avoid as they may be perceived as arrogant and closed in their views. He is unlikely to command the court's respect. One caveat is the expert who is an acknowledged authority by his peers and perhaps derives his overconfidence from that position bestowed on him by his colleagues.

However, beware the biased expert who steadfastly holds an opinion to support a party's case but lacks balance and refuses (or cannot see) the opposing view. This does no service to the relying party or to the court.

Or as Justice Evans said about the defendant's expert in *Williams v Jervis*,

> "...*he approached the case with a set view of the claimant and looked at the claimant and her claimed symptomology through the prism of his own disbelief. ...he unfortunately lost the focus of an expert witness and sought to argue a case.*"

The net result was that the judge placed no reliance on that expert. Equally an expert who makes a bad point undermines his credibility when he makes potentially better points.

In seeking out a 'good' expert, one who practises in the specialism for which s/he is instructed, understands his/her role as an expert under

Part 35 and undertakes medico-legal work for both sides is a good starting point. But it's worth checking with counsel or bodies such as APIL or AvMA who maintain a list of experts who have been 'tried and tested' by claimant lawyers. For those on the defendant side, the same criteria apply, although approaches to bodies such as FOIL will be appropriate.

Care should be taken in instructing an expert who has retired or who concentrates on medico-legal practice to the exclusion of clinical practice. This was exemplified in the case of *Melhuish v Mid-Glamorgan Health Authority* [1999] MLC 00145 where the court preferred the evidence from the defendants' experts. That may have arisen from the lack of knowledge about a seminal work by one of the claimant's experts, but it may also have been because of the perception that they lacked independence as deriving their income from medico-legal practice.

What an expert needs to demonstrate if they are to persuade the court are qualities demonstrated in *Morwenna Ganz v Dr Amanda Jillian Childs, Dr John Lloyd, Kingston Hospital NHS Trust* [2011] EWHC 13 (QB) when the judge said of the claimant's expert: '*I thought she was authoritative when she felt she could be, cautious when she felt she had to be and entirely thoughtful and well-balanced in her approach...I detected no basis for thinking that she was partisan or that she was attaching herself to some document or piece of information because it suited her case*'.

The expert must know and comply with the Civil Justice Council's 'Guidance for the instruction of experts in civil claims'. This sets out best practice for complying with **Part 35** and court orders.

Consideration must be given to the possibility that the court might be minded to order a single joint expert in a claim that is relatively straightforward (if such a case exists) (**Part 35.7(1)**).

3.3 Hearsay evidence

Civil Evidence Act 1995

3.3.1 It is easier to say what it is not, namely it is the absence of the maker of the statement giving oral evidence at trial.

It is either a disclosed witness statement upon which reliance is placed, without calling the maker to court for cross-examination;

Or it is the repetition by a witness of what a third party has previously said in order to prove a fact is true (by that third party). So it relates to facts not within the witnesses own knowledge.

Equally it applies to the witness previously having made a self-serving statement.

The point is that the evidence will not be admissible unless there is compliance with **section 1 CEA. PD 33.2**:

Inform the other parties that the witness is not being called to give oral evidence, and give the reason why the witness will not be called

The Act enables you to:

1. Ask a witness to tell the court what somebody else has told him about the facts.

2. To put in front of the court the statement of the matters in dispute.

Such evidence is admissible so as to prove the facts contained within the statement.

By **Section 2(1)** of the Act:

In any civil proceedings, a statement made, whether orally or in a document or otherwise, by any person, whether called as a witness in those proceedings or not, shall, subject to this section and to rules of court, be admissible as evidence of any fact stated therein of which direct oral evidence by him would be admissible.

3.3.2 Giving notice of proposed hearsay evidence

The procedure is to serve a hearsay or civil evidence Act notice.

The hearsay notice must be served on the opponent no later than the date for serving witness statements (or the expert report). This is not always feasible, for example where the witness has become too ill to attend trial. An application to the court will be necessary in those circumstances seeking permission to rely upon the hearsay evidence.

The contents of a hearsay notice under section 2 CEA requires details of the circumstances in which the hearsay statement is made and that the maker cannot be called to give oral evidence:

> (a) the time, place and circumstances at or in which the statement was made;
> (b) the person by whom, and the person to whom, the statement was made;
> (c) the substance of the statement or, if material, the words used; and
>
> 1. that the maker is dead.
> 2. that he is beyond the seas.
> 3. That he is unfit by reason of his bodily or mental condition to attend as a witness.
> 4. That despite the exercise of reasonable diligence it has not been possible to identify or find him.
> 5. That he cannot be expected to have any recollection of the matters relevant to the accuracy or otherwise of the statement to which the notice relates.

An example of a hearsay notice appears at chapter 11.

Evidence which is not contained or exhibited to a witness statement - such as documents, plans, photographs or models – require service of a hearsay notice under **Part 33.6**. Notice is to be given no later than the latest date for serving witness statements.

A later time period of at least 21 days before the hearing applies where there are no witness statements or the document etc is used to disprove an allegation made in a witness statement. This time limit also applies where the evidence that is relied upon is for any reason that is not factual or expert evidence.

WARNING!

If there is a failure to serve a civil evidence Act notice relating to documents, then unless the court orders otherwise, the evidence shall not be received in evidence (Part 33.6(3)).

3.3.3 Admissible hearsay records

Certain documents do not require a notice under 33.6 where they form part of a record compiled by a person acting under a duty from information supplied by a person having personal knowledge of the information supplied.

Under **Section 4(1) CEA** the record must be in documentary form and must constitute a 'record'.

Therefore medical records or an employer's risk assessments or training records or Inquest statements or reports would be admissible by virtue of **section 4(1)**. However, whilst the records are admissible evidence of the facts contained in them, they may not be admissible evidence of any opinion stated in them.

So in the case of medical records, where a clinician has expressed an opinion of the likely diagnosis, reliance on that opinion would be unwise although it would be perfectly proper for your own expert to comment on another medical opinion.

Hearsay notices are not necessary for interim hearings.

3.3.4 Serving a counter notice

The opponent who wishes to attack the credibility of the hearsay evidence must serve a counter notice within 14 days of receipt of the hearsay notice.

If the opponent wishes to cross-examine the witness in which a hearsay notice has been served, then they may apply to the court under 33.4 permitting them to call the maker of the statement. Unless they attend voluntarily, resort to a witness summons will be necessary.

3.3.5 Failure to comply with notice requirements

If there is a failure to serve a hearsay notice, it does not render the evidence inadmissible under the Act as the court has discretion under sections 2 or 4 of the CEA to allow a hearsay statement to be admitted. However, it is a breach of the rule. If the opponent objects to the admissibility of the evidence, then the court has wide powers under case management and by application of sanctions and wide powers to manage evidence under **rule 32.1**.

The failure to give notice goes to costs and weight.

In particular the court may have regard to **Part 32.19** where a document has been disclosed under standard disclosure. The recipient is deemed to admit the authenticity of a document unless he serves notice that he wishes the document to be proved at trial.

So if the document goes unchallenged as to its authenticity, the court may admit the document as hearsay.

But if a hearsay notice has not been given and the opponent takes issue with it, the best course of action is to apply to the court for permission to admit it and to seek relief from sanction if necessary. This is best dealt with in an interim application rather than trial.

The weight of a hearsay statement

As the witness is not available to be cross examined on their statement, the weight that the court attaches to it is likely to be significantly less than if the maker was called to give oral evidence.

Section 6(3) sets out the rules to be applied as to the weight to be attached. The court must have regard to all the circumstances in which the statement was made, such as whether it was made contemporaneously with the facts stated or after a long period of time had elapsed or whether there was any motivation to misrepresent the facts.

- Was it reasonable and practicable to produce the maker of the statement?
- Did the maker have a motive to conceal or misrepresent?
- Was the statement made in collaboration with another person?

3.4 Conference with counsel

3.4.1 In low value claims, it will be difficult to recover counsel's fees or if they are recoverable, will enable the defendant to argue that delegation renders a lower hourly rate and grade of fee earner.

Ideally counsel should be instructed early on but this may be tempered by the wish for review of D's witness statements to avoid unnecessary and irrecoverable costs. Clearly in a claim of maximum severity where consideration of a voluminous bundle of medical records may be required, before instruction of a medical expert then an early conference and thus instructions is desirable.

3.4.2 What to include:

- A sorted and paginated set of medical records
- CTG traces in a birth injury claim
- Initial witness statement
- Initial medical report (on breach of duty in clinical negligence)

Counsel will need to have a brief synopsis of the case, the factual or medical issues, the progress in the claim, i.e. whether the letter of claim or pre-action letter has been sent and any response, including whether there has been any admission or partial admission or the basis of the denial. The issues that you consider are relevant should be detailed and counsel asked what he is instructed to do, whether it be to advise on the expert evidence or on merit generally. If a conference is to be arranged then counsel will wish to await the conference.

If the conference is about a clinical negligence claim, then it will concentrate on the expert medical evidence opinion. It would be ideal if the expert(s) is available preferably in person or video conferencing or at the end of the telephone. The purpose is to clarify and test the evidence. Has the expert appended peer reviewed scientific or medical literature to support his proposition? Is the opinion over-cautious? Has the expert understood Bolam and Bolitho? Are there factual errors in the report?

Where there is room for doubt, has the expert expressed alternative views. Experts who are very sure of themselves and leave no room for alternative scenarios are often not the best experts. Those who consider competing explanations but are able either to distinguish their opinion from those of the opponent or able to advise on the balance of probability why their view should be preferred are often more effective experts than those who are not driven to reflect on the opposing view. This is the opportunity to explore any weaknesses in the case and the experts!

What should be done if one of the experts is not on side by which we mean unsupportive of an element in the case. If this goes to the crux of breach of duty or causation, then consideration will need to be given to obtaining a second expert opinion, assuming that there has been no disclosure of the report. Clearly there are cost implications that the client will need to understand and approve of instructing a new expert. In all likelihood they will have to bear the cost of the unsupportive expert.

Depending on the stage of the conference, there may be many experts advising on liability. For example in a cerebral case, you may have expert: Neonatician, Obstetrician & Gynaecologist, Midwife and engineer in CTG tracings present. Is their evidence consistent and supportive of the others? Do they understand the legal principles? This should have been set out in the instruction letter. It is the opportunity to have a mock trial to determine how the experts would come across at trial. Are they familiar with the medical records and are those records complete. Are there any missing traces and if so, why?

Once the particulars of claim have been drafted, consider asking the expert to review. This is particularly pertinent in a complex medical claim where timings of treatment are crucial.

3.4.3 The client's role

Ideally the conference should be divided into segments dealing with proving the claim involving mostly the experts in clinical negligence and then in answering the client's concerns and going through their witness statement. Does the client understand the expert reports and the issues relevant to proving negligence. There are occasions when clients have a very clear view as to what they consider are the errors in treatment that may not touch on breach of duty. They may not appreciate the test for proving negligence so time will need to be spent ensuring that they understand the issues germane to proving the claim.

In a workplace accident, the client's involvement will be centre-stage in explaining their training and the process

The conference with counsel should be treated as a 'dummy run' for the trial. Experts should be challenged and assessed for how they may stand up to cross-examination.

A note of the conference should be taken by those attending and sent to counsel shortly afterwards for checking. It is also helpful to send to the expert to act as a reminder of any issues that arise and correction to their report if necessary.

Following the conference, any revisions to the reports must be undertaken and then sent to Counsel if s/he is to draft the Particulars of Claim.

Key points

- Keep the client's statement succinct. Use headings.

- Do not include opinion evidence.

- Use the witness' own words and terminology.

- Tell the witness' story.

- Do not stray into matters to be addressed by an expert.

- Think about the facts in issue and how the judge will try the case to make findings.

- Try and reach agreement with the other side on hearsay evidence to avoid having to serve a notice.

- Examine an expert's CV carefully. Obtain recommendations from other solicitors or counsel or from AvMA.

- Make a detailed note of the clinical records and send to the proposed expert. You may get an indication from them which may affect your decision to instruct them.

- If the expert's report needs revising, ask them. Perhaps they have misunderstood or not applied the Bolam test. But never ask them to change their opinion.

- Consider whether different experts are required for breach, causation and condition & prognosis (most likely).

- Should Part 35 questions be put to the other side's expert for clarification or is it better to leave to the experts' meeting.

- Arrange a conference between the expert and counsel.

CHAPTER FOUR
CASE AND COSTS MANAGEMENT

CPR Part 3 and Parts 26-29

4.1 The court's case management only takes effect once proceedings have been issued so it is important that the relevant pre-action protocol for personal injury or clinical disputes has been complied with as the court will wish to establish whether there has been compliance, namely in exchange of information and documents relevant to the claim. This is a question asked in the Directions Questionnaire and requires an explanation if there has been non-compliance with the protocol.

The court's wide powers of case management will increasingly be influenced by its desire to ensure that costs are kept under check via costs budgeting and by the exercise of proportionality that will be applied to provisional or detailed costs assessments.

4.2 Costs management will apply to all cases outside the fixed costs regime, except those cases involving children or where the value exceeds £10 million [**CPR 3.12**].

So, many of the orders that the court will make will be viewed through the prism of cost effectiveness.

The overriding objective, **CPR 1.1**:

> *These rules are a new procedural code with the overriding objective of enabling the court to deal with cases justly and at proportionate cost.*

It is worth remembering that when the court issues its case management directions that they must be followed implicitly if sanctions are not to apply.

At **1.1(2)**, dealing with a case justly and at proportionate cost includes the power of the court of:

(f) enforcing compliance with rules, practice directions and orders.

4.3 It will be difficult for a party to argue that the incurrence of significant costs is warranted for a particular step – whether for disclosure, proofing many lay witnesses or for expensive expert reports. Clearly it is necessary to obtain a 'just' result, although the court may say that the overriding objective has never been subject to an overarching consideration of securing justice in an individual case.

The robust approach to rule compliance and proportionality of costs is the new vanguard for furthering the overriding objective.

4.4 The starting point for the court's case management is the Directions Questionnaire (DQ) sent to the parties on receipt of the defence. A court officer will provisionally allocate the claim to the track - almost certainly multi-track and notify the parties in the notice of proposed allocation. Virtually all personal injury and clinical negligence claims will be allocated to the multi-track as those issued as a Part 7 claim will exceed the current threshold of £25,000 below which fixed costs apply for personal injury cases (and may soon do so for clinical negligence claims). The complexity of clinical negligence claims should justify their allocation to the multi-track irrespective of their value.

Part 26.8 sets out the criteria for allocation to a track, namely: (a) the financial value of the claim (b) the nature of the remedy sought (c) the likely complexity of the facts, law or evidence (d) the number of parties (e) the value of any counterclaim or Part 20 claim and its complexity (f) the amount of oral evidence required (g) the importance of the claim to non-parties (h) the views expressed by the parties (i) the circumstances of the parties.

4.5 The Directions Questionnaire (DQ)

This is form N181 for fast track and multi-track claims. This requires the parties to file directions for the management of the proceedings. Preferably they should be agreed but if not, it is likely the court will list for a Case Management conference (CMC). The court may impose costs sanctions if one party refuses to cooperate with the other. This is unlikely to arise given that standard and model directions are the default position — see www.justice.gov.uk/courts/procedure-rules/civil/standard-directions — which provides templates for multi-track cases. These will increasingly be composed online and completed by the District Judge at a case management hearing. Two templates, one for clinical negligence, the other for personal injury appears at Appendix II.

The DQ must be filed with the court within 28 days of being served by the court. Also draft directions must accompany its return together with a costs budget where the claim is less than £50,000.00. Any application, such as for summary judgment should also be filed at this stage.

WARNING!
CPR 26.3
(7A) or (8)

A failure to serve the DQ by the date specified in the notice of proposed allocation is likely to result in an unless order requiring service of the DQ and required documents within a further 7 days. If the defaulting party fails to comply with the notice, then either the claimant's statement of case will be struck out or the defendant's defence will be struck out and judgment entered against them.

WARNING!
CPR 3.7(6)

A court fee is payable by the claimant on filing his DQ (unless an application has already been made for a fees remission).

If not paid, the court will send a warning notice and if payment is not made by the date stated, then the claim will automatically be struck out and the claimant will be liable to pay the defendant's costs.

The DQ requires the following questions to be completed:

Part A

This concerns potential settlement and a request for a one month stay. Given that liability will have been denied, the defendant is unlikely to request a stay as this might indicate that they are receptive to exploring a settlement or of considering Alternative Dispute Resolution. It is suggested that it is always desirable for the claimant to agree to a stay to explore ADR. If the defendant refuses then that is likely to place the defendant on the back foot when costs are determined as the courts do not look kindly on parties refusing ADR – and particularly mediation.

Part B

Concerns venue – High Court or County Court and Hearing Centre. A District Judge will only be receptive to a request for transfer to the High Court/District Registry if the claim has significant value and complexity. They will be mindful of the increased costs incurred in the High Court. Care should obviously be taken in making a request for transfer not to imply that the claim is too complex for a County Court Judge.

If the claim was commenced in the High Court, consideration may be given by a High Court Judge as to whether the case is suitable for being tried by a section 9 Circuit Judge. Complexity (expert evidence), value and costs will be uppermost in Her Ladyship's mind.

Part C

Requires confirmation that you have complied with the pre-action protocol. If you have not, expect a sanction unless there is an exceptional excuse. If the opponent has not complied, such as failing to serve a letter of reply to the letter of claim then mention it.

Part D

There are three questions. Firstly, about case management information and whether any application been made. It invites you to consider whether any issues can be disposed of at this stage and appropriate directions requested. Some issues to consider are set out below. Secondly, about the allocation to track. The vast majority of claims will be multi-track by reason of their value. The third question is about disclosure of documents. Is there likely to be electronic disclosure. If so then PD 31B applies requiring a spreadsheet, identifying the document, the author and the recipient. Non-electronic documents are most likely to be standard disclosure via a list of documents in accordance with **Part 31.6.**

Issues to consider in making an application:

• Limitation

Has limitation been raised by the defendant. Typically this may arise by late issue of the claim form or in an historical abuse or in an industrial injuries' claim or by a failure to pay the actual court fee by undervaluing the claim at issue.

• Split trial

If liability is disputed, is it appropriate in a high value claim to consider a split trial? This is more likely in a serious injury claim with complex quantum calculations that will require expert evidence. It is difficult to know whether a split trial really benefits either the claimant or defendant. From the perspective of funding the claim, it might be said that they favour claimants because the costs of quantum evidence are saved until the outcome of liability and causation are known. If successful, then an early interim payment may be sought and this may help if agreement is reached with the claimant on funding future care and also some disbursements.

It may be argued that defendants are less ready to settle but the claimant may not have all their evidence ready to settle anyway and once liability/causation is determined, then the defendant is far more likely to be receptive to settlement overtures.

Of course, the parties may be more willing to compromise so as to reach an agreement on liability and causation, especially if one of the parties, but more usually the claimant, has put forward a Part 36 offer to settle at a percentage of the total value of the claim. This has some disadvantages, notably the defendant will not know the amount of financial exposure they face, but then one can say if that avoids a split trial, then potentially it can save them substantial costs if they were at a risk of losing.

Ultimately, the desirability of a split trial is likely to come down to the assessment of risk and costs. For claimants, there can be a significant saving if they lose on liability. In all likelihood the claimant is likely to have an after the event insurance policy so the insurers will be keen to ensure that they are not faced with a large bill to cover the claimant's own disbursements. Under one way qualified costs shifting, there is no liability to pay the defendant's costs. But if the claimant succeeds on liability, they are in a far more comfortable and stronger negotiating position. But ultimately costs will increase as there may potentially be two trials instead of one.

How will the court consider a contested application for a split trial?

Assuming the claim is high value and complex with several expert witnesses necessary for liability/causation and also quantum, then one can expect the judge to be receptive to an application for a split trial when giving effect to the overriding objective as it will save court time and expense.

Factors that the court may consider in determining the issue are:

- Are there allegations affecting the credibility of the claimant? For example, concerning quantum. Is there a suggestion that the special damages claim is wildly exaggerated or the extent of the injury or incapacity exaggerated. This may have an impact on whether credibility affects a liability trial such that all matters are heard together.

- Whether the same experts are likely to opine on liability/causation and quantum. This would tend to indicate that a saving in costs would be achievable in having only one trial. But if there are a substantial number of other quantum experts such as care and therapists then this may favour a split trial.

- The extent of the claimant's injuries; is the prognosis known. If not, a split trial is more likely to be ordered.

- If a partial admission has been given, for example breach of duty is admitted whilst causation is partially admitted, then the court is more likely to order one trial as it will be clear that some damage is admitted and a quantum trial will be inevitable.

Other considerations that may apply are applications for summary judgment or pre-application disclosure or relief from sanctions, for example. These are considered in Chapter 7 covering interlocutory applications.

Part E

Covers the instruction of experts. Permission is required from the court under **Part 35.4** to rely on expert evidence.

It shall be restricted to that which is reasonably required to resolve the proceedings (**Part 35.1**).

In all cases by the time of issue, the claimant will have some expert evidence and will have disclosed at least one report on condition & prognosis. In clinical negligence, a report on breach of duty and perhaps separately on causation will also have been obtained. In catastrophic claims, many more experts will be needed. In the event that the parties cannot reach agreement between themselves, it may be helpful for the claimant to provide a case summary identifying the issues and why particular experts are required. Given that a costs budget will either be filed with the DQ for claims under £50,000 or 21 days before the CMC, the court will need to be persuaded that they are necessary, reasonable and proportionate.

The danger for the claimant is that by the time of filing the DQ, several expert reports may have already been obtained and it does not follow that permission will necessarily be given for reliance on all of them. If not, then the cost of such disallowed report will not be recoverable. However, the first condition & prognosis report may helpfully identify other medical experts on quantum. Counsel may have given an advice and whilst this would not be disclosed to the court, the contents might be helpful in preparing a case summary.

When the disciplines have been identified, it is not wise to name the experts in the DQ or draft directions (especially if their reports have not yet been obtained) because you may not wish to rely upon them. Permission to rely upon a different expert will be difficult to justify unless the expert has failed in his Part 35 duties. The report would have to be disclosed and that would undermine that party's position, especially if the opinion proffered was unfavourable. That alone would be insufficient to persuade the court. Inevitably costs of that expert would not be recoverable if the court did give permission. Therefore do not name experts whose report is yet to be obtained.

Separate or joint expert

A single joint expert on condition & prognosis in a personal injury claim of say under £50,000.00 might be appropriate but less so in a clinical negligence claim where liability and/or causation are in dispute. Effectively, the outcome of the case would be determined by the opinion of a single expert, without recourse to a trial.

The claimant will have served a medical report with the particulars of claim so will wish to rely upon that expert. It does not follow automatically that they will be given permission; the court has the power under **Part 35.7(1)** to direct that evidence be obtained from a single joint expert. Inevitably the defendants would object to the appointment made by the claimant without a joint instruction or their approval of that expert.

The parties might be agreed on separate experts for liability issues as there is every probability that the defendant either has or is in the process of obtaining its own expert evidence. The more likely scenario where the court may impose its power on a single expert is on quantum evidence in more modest value cases where proportionality is more pertinent.

Where the court does impose a single joint expert on the parties, either the parties must reach agreement on a jointly instructed letter, or they will compose separate instructions and send a copy to the opponent. If one party (or both parties) is dissatisfied with the conclusions reached by that expert, then according to Lord Woolf in *Daniels v Walker* [2000] 1 WLR 1382, the first step is to ask questions of that expert pursuant to **Part 35.6**. If that does not resolve the dispute, then that party may instruct another expert as they do not need permission of the court. But they will need permission if they wish to rely upon the separately instructed expert. The other party will need to be informed so that they can consider their position and whether they wish to obtain their own expert opinion.

It is suggested that objecting to a single joint expert is fraught with difficulties for the dissatisfied party. They will incur further fees of another expert. The opponent may get a second opinion as well. That may support the initial opinion thus giving them two supportive opinions. The court may be more persuaded to prefer the first expert against a new opinion from an expert for the dissatisfied party.

The court has power to direct discussions between experts for the purposes set out in the rules – **Part 35.12**. This is a standard direction provided for so as to identify and discuss the expert issues in the proceedings, to reach agreed opinions on those issues, or if not possible, to narrow the issues. Ideally an agreed agenda should be sent to the experts

Part F

Witnesses. The identity of lay witnesses should be named and the facts to which they depose should be set out here. The court will direct (usually) that there be a simultaneous exchange of witnesses of fact. It may give directions as to the order in which they are to be filed.

There may be some debate on whether a medical practitioner that has provided treatment to the claimant is actually an expert witness although described as a factual witness. It is therefore important to distinguish between factual and expert evidence. Permission is not required to rely upon factual evidence, although the court may limit the number of factual witnesses.

The Court of Appeal looked at the distinction between factual and expert evidence in *Kirkham v Euro Exide Corporation (CMP Batteries Limited)* [2007] EWCA Civ 66. The claimant suffered personal injuries in an accident at work. He had a relevant medical history and had received treatment from an Orthopaedic Surgeon. Post accident, the claimant had an above-knee amputation of his right leg. The defendant raised causation, arguing that the outcome would have been the same irrespective of the work accident. The claimant sought to call the Orthopaedic Surgeon as a factual witness. At a case management conference, the District Judge refused permission to rely upon the treating surgeon's report but did not exclude him as a possible witness of fact. The claimant then sought to separate out the factual aspects from the expert aspects in a revised statement. The defendant appealed to the Circuit judge who allowed the appeal, holding that the issue was one of admissibility of evidence to be determined before the hearing and not by the trial judge. It went to the Court of Appeal that held that the object of equality of arms must not be regarded as an absolute rule that in every case the parties should be limited to calling the same number of experts. They dismissed the appeal, finding that the treating surgeon was simply saying what he would have advised the claimant to do. He was not advising on the correctness of that advice or seeking to justify it. It was a matter for the trial judge to determine whether the surgeon was expressing an expert opinion.

It is not unusual for defendants in clinical negligence claims to proof treating doctors or surgeons. Not surprisingly their statements support the defence and will be consistent with the expert opinion. The claimant must be alive to professional witnesses seeking to bolster expert opinion. If they go beyond their own factual account, the claimant should consider applying to the court for that witness statement to be ruled inadmissible and/or the oral evidence of that witness be disallowed. If the court is not persuaded to disallow, alternatively the offending paragraphs could be redacted.

Part G

This section requests an estimate of the length of trial and availability of expert or other essential witnesses. If the trial is stated to last less than one day, this tends to suggest suitability for allocation to the fast track, though value is clearly significant. The final decision may be made at the CCMC or of the court's own motion. In those personal injury cases where quantum is less substantial, written directions may be given by the court pursuant to **PD 29, para 3.3**. The court does have the power to hold an allocation hearing via a telephone conference (**Part 26.5(4)**). This may be more likely where liability is admitted and allocation concerns the length of the assessment hearing to quantify damages. The answers given will assist the court when a trial date or window is set during case management.

Part H

This requires a costs budget to be filed with the DQ if the claim has a value under £50,000.00 or 21 days before the first Case Management Conference (**Part 3.13(1)**). The exception is a litigant in person who need not do so.

WARNING!

If a party fails to file its budget on time or not at all, then they will be treated as having only filed a budget comprising only the applicable court fees (**Part 3.14**). This is the *Mitchell* sanction so the parties should be thinking about the budget at the time they are preparing their particulars of claim or defence. If the role is to be delegated to a costs draftsperson, sooner rather than later is key. Don't wait until you receive the DQ – send your file after receipt/filing of the defence.

The budget should be signed by a senior legal representative, accompanied by a statement of truth.

Part I

The final question asks whether any applications will be made in the future so similar considerations apply as in Part D. The difference being that Part D was asking about applications already made.

This section invites you to set out any other information that will help the judge manage the claim. This could cover areas such as proposed allocation, giving an opportunity for you to advise why you consider the allocation is wrong.

It may be to anticipate difficulties in contentious areas of evidence; for example the appointment of a case manager on behalf of the claimant in a serious injury claim. The case manager's role is to identify rehabilitation needs and a care package for the claimant. Initially they will prepare an assessment report with their recommendations after interviewing the claimant (if possible). The defendant may suggest a joint instruction but the case manager is not an expert but acts in the claimant's best interest. The claimant may wish to call the case manager as a factual witness. Their assessment report is disclosable to the defendant but all communications between the claimant's legal representative and the case manager are subject to legal professional privilege.

Other areas that may need to be addressed here include whether it is the intention to claim periodical payments.

4.6 The Case Management and Costs Conference (CCMC)

After consideration of the Directions questionnaire, the court is likely to list for a CCMC.

Part 3.12(1) provides that costs management applies to all **Part 6** multi-track cases except in cases: exceeding £10 million; where a claim is commenced after 6.4.16 on behalf of a child; where fixed costs apply and where the court orders otherwise (such as in a mesothelioma case with short life expectancy).

This means that you will need a costs budget prepared in good time in advance of the CCMC. It is suggested that on receipt of the notice of allocation, the budget is prepared then or sent to costs draftsmen for them to draft the budget.

Case management is covered in **Part 29** and determines the direction of travel of the case by issuing directions. The starting point will be the model directions for clinical negligence claims and standard directions for personal injury actions. The court will use these directions as a template and adapt as appropriate to the circumstances of the case. Sample directions appear in both types of case at Appendix II.

The court will determine whether it wishes to deal with the costs budget firstly (which is more likely) and then deal with the case management directions. It is possible that some courts will give directions based on the DQ and the draft directions submitted, avoiding the parties' attendance. This leaves only the costs budget to be dealt with at court. Alternatively, and more usually, a case management conference to cover both aspects will be listed.

4.7 Case management

Howsoever the court addresses case management, preparation is important as consideration must be given to the issues likely to arise during the hearing. The court will want to ensure that the necessary evidence is prepared and disclosed.

If counsel is instructed to advise on evidence, it may be timely to discuss the extent of expert evidence required in a high value claim. If a substantial number of experts are anticipated, a skeleton submission may be required for the case management conference if the managing judge is to be persuaded of their need. The court will be looking to contain the number of experts at all costs. You may wish to run your draft DQ past counsel as that will identify your proposed experts.

In a complex case, consider whether a case management bundle is required. This might include a case summary, draft directions, costs budget, skeleton argument and application notice. A case summary should not exceed 500 words. It should give a brief chronology of the claim and state the factual issues that are agreed and those in dispute, and the type of evidence required to prove them.

4.8 Conducting the hearing.

4.8.1 Hopefully you will feel confident in advancing the case concerning directions. But costs budgeting requires some different skills as you will need to be agile with mental arithmetic. Even if you are confident, there is every possibility that your opponent may have engaged a costs draftsperson to deal with the budgeting aspects. If you do decide to instruct a costs lawyer, then be prepared to justify why some particular work is necessary. You may have to act as a 'tag team' with your costs lawyer in fielding questions from the judge. Before the hearing starts, do check with the judge how you propose to address the court on the different aspects of the CCMC.

4.8.2 Before you attend the hearing, ensure you have the authority of your client to attend and make representations, particularly on the evidence required, and any concessions should the court rule against certain expert evidence being allowed. Be prepared to make an oral application for permission to appeal should the need arise.

4.8.3 The draft directions order may effectively be used as the agenda. In the unlikely event that the parties can reach agreement on the directions and the respective costs budget then the court may approve them without a hearing (**rule 29.4**).

Some issues that may arise are set out as follows.

4.8.4 Issues

4.8.4.1 Under **Part 32.1** the court has power to give directions limiting the issues and the evidence that will be adduced at trial.

Some key issues are liability, causation and quantum. Limitation arguments may feature in an industrial disease case or historical abuse or perhaps simply because the claimant has delayed bringing the claim.

Liability involves consideration of breach of duty and causation. In personal injury cases, reasonable foreseeability is also a factor. Has there been an admission, albeit limited in the defence. Are there grounds for seeking a judgment on that admission. Should there be a split (or liability) trial to deal with liability as a preliminary issue. The court will be considering costs efficacy and whether the same or similar number of experts would be required in a liability and a quantum trial. If there is a considerable overlap between the evidence on liability and quantum, this may militate against a split trial.

4.8.4.2 The court will need to know the identity and number of proposed experts, whether they are single or joint. As permission is required, the court will need to know whether they are 'reasonably required' under **Part 35.4.** In a complex case with more than two experts for each party, it would be helpful to set out reasons for each expert in a case summary. In lesser claims, be prepared for the court to enquire why a single joint expert should not be instructed. In clinical negligence claims, it should be clear when the factual evidence is in dispute. Where a report on condition and prognosis is required, it may be less obvious.

4.8.4.3 A split trial. The parties will have similar considerations as to whether a split trial is desirable. For claimants, costs will be saved in investigating quantum. There are tactical benefits if liability and causation can be established earlier than otherwise would be the case, as the claimant would be looking for a substantial interim payment which may be used to fund future litigation, a care regime and accommodation, for example.

4.8.4.4 There are potential disadvantages too for claimants if the case is weak (or is considered weak by the defendant). The defendant will be reluctant to settle on a full liability basis and any offer may be considerably discounted to reflect their assessment of risk. The defendant may seek to obtain their own valuation evidence anyway if they are minded to look to settle. This would require the claimant to obtain its own valuation evidence should there be any settlement negotiations. However, the claimant may well decide to oppose any application for examination facilities given that one of their objectives in having a split trial is to save costs.

If a split trial were ordered, it may persuade the parties to consider a settlement on liability on a percentage basis. Part 36 offers will play an important role at this stage (see Chapter 6 for further details).

4.8.4.5 Generally defendants are less enthusiastic about split trials unless they believe the claim will be defeated. Causation is likely to be in issue in a clinical negligence claim so it will be difficult to evaluate their liability. They cannot place an accurate reserve on the value of the claim as a detailed schedule of loss will not have been served at this stage. For the opposite reasons advanced by the claimant, a defendant will wish to avoid a request for a substantial interim payment.

4.846 If one party seeks a split trial, how will the District judge approach the request?

Are there any admissions on liability and causation? If there is a partial admission and some damage was caused, then this would be good reason for proceeding to a full trial on all issues. The reason being that quantum evidence would need to be called and two trials will be more costly than one trial.

In a claim where the prognosis is not certain and therefore is not capable of quantification in early course, then a split trial is more attractive to the court. The court will wish to ascertain the complexity of quantum evidence and the likely number of witnesses. Is there a clear demarcation between expert witnesses on liability and quantum because where there is some overlap, a split trial would require their attendance at both.

The court might suggest that where there has been an admission on breach of duty but causation is in dispute, a short trial on causation might assist. The court will wish to explore all options that might save the court's resources consistent with the overriding objective. So if causation is the major problem and can be resolved at trial, the prospects of settlement might be achieved without incurring the resources of a full trial.

If the court is moved to order a split trial, then it will adopt the model directions for determining a preliminary issue:

> *A preliminary issue should be tried between the claimant and the defendant as to whether or not the defendant is liable to the claimant by reason of the matters alleged in the Particulars of Claim and, if so, whether or not any of the injuries pleaded were caused thereby; if any such injuries were so caused, the extent of the same.*

4.8.4.7 Other areas that the court will examine are whether any amendments are required to the particulars of claim or the defence. This will have been flagged up in the DQ at paragraphs D or I; what disclosure of documents is necessary; what expert evidence is reasonably required in accordance with **rule 35.1**, and how and when that evidence should be obtained and disclosed; what factual evidence should be disclosed; any requests for further information of the statements of case; and updating schedules of loss.

The question of factual and expert evidence will arise during case management and could be contentious so you need to be prepared for any questions the District judge throws at you.

4.9 Costs management

4.9.1 The ideal situation is that the parties' costs budgets are agreed as then the court is unlikely to interfere with them. Reaching an agreement on all phases of the budget is unlikely. The claimant's budget almost certainly will exceed the defendant's budget for the simple reason that the claimant will have done more work and over a longer period. The test that the court will apply is set out in **PD 3E, para 7.3**, which is to approve costs that fall within the range of *reasonable and proportionate* costs. Each phase of the proceedings is examined but only for those costs that are to be incurred. Those costs already incurred are not subject to budgeting, but the court may record its comments and take them into account when considering the reasonableness and proportionality of all subsequent costs (**PD 3E, para 7.4**).

4.9.2 The budgets are likely to be viewed in the prism of the case management order that will have gone before it. Equally the contrary situation applies should the court deal with the budget firstly, as **Part 3.17** provides that the court will have regard to the costs involved in each procedural step when giving its directions. The costs budget will underpin how the claim is progressed so it is worth having a case summary detailing why certain expert evidence is required and why it costs so much.

4.9.3 The decision of <u>GSK Project Management Ltd (in liquidation) v QPR Holdings Ltd</u> [2015] EWHC 2274 is a lesson as to how courts will address disproportionate costs. The claimant's costs budget came to over £800,000 in a claim for damages of similar value, of which some £300,000 had already been expended. The judge considered proportionality and reasonableness of the costs together with the options available to him, including ordering a new budget, declining to approve the budget, setting budget figures or refusing to allow any further costs. The judge ruled that the case was not exceptional in any material respect. He accepted that the defendant's budget was an indicator of the requirements of the litigation. He declined to approve the claimant's costs budget as the costs already incurred amounted to the total costs that were assessed as reasonable and proportionate as a whole. The judge noted that **Part PD 3E, para 7.4** – which covered incurred costs - did not address the situation where they were disproportionate that could be reflected in assessing future costs. The court was entitled to say what total costs it would have approved.

The clear message from that case was that claimants pursuing cases where costs may be disproportionate run the risk of non-recovery even at the costs budget stage.

4.9.4 When drafting a case summary, state why costs may be disproportionate – is the case complex, has there been delay or extra work because of the opponent's conduct. Why is there a disparity from the opponent's costs. Is there a danger that one party, perhaps more so the defendant who is unlikely to recover their costs under QOCS, has underestimated actual costs. Historic data from previous cases may prove useful if appended to the case summary.

Before the court starts the costs budgeting process, the claimant's legal representative may wish to address the court on reasons about any particular difficulties in the case. Perhaps extensive investigations were necessary to identify the correct defendant or there may have been problems in obtaining disclosure under the protocol. This will help to defray any concerns about proportionality.

4.9.5 Layout of a costs budget

This must be in the prescribed format of Precedent H. This is the summary page.

Work done/to be done	Incurred		Estimated		Total
	Disbursements	Time costs	Disbursements	Time costs	
Pre-action costs					
Issue/statements of case					
CMC					
Disclosure					
Witness statements					
Expert reports					
PTR					
Trial preparation					
Trial					
ADR/Settlement discussions					
Contingent cost A: [explanation]					
Contingent cost B: [explanation]					
GRAND TOTAL (including both incurred costs and estimated costs)					

This estimate excludes VAT (if applicable), success fees and ATE insurance premiums (if applicable), costs of detailed assessment, costs of any appeals, costs of enforcing any judgment and [complete as appropriate]

Statement of Truth

This budget is a fair and accurate statement of incurred and estimated costs which it would be reasonable and proportionate for my client to incur in this litigation.

Signed

Position   Date

Key points

- Diarise key dates for submission of Directions Questionnaire and Costs budgets, otherwise sanctions apply. A late budget means a claimant recovers only the court fees.

- Consider instructing a costs lawyer for the budget and think about doing so after issue of proceedings. Up to £1,000 is allowable for these costs.

- Try and agree directions for the CMC and ideally the budgets. Be prepared to fight over the claimant's budget. Even so some phases may be agreed. Courts may require a position statement with areas of agreement and disagreement filed with the costs budget.

- If a complex case – perhaps needing several experts or costs are expected to be disproportionate, draft a skeleton argument. This should attempt to justify the costs by reference to the issues, complexity, witnesses, grade of fee-earner and conduct.

- Consider a two-pronged approach at the hearing, lawyer for the case management, costs draftsperson for the costs budget.

- For costs under £25,000 only the front page summary is necessary, otherwise the whole Precedent H must be submitted.

CHAPTER FIVE
ALTERNATIVE DISPUTE RESOLUTION

5.1 *What is ADR?*

CPR 3.1(2)(m)

The court's case management powers specifically refer to the court's ability to order the parties to consider ADR.

> *Take any other step or make any other order for the purpose of managing the case and furthering the overriding objective, including hearing an Early Neutral Evaluation with the aim of helping the parties settle the case.*

It encompasses methods by which a dispute may be resolved either before litigation or to avoid a trial. Frequently this involves a round table meeting, mediation or arbitration, the latter being less widespread as it imposes a decision on the parties by the arbitrator.

5.2 The clinical negligence model directions contains a provision for ADR requiring the parties usually about 3 months before the trial window opens to consider whether the case is capable of resolution by ADR. It is suggested that this may be a useful provision to include in the standard directions for all personal injury claims.

The need for ADR is emphasised in paragraph 5 of the Pre-Action Protocol for the Resolution of Clinical Disputes. It reminds the parties that litigation should be a last resort and that they should consider whether negotiation or ADR may resolve the dispute. This may include discussion and negotiation, possibly including Part 36 offers; mediation, a third party facilitating a resolution; arbitration, a third party deciding the dispute; early neutral evaluation, a third party giving an informed opinion on the dispute; and Ombudsman schemes.

Ideally both parties would indicate in the letter of claim and reply that they are amenable to ADR. Some - especially defendants, may consider that an early reference to ADR might be construed as a weakness in their position. But of course a willingness to engage in discussions does not imply the outcome, other than an intention to resolve the dispute.

The sting in the tale for a party refusing ADR is of course costs. So the directions will often remind the parties that if they consider the case is unsuitable for ADR, then they will need to justify their decision before the judge at conclusion of the trial.

5.3 An unreasonable refusal to consider ADR may be met with a sanction.

The typical directions state as follows:

The parties shall by [a date usually about 3 months before the trial window opens] consider whether the case is capable of resolution by ADR. If any party considers that the case is unsuitable for resolution by ADR, that party shall be prepared to justify that decision at the conclusion of the trial, should the judge consider that such means of resolution were appropriate, when he is considering the appropriate costs order to make.

Such means of ADR as shall be adopted shall be concluded not less than 35 days prior to the trial.

The party considering the case unsuitable for ADR shall, not less than 28 days before the commencement of the trial, file with the court a Witness Statement, without prejudice save as to costs, giving the reasons upon which they rely for saying that the case was unsuitable. The Witness Statement shall not be disclosed to the trial Judge until the conclusion of the case.

['ADR' includes 'round table' conferences at which the parties attempt to define and narrow the issues in the case, including those to which expert evidence is directed; early neutral evaluation; mediation; and arbitration. The object is to try to reduce the number of

cases settled 'at the door of the court', which are wasteful both of costs and judicial time.]

Either party may be reluctant to agree to mediation in the early stages when evidence is being assembled. Neutral evaluation on breach of duty may be of considerable assistance when both parties have obtained an initial breach report but the will has to be there. This might include the instruction of an independent expert to act as the facilitator or counsel. It can be less formal than mediation and would benefit from early involvement but it is not obligatory. One could say that the parties' legal representatives should always give thought to how the case may be resolved without placing any barriers in the way.

The reality in a large claim requiring many experts is that both parties may simply not be ready to consider settlement overtures in the early stages of evidence gathering. Each will wish to assess the respective strengths and weaknesses and that cannot happen until after exchange of expert reports. It is suggested that waiting until after the joint experts' meeting is not essential because by that time, one or other party's position may become emboldened or entrenched and the desire to compromise become less.

The claimant's lawyers have perhaps the more difficult balancing exercise between aiming to achieve a good settlement for their client in circumstances when there may be pressures on them to settle, perhaps prematurely when not all quantum evidence has been obtained. The lawyer may apply undue pressure on his client to reach an early settlement if an offer has been made that might represent an undervalue. There could be pressure applied by the defendants to engage early in ADR. That may not be a bad thing if it starts focusing the parties on settlement. It may not be possible to settle at that stage but it can do no harm for the parties to meet and set out a timetable or action plan with a view to reaching a common goal, namely to avoid a trial.

5.4 The options

5.4.1 Round table meeting

A face-to-face meeting usually has lawyers for both sides and often the claimant. This provides an opportunity for the claimant to express his views. This may be particularly helpful if the claim concerns a family member who has died. It is an opportunity to air grievances and speak directly to a representative of the trust if they attend. Usually beneficial where quantum only is in dispute and the usual avenues of direct negotiations have broken down or reached a stalemate.

Advantages: The potential to narrow the issues and reach a settlement if the parties are open and willing to settle.

Disadvantages: If one party restricts the ambit of the discussions, for example that no or no increased offers by the defendant, or the claimant will not accept less than they are claiming, then necessarily the nature of any discussions is likely to be fraught and more liable to retrench positions and lead to failure.

5.4.2 Joint Settlement meeting

These tend to take place in the later stages of the claim when all expert and factual evidence has been exchanged together with schedules of loss. An agreed bundle is helpful. Often the JSM will take place at either office of the solicitors or counsel's chambers. It is beneficial for there to be separate rooms for each party. Frequently the defendants wish to meet the claimant, and this will be the first time that they do so. The claimant's lawyers need to decide whether that is wise as it should not be an opportunity for the defendant to try and cross-examine or to make perhaps a rash judgment as to the claimant's fitness and general health. After all, the prime objective is to reach an agreement on quantum and the claimant's condition and prognosis detailed in the medical reports may well be challenged.

Prior to the JSM, the parties should set out some ground rules to ensure that both parties' expectations of what can be achieved are realized:

- A commitment from both to move from any previous offers made, i.e. that the claimant is willing to accept less, the defendant willing to offer more;

- An agreement reached on bearing the costs of the JSM, usually for costs to be in the case. If this presents a difficulty, then the parties may accept that no costs are incurred by attending the JSM.

- That the meeting addresses only damages and not costs (as they will follow the event). A defendant may find it more attractive to wrap up damages and costs in an inclusive Calderbank offer. The parties may not wish to be constrained on the structure of any settlement offers.

- That the parties have authority to settle. There is nothing more infuriating for the parties to skate around each other on quantum and for an offer to be made that is met with the riposte that instructions need to be taken. It is often thought by those who indulge in such a tactic that it represents a strong negotiating hand, when really all it does is to alienate the offering party. If previous authority has not been obtained then the parties should ensure that those who do have authority, namely the claimant and the defendant's insurer or representative of NHS Resolution are present.

- All discussions are to be without prejudice and not to be recorded. This may allow the parties to speak freely about a joint expert report and schedules of loss.

- An outline of the type of agreement that may be reached, so if the format is to be a Tomlin Order, then a standard draft may be circulated to each party in advance, obviously leaving blank the proposed settlement sum and any form of apology.

5.4.3 Mediation

5.4.3.1 This is similar to the joint settlement meeting but with the obvious inclusion of a third party engaged by the parties to act as the mediator. The recommendations by the mediator are not binding, though the mediator tries to steer a course that both parties, even if unwilling at the outset, may find acceptable. Compromise is the name of the game.

Either party may be resistant to mediation, notwithstanding the costs repercussions and seek to procrastinate, either by arguing that further evidence is necessary or by suggesting some other form of ADR but seeking to impose restrictions on the ambit of discussions. That is not a satisfactory position to adopt if the intent is to really attempt settlement, rather than window dressing for the court to show an attempt at ADR.

Both parties should be aware of the costs implications and therefore need to be committed to the process on the understanding that a settlement is likely to save costs for both parties. No egos are required to fetter the prospects of settlement.

5.4.3.2 There may be resistance to the type of mediator proposed or some belief that s/he is not neutral or seeks to impose his/her will against an intransigent party. That misunderstands the professionalism and role of the mediator and if such concerns are raised, then one need only suggest that a mediator with expertise in the type of case to be mediated is appointed by CEDR or Trust Mediation Ltd or some such similar body. Cost may present a stumbling block but as costs would normally be borne equally, then it can be argued that if a settlement is achieved, then substantial costs will be saved (even at a late stage of the proceedings with an imminent trial ahead), if only by the saving of calling expert witnesses. And this is before one even considers the costs of the advocates and other attending lawyers.

What may need to be overcome is the erroneous belief by one party – often it has to be said the defendant – that their position on liability is unmoved and any offer made reflects their assessment of risk and that no increased offer is forthcoming. It can be difficult to dissuade a party from this type of thinking. It is often the case that the opposing party may consider that their case is strong and that they too are in possession of supportive expert evidence – hence the impasse. But as we all know, litigation risk is present in all cases and no one can be sure how one's expert will perform on the day or the view that the judge takes. This is before we consider the substantial costs that the parties will have by indulging in their 'day in court'. If one is not careful, the talk of principles and the belief in maintaining a robust demeanor obscure what is often more important and that is to attain a fair result which both parties can live with at proportionate cost.

This is why mediation can be so significant because a neutral party presents a collaborative, problem-solving approach with none of the baggage that may have developed over the years that the case has been fought. The mediator does not make a decision – s/he facilitates settlement.

5.4.3.3 Similar ground rules apply to a planned mediation as to a JSM. The parties should also be guided by the appointed mediator on his/her requirements. A joint bundle will need to be prepared together with position papers from each party setting out the issues in dispute whether it be liability, causation or quantum. A decision must be made between the parties whether the position paper should be disclosed to the other party because if so, it would be better if the expectation of damages is omitted. Alternatively, there might be two position papers, one for disclosure and the other containing confidential information for the mediator's eyes only. This would be particularly appropriate if some expert evidence has not yet been exchanged. The potential problem is that withholding of expert evidence arises because it is not especially beneficial to one party so it is likely that it may be withheld from the mediator. The parties may feel more relaxed if the second position paper is not disclosed at least until the mediation (or not at all) but the contents disclosed to the mediator part way through the mediation. It may be expected that a level of trust needs to be established with the mediator as concerns may arise (almost certainly unfounded) that the mediator will be looking to reach an early settlement and play one party off against the other.

5.4.3.4 *The process*

The opening meeting or plenary session starts with the mediator and all parties and their lawyers in the same room. The mediator explains the objectives and how the day is planned, that all discussions are confidential and without prejudice. Each party is encouraged to set out in the private session their high watermark position on damages safe in the knowledge that it will not be disclosed to the other party.

Normally each party through their lawyer makes an opening address in an informal manner. The claimant may wish to speak, particularly if an insurance representative or someone from NHS Resolution is present. It may be that one of the clinicians from the Trust is present. This can be quite an effective way to break the ice and allows the claimant to express their concerns.

Following the opening session, each party returns to their own rooms during which the mediator alternates between the two.

In private, each party must determine what is provided to the mediator and whether this is disclosable to the other party. Ideally this will have been covered in a meeting with the client in advance of the mediation. Sometimes a mediator will ask at the outset what is the top line claimed for damages and the bottom line. Whilst a legitimate question, the lower figure should not be given at least until negotiations are underway. Invariably there will be considerable 'toing and froing' by the mediator when figures are discussed. It is important from the agenda agreed with the mediator whether he is invited to express an opinion on merit. This is unlikely to be the case as it will obviously create discord and distrust with the other party. However, it may be useful if for example a particular head of loss is unrealistic that the mediator is permitted to give his views, even if they are not discussed with the other party.

What of the situation that seems intractable, perhaps the defendant will not move on liability and no offer seems likely. If that does occur, then the parties should try and reach an agreement on some other issues; that may be agreeing some of the issues in the expert reports on life expectancy for example or reaching agreement on heads of loss.

Even if settlement is not achieved at the meeting, the parties should be encouraged to leave offers open for say 7 days to allow some mulling over and the realization that this may be the last opportunity before trial to resolve the case.

5.4.3.5 *Reaching an agreement*

A draft template should have been made available to the mediator before the day of the mediation.

Advantages:

- Flexible. Format tailored to the parties' wishes. So round table, by telephone or online. Choice of mediator to be agreed or no mediator.

- Confidential, without prejudice and non-binding. Nothing discussed leaves the meeting unless offers are made for later consideration.

- If it takes place early in the litigation, substantial costs are saved. Changes the mindset from one of formal proof and denial to trying to achieve a deal. NHS Resolution (or the insurer) should pay for the costs of mediation.

- Allows the client to be part of the process and to take a more centre-stage role (as they wish). A claimant may express grievances and seek assurances that are lost on paper and not available at court.

- The parties make the decision so are in control, thereby avoiding imposition of a decision by a court or through lawyers. The mediator listens and facilitates but does not decide.

- There is no pressure to reach a settlement. Where the parties cannot agree on some of the principle issues, Early Neutral Evaluation may be apposite. An independent expert, usually a lawyer, perhaps a retired judge examines the issues in the claim and gives a view. It is non-binding but may cause one or both parties to move away from entrenched views. It may be considered as an alternative or adjunct to other forms of ADR (round table conferences, mediation, arbitration etc).

- As mediation is more formal than a round table meeting, extra preparation is required which may focus minds more and cause the parties to be more committed.

Disadvantages:

- Early disclosure of expert evidence may not be ideal if some concessions are revealed and mediation fails. A joint experts' report, whilst privileged, may affect the experts' thinking when a further joint report is prepared for trial. To address that, a single joint expert only for the mediation would be required.

- If a party is determined to have their day in court, mediation serves only to increase costs.

5.4.4 Arbitration

Arbitration works on a similar level to mediation save for the fact that the decision imposed by the arbitrator is binding on the parties. It is suggested that the vast majority of claims will be dealt with via mediation because of the ability to proceed to court if necessary.

So both parties should embrace ADR but what of the recalcitrant party who refuses. The courts cannot force a party to engage but merely encourage and punish! Yes, by striking a party where it hurts – in making costs orders against them.

Consider *PGF II SA v OMFS Co 1 Ltd* [2013] EWCA Civ 1288. The defendant ignored an offer to mediate and despite the claimant accepting a Part 36 offer out of time, the defendant was refused its costs from the date of expiry of the relevant period. Why? – their unreasonable conduct in refusing to mediate.

It would be an unwise party that boldly refuses ADR. More likely they will say it will be considered – but not yet - until there has been disclosure or a joint experts' meeting or a conference with counsel or whatever other reason can be summoned to prevaricate. Or in questioning its benefits, they will maintain that a Part 36 offer has been made or that the parties are too far apart, or - and this is the best one, that they will agree to ADR but they have made their best offer so damages and costs will not be up for discussion.

If you are experiencing problems with an incalcitrant opponent, they may well mark their correspondence as 'without prejudice' in the mistaken belief that such correspondence is safe from the judge's eyes, thus not revealing their reticence or refusal to agree to ADR. They would be wrong. The court is entitled to see any correspondence, and in particular when the issue of ADR is concerned unless such correspondence is intended to represent settlement proposals. It is trite to say that it is the content of the correspondence that dictates whether it is privileged from disclosure and not whether it is marked 'without prejudice' or not – see the case of *Northrop Grummon Mission Systems Europe Ltd v BAE Systems (Al Diriyah C4I) Ltd* (No 2) [2014] EWHC 3148 (TCC).

Key Points

- Claimants should always propose ADR – in the letter of claim. And keep repeating the offer at regular intervals if needs be.

- Know your case law on costs sanctions for refusal to engage in ADR.

- ADR gives wider opportunities for redress than available in court – compensation, admission, apology in person and explanation for how injury happened.

- NHS Resolution offers a mediation service provided by two independent companies. The cynical view is that it is offered only where they admit fault but are less persuaded to engage where there is a denial.

- Where expert evidence is disputed, consider expert evaluation or neutral evaluation by a facilitator. A facilitator may have an overarching remit over the course of the case or be engaged to resolve a particular problem, say a causation issue or an accommodation problem for a seriously injured claimant. The parties may benefit from a without prejudice, objective evaluation of the merits of each parties' case.

CHAPTER SIX
TACTICS

In this chapter, we will consider various tactical measures to advance the claim to your advantage. This is not achieved through sleight of hand but by applying provisions under the civil procedure rules. We will consider the following:

6.1 Part 36 offers
6.2 Calderbank offers
6.3 Requests for further Information, Admissions and Notices to admit
6.4 Interim payments
6.5 Summary judgment or dismissal
6.6 Exit opportunities from the personal injury portal
6.7 Know your limitation(s)

6.1 Part 36 offers

6.1.1 Part 36 should be read in conjunction with Part 44 when considering offers to settle.

Offers to settle, whether for damages or issues on liability, made under Part 36 have costs consequences designed to encourage out of court settlements.

They are probably the most significant armoury that the parties possess to exert some pressure on the opponent to settle – provided of course they are realistic and well judged.

So, consider making admissible offers, whether under Part 36 or as a Calderbank offer, without prejudice save as to costs.

Care must be taken to follow the requirements necessary in order to make a valid offer and to appreciate the differences between Part 36 and a Calderbank offer, to avoid any unintended consequences or even potential negligence.

Part 36

6.1.2 Changes to Part 36 Offers

The ability of the parties to make early and effective offers so as to save costs is without doubt the most effective means of putting some pressure on the opponent to consider settlement. But the offer must be pitched at the right level so as to cause the other party to seriously reflect on whether it should be accepted or rejected. It must also be compliant with the rules if it is to be valid.

Part 36 of the civil procedure rules is a self-contained code designed to encourage out of court settlements by imposing cost sanctions on a party who declines an offer then subsequently fails to obtain a better result. The rules are highly prescriptive so must comply with CPR 36.5 if they are to be effective.

Offers may be made for settlement of damages or issues, principally for the assessment of liability. They may be made as part of the claim or counterclaim or other additional claim or in an appeal or cross-appeal.

The Part 36 rules substantially changed after 6 April 2015 under the Civil Procedure (Amendment No 8) Rules 2014. After this date, provision may be made for time limited offers that are automatically withdrawn after 21 days. Also the original offer may be varied to be more generous to the recipient (or offeree) BUT retaining the costs protection of the original lower offer.

Very high claimant offers permit the court to consider 'whether the offer was a genuine attempt to settle the proceedings' when deciding whether ordering costs would be unjust. This aims to prevent cost consequences arising where the claimant makes an offer for the whole or nearly whole amount of the claim that is rejected but the claimant succeeds at trial.

Part 36 offers now apply in equal status to counterclaims or additional claims.

A saving provision applies under 36.23 where a party's costs are limited to only the court fee for failing to provide a budget on time. If a party beats its own Part 36 offer, then he shall recover 50% of the costs assessed.

6.1.3 *36.5 Form and Content of a Part 36 offer*

(a) The offer must be in writing;

(b) make clear that it is made pursuant to Part 36;

(c) specify a period of not less than 21 days within which the defendant will be liable for the claimant's costs in accordance with rule 36.13 or 36.20 if the offer is accepted;

(d) state whether it relates to the whole of the claim or to part of it or to an issue that arises in it and if so to which part or issue; and

(e) state whether it takes into account any counterclaim.

The relevant period is usually 21 days but can be more but not less.

In order to ensure compliance in making a valid Part 36 offer, the above contents must be included. Alternatively, use the standard form N242A – reproduced in chapter 11.

The rules are a self-contained code, requiring the offer to state that it is made pursuant to Part 36. The last revisions came into force on 6 April 2015 and changed the 2007 rules to include a 'sunset clause' allowing for automatic withdrawal after 21 days. Also under the old rules, an offeror (person making the offer) could withdraw an offer or change its terms (with permission of the court) even when the offer had been accepted.

6.1.4 Withdrawing or changing the terms of a Part 36 offer

A series of Part 36 offers may be made without withdrawing the original offer. So more generous offers may be made to the offeree (recipient of offer) without withdrawing the original offer – **CPR 36.9(5)(a)**.

Part 36 offers may be withdrawn or changed before expiry of the relevant period provided the offeree has not served notice of acceptance. If the offeror does that, then they do not benefit from the potential cost consequences. Rule 36.17(7) covers this situation. Also, if the offer has been changed on terms less advantageous to the offeree which is beaten, then the costs benefits do not accrue to the offeree.

The terms of the offer may provide that after, say 21 days (or such longer period), the offer is deemed withdrawn. Or if the offer is open for 21 days and not accepted, the offeror may serve notice on the offeree withdrawing the offer.

6.1.5 A defective Part 36 offer

If a purported Part 36 offer does not comply with **Part 36.5**, then it will not have the consequences on acceptance or following judgment set out in rules 36.13, 36.14 and 36.17.

In determining whether an offer is defective, it was held in _Gibbon v Manchester City Council_ [2010] 1 WLR 2081, that the offer should be interpreted as it would be read by a reasonable solicitor.

So a time limited offer is inconsistent with **Part 36.11(2)** that provides that a Part 36 offer may be accepted at any time unless it has already been withdrawn.

If an offer is expressed in terms that the claimant will only receive part of his costs or that the offer incorporates damages and costs, then these provisos do not comply with 36.5(1)(c) and 36.13 so it will not be a valid Part 36 offer. An offer to discontinue is not a Part 36 offer as held in _AB v CD_ [2011] EWHC 602 (Ch).

6.1.6 *Challenging a defective offer*

If the offeree considers the offer does not comply with Part 36, they may be wise to raise this with the offeror. The offeror may make an offer and invite the recipient to raise any issue if they considered it was defective in any way. If silent, the lack of challenge may be considered relevant as in *Seef v Ho* [2011] EWCA Civ 401.

If a purported Part 36 offer is materially defective, then the beneficial costs consequences of a valid Part 36 offer do not apply. But the court may still take into account a non-compliant offer when deciding the question of costs. It will be necessary to decide if the offer is admissible and made as a Calderbank offer. If so, costs are determined under Part 44.2 applying the court's discretion as to costs.

Part 44.3(4)(c) requires the court to have regard to all the circumstances, including any admissible offer to settle made by a party which is drawn to the court's attention and which is not an offer to which cost consequences under Part 36 apply.

Offers that are made on a 'without prejudice' basis will not be admissible, even if a party wishes to rely upon it in connection with a claim for costs. This dates back to *Walker v Wilsher* (1889) 23 QBD 335, which was cited in *Reed Executive plc v Reed Business Information Limited* [2004] EWCA Civ 159.

Offers marked 'without prejudice' may only be referred to a court once a binding settlement has been reached as evidence of that compromise, perhaps to enforce the agreement.

There is no benefit to a party making a 'without prejudice' offer as it is not referable to the court on costs and no costs benefits flow from it. The only time this discussion may arise is in the context of a defective Part 36 offer and whether it is admissible, either as a Calderbank offer or inadmissible as a without prejudice offer.

If the defect is minor then the court may rectify it and allow the offeror the same costs benefits as if no error had arisen.

The court's discretion under **Part 44.2(4)** was tested when construing a Part 36 offer in *Huntley v Simmonds* [2009] EWHC 496 (QB). The offer was one for future pecuniary loss where the defendant failed to state under **Part 36.18(4)(d)** that periodical payments would be funded such that continuity of payments would be assured. There was no prejudice as the claimant understood the offer. In exercising discretion, the court interpreted the offer as having the same effects as a Part 36 offer.

6.1.7 Effect of CRU – **CPR 36.22**

The parties must appreciate the terms of the offer and relationship with the Compensation Recovery Unit (CRU).

In order to beat a Part 36 offer it is the **net** figure that is crucial – **Part 36.22(8)**, i.e. after deductions of CRU benefits.

This was tested in *Crooks v Hendricks Lovell* which went to the Court of Appeal which held that the defendant's Part 36 offer described as net of CRU and without regard to any liability for recoverable benefits was valid. It was made under **CPR 36.15(3)(a)** (which is now **36.22(3)(a)**) and therefore did not need to state the gross amount of compensation under (now) **36.22(6)(a)**. The second issue concerned whether costs should be deferred until the outcome of an appeal to the CRU certificate (as argued by the claimant) or on the day judgment was given (as submitted by the defendant). The appellate judges held it was correct to await the CRU appeal. Thirdly, in determining the winner following a reduced CRU certificate, it is the amount the claimant receives as compared to the offer made in determining whether he had bettered the Part 36 offer.

6.1.8 Clarification of a Part 36 offer – **CPR 36.8**

On receipt of an offer, clarification may be sought within 7 days by the offeree. This would be appropriate if the offer appeared non-complaint or if there was inadequate information about CRU benefits as required under **Part 36.22**. It would be a misreading of this rule to use it as an opportunity to interrogate the offeror about their thinking behind making the offer, perhaps as to how they apportioned general and special damages. By all means make the request, but be prepared for a refusal as there is no obligation to provide such information.

Should the receiving party not provide clarification, then an application may be made to the court within 7 days of receiving the request.

6.1.9 *Advantages of a well-pitched Part 36 offer:*

For claimants who beat their own Part 36 offer following judgment

6.1.9.1 Under Part 36.17(4), unless unjust*, the claimant will receive:

(a) interest up to 10% above base rate on damages for some or all of the period following expiry of the Part 36 offer;

(b) costs on the indemnity basis (see next bullet point below);

(c) interest on those costs at a rate not exceeding 10% above base rate; and

(d) an additional award up to 10% of their damages up to £500,000 and thereafter at 5%, subject to a limit of £75,000.

By reason of CPR 47.20(4), Part 36 applies also to detailed assessment proceedings. This was tested in *Cashman v Mid-Essex NHS Trust* (2015) EWHC 1312 (QB), when on appeal to the High Court, it was confirmed that as the claimant beat his own Part 36 offer, he was entitled to the additional 10% on costs as the uplift was intended to be punitive.

6.1.9.2 To recover costs on the indemnity basis rather than the standard basis. This sidesteps budgeted costs and avoids the proportionality test. Under CPR 44.3, a standard basis assessment requires a two-step approach. Costs will be assessed as reasonably and necessarily incurred and then reviewed to determine whether they are proportionate by reference to the amount of damages, the value of any non-monetary relief, the complexity of the case, any additional work generated by the conduct of the paying party and any wider factors such as reputation or public importance.

6.1.9.3 Recovering <u>more than fixed costs</u> (which apply under CPR 45). In cases where fixed costs are payable under the RTA or EL/PL Protocols, claimants will be entitled to indemnity costs (see the Court of Appeal decision in *Broadhurst v Tan* [2016] EWCA Civ 94. Part 36 trumped the fixed costs provisions such that a 'good' offer incurred indemnity and not fixed costs). This will also apply to cases that settle before going to trial.

6.1.9.4 To <u>undo the 'Mitchell'</u> sanction of being deprived of costs, only limited to court fees on account of CPR 3.14. Under Part 36.23, a winning party may recover 50% of their costs.

* In determining whether it would be unjust to make such an award, the court will take into account all the circumstances under **CPR 36.17(5)**, namely:

(a) the terms of any Part 36 offer;

(b) the stage in the proceedings when any Part 36 offer was made, including in particular how long before the trial started the offer was made;

(c) the conduct of the parties with regard to the giving of or refusal to give information for the purposes of enabling the offer to be made or evaluated; and

(d) whether the offer was a genuine attempt to settle the proceedings.

6.1.9.5 In the case of *Jockey Club v Wilmott Dixon* (2016) EWHC 167 (TCC), consideration was given to paragraph (d) above when an offer to settle at 95% of the full value of the claim was adjudged as a genuine attempt to settle because the 5% given away amounted to £40,000 and was therefore not a '*derisory*' sum. It therefore did not matter that the offer represented an unlikely outcome.

Significantly, this will apply to cases where some causation of loss or injury is proven even if many allegations are not sustained.

This case leads on to making an issues based Part 36 offer.

6.1.10 *Issues specific Part 36 offers*

There is a clear benefit to a party making an offer on liability as in *Jockey* because of the cost consequences that apply in **CPR 36.17**, although the most attractive penalty applies if the case goes to trial - 36.17(4)(d) where damages of up to 10% may be awarded up to a claim of value of £500,000.

An offer on liability may be made even if the quantum claim has not been pleaded. Therefore consideration may be given to making an early offer on liability and at a later date on quantum when further evidence has been obtained. It may be particularly helpful in clinical negligence claims where there are multiple allegations on breach of duty with alternative cases put on causation, some of which may prove unsuccessful. Nevertheless a win is a win for the purposes of Part 36.

Where a claimant is successful on some allegations and not others, and had made a Part 36 offer on liability, was tested in the clinical negligence claim of *Webb v Liverpool Women's NHS Foundation Trust* [2016] EWCA Civ 365.

The claimant had made a Part 36 offer to settle liability on the basis that the claimant receive 65% of the damages that would accrue on a 100% basis. The claimant won 100% at trial but failed on some of the substantive issues. The trial judge held that a successful Part 36 offer did not mean the court was unable to make an issue based or proportionate costs order. Therefore he limited the claimant's costs to a percentage of time expended on establishing the first limb of her claim.

The claimant appealed successfully to the Court of Appeal on the costs order. It held that the claimant should not be deprived of her costs in pursuing the second allegation of breach of duty (that ultimately was unsuccessful). The claimant therefore recovered her costs on the indemnity basis from the effective date of the offer.

The ratio was that Part 36 is a self-contained code and in deciding what costs order to make under Part 36.17, the court did not first exercise discretion under Part 44, as the only discretion is that conferred by Part 36 itself.

So, Part 36 trumps Part 44. But the court did say that it was subject to whether it would be unjust for the claimant to be awarded all costs (echoing 36.17(3)), to be determined having regard to all the circumstances of the case. In exercising discretion, the court must take into account that the unsuccessful defendant could have avoided the costs of the trial if it had accepted the claimant's Part 36 offer.

6.2 Calderbank Offers

Calderbank

6.2.1 These are more often than not made by defendants, frequently offering an inclusive sum for damages and costs. They may not quantify them separately. They are described as without prejudice save as to costs, or as a Calderbank offer following the family case of *Calderbank v Calderbank* [1976] Fam 93. The offer is a contractual one so it can contain any terms and is not as prescriptive as a Part 36 offer as it does not have those cost consequences. There is no presumption that costs will be paid. If an offer of £X damages is made in full and final settlement and is silent as to costs. Then an acceptance leads to a concluded settlement. The offer can also be subject to strict time constraints, thus open for acceptance within 7 days. The reality is that the offeror may withdraw the offer at any time and before any deadline has elapsed.

The point is that it may be attractive to a party to attempt to leverage some pressure on the opponent to try and settle the case – and resolve costs in one fell swoop without further delay. They therefore make a Calderbank offer.

It can be said that having defended a case almost to the doors of the court, the defendant then faced with the reality of trial but having no appetite to pick up a significant costs tab, may be willing to entertain an inclusive settlement that may represent a significant discount from the full exposure of damages and costs.

6.2.2 Of course it can work the other way too. The claimant may have rejected a modest – or what they perceived as a modest Part 36 offer some considerable time back and the case progressed and significant costs incurred by both parties. The complexion of the case may have changed, either following a joint experts' meeting or late disclosure of documents or following a conference with counsel. The claimant may be getting decidedly uneasy about the prospect of a trial, or that his insurers will increase the premiums, such that that an earlier Part 36 offer does not look so bad after all. But seeking to accept a Part 36 offer out of time will inevitably lead to the claimant paying the defendant's costs incurred from the date on which the relevant period expired. Making another Part 36 offer may be ineffective as the defendant is not minded to settle. This is where a Calderbank offer may prove beneficial as it resolves the liability of both parties' costs in a package that both accept.

From the claimant's lawyer's perspective, it is important to be clear with the claimant as to the realistic valuation of damages, taking into account the litigation risks. Otherwise there is a danger of the perception of self-interest which would represent an obvious conflict of interest with the client. In a modest value claim, costs may exceed damages and it may be difficult for the client to understand why he gets a smaller slice of the pie. This difficulty is clearly avoided where there is a Part 36 offer for a discrete amount of damages.

6.2.3 The interplay between Part 36 offers and Calderbank offers must be appreciated so as to avoid difficulties in rejection. The opponent's Part 36 offer may be rejected or a counter Part 36 offer made in response. Indeed, a Calderbank offer could be made in reply. If the counter offer itself is rejected, one could then proceed to accept the opponent's Part 36 offer at any later stage – with the appropriate costs consequences. This is because Part 36 is a self-contained procedural code – CPR 36.1.

Therefore, parties can make a series of Part 36 offers and counter Part 36 offers knowing that an earlier one may be accepted at a later stage if needs be. Sometimes in the heat of negotiations, with Part 36 offers flying backwards and forwards, one party may respond to a Part 36 offer that an increased offer of £X will settle the claim (plus payment of costs on the standard basis). The opponent then requests if their Part 36 offer is rejected. Tell them yes. Because you may accept it at any later time and within 21 days (or whatever timescale has been provided), if you wish to avoid adverse costs consequences. So the request is really an unnecessary one. You either accept within 21 days (or whatever timescale is provided) or face the cost consequences.

6.2.4 The same principle of rejection does not apply to Calderbank offers. So if the opponent makes a Calderbank offer which is rejected, that's it. There's no obligation for the offeror to reinstate it. Even if one counters with a Part 36 offer or another Calderbank offer, these also amount to rejection. This is because without prejudice save as to costs offers are contractual. They follow the precepts of offer, consideration (damages and/or costs) and acceptance. This constitutes a contract that is enforceable. Likewise rejecting an offer is final. So trying to accept the offer following a previous rejection is misconceived.

This was tested in the case of *DB UK Bank v Jacobs Solicitors*. The Deputy High Court Judge confirmed the contractual basis of Calderbank offers and that a party who made a Part 36 offer in reply to a without prejudice save as to costs proposal had in law rejected the offer.

6.2.5 The conclusion to be drawn is that Calderbank offers are much more flexible than Part 36 offers, both as to their content and timing. They may often be used in situations when the parties have reached an impasse over costs particularly as the trial approaches. Where they lose some flexibility is that a rejection of one offer is final so the parties are unlikely to be trading many such offers. Whilst they offer certainty as to payment of the claimant's costs, such costs are likely to be lower than would be recoverable at assessment (on the assumption that there are no adverse costs payable). However one could say that the tide has been changing against claimants' costs recoverability for some time so taking the risk at an assessment may not be an attractive one.

> **Key Points**
>
> - Make a Part 36 offer on damages. The claimant may lose their QOCS shield. The defendant may have to pay costs on the indemnity basis – even in a fixed costs case as in *Broadhurst*.
>
> - Make a Part 36 offer on liability.
>
> - Make a Part 36 offer on costs in detailed assessment proceedings – if beaten – enhanced costs are recoverable. Obligatory if 'Mitchelled' and limited to court fees only under CPR 3.14.
>
> - Understand the terms of withdrawal of a Part 36 offer under CPR 36.9 and 36.10. If the offer is stated to be open for (generally) 21 days, the offeror may withdraw the offer before expiry of this period – no grounds or reasons are required. If the offer is good, accept without delay.
>
> - The offeree may reject a Part 36 offer either by word or making a counter Part 36 offer. But the original offer is still capable of acceptance.
>
> - Rarely should claimants consider accepting defendants' issue based costs offers during negotiations.
>
> - Ensure compliance with CPR 36.5 for a valid Part 36 offer.

- Ascertain any CRU liability. Is the defendant's Part 36 offer net i.e. in the claimant's hand under 36.22(3)(a); or gross by including deductible benefits under 36.22(3)(b).

- If the opponent's offer is non-complaint, decide whether it is in your client's interests to raise this fact. If intended to accept, certainly raise it for correction – so that cost consequences flow from acceptance. If the offer is not acceptable, consider remaining silent as no costs benefit accrues to the offeror if the purported offer fails to be beaten. Note that a minor defect may be interpreted as valid and remaining silent may be considered as acquiescence.

- Make use of Calderbank without prejudice offers – write your own terms. Typically beneficial where there is entrenchment because of costs build up.

6.3 Requests for further information, Admissions and Notices to Admit

CPR 18, 14 and 32.18

It may seem that these three areas of the CPR are quite disparate but all concern the state of written factual evidence. A party may use the procedures to extract further information to assist in the progression of the claim or the defence where the other party is reticent about a piece of information or drafts an inadequate pleading.

6.3.1 Requests for further information – CPR 18

6.3.1.1 This is now little used in seeking clarification of matters in dispute as post Woolf, the parties should provide detailed statements of case. Although this topic appears on a chapter about tactics, the courts will not permit requests for further information where the other party's case has been sufficiently well set out. So if it is done for tactical reasons, fishing for evidence or enquiring about the opponent's legal arguments, then these reasons will represent an abuse of process and any application is likely to be dismissed, possibly with an adverse costs order on the indemnity basis.

What is permitted is a legitimate request for more detail of the particulars of claim or defence which is inadequately particularised, provided such request is necessary and proportionate (**PD18, para 1.2**). If no cause of action is revealed in the claim or there has been an apparent fundamental misunderstanding about the import of a statute, then it is permissible and proportionate to request further information, perhaps as a prelude before an application to strike out is made.

6.3.1.2 A request should be concise and relate to matters that are necessary and proportionate to enable the party to understand the other side's case better and what can be achieved by such a request. They are particularly useful where the opponent's statement of case is vague. But it can have the effect of causing the opponent to review their pleading and improve it!

Part 18.1 provides that:

(1) The court may at any time order a party to –

(a) clarify any matter which is in dispute in the proceedings; or

(b) give additional information in relation to any such matter, whether or not the matter is contained or referred to in a statement of case.

6.3.1.3 So the request need not confine itself just to the pleadings. It may come in response to an allegation or statement of fact in a letter of claim or arising from an assertion or admission in a letter of response. For example there may be what appears to be a partial admission to breach of duty and causation but a failure to address other allegations. The claimant may wish to tease out the extent of the admissions before deciding whether an application for judgment should be made.

A Part 18 request is likely to arise in the following circumstances:

- To obtain further information of particulars in a statement of case.
- Establishing facts prior to disclosure or concerning the letter of claim/response before instructing an expert or issuing proceedings.
- Following exchange of witness statements.

6.3.1.4 By asking questions early on may box in your opponent on evidential and legal matters. This would clearly be opportune before exchange of witness statements.

The subject matter for the request does not have to be in dispute such as in *Harcourt v Griffin* [2007] EWHC 1500 (QB) where the claimant requested information about the nature and extent of insurance cover available to meet the claimant's claim. This was a personal injury claim where the claimant was seriously injured and liability had already been agreed. The court was persuaded to make the order for disclosure in order to determine whether further litigation would be useful or a waste of time and money.

The procedure is that the party seeking clarification or information should firstly make a written request stating a date, allowing a reasonable time, by which the response should be made (**para 1.2 PD18**).

6.3.1.5 *How to reply*

If the request goes beyond clarification or no such clarification is necessary, the respondent may wish to deny the request, arguing that it is more akin to an interrogatory and does not further the overriding objective. But caution should be exercised in the reply as the courts will expect the parties to communicate before launching in to an application. A failure to co-operate may have costs' consequences.

In a pre-CPR case of <u>Hall v Sevalco Limited</u> [1996] PIQR 344, the Court of Appeal adopted the *necessity* test in determining whether interrogatories (as they were known) were necessary to obtain information or admissions which were likely to be contained in pleadings, medical reports, disclosure or witness statements.

In responding to the request, the same format should apply, so if by letter then this will suffice or by formal document if necessary.

The form of objection to an unnecessary request should state some or all of the following points, as appropriate:

(a) that it is a request for information or clarification that is unnecessary, irrelevant or improper;

(b) that he is unable to provide the information or clarification requested;

(c) that insufficient time has been given to him to formulate a reply;

(d) that the request can only be complied with at an expense which is disproportionate to the claim, or is otherwise contrary to the overriding objective;

(e) that he is protected from answering by privilege.

6.3.1.6 *Making the application to the court*

The application notice, N244 should set out the order sought and that it is pursuant to **Part 18.1.** The letter or document making the request should be appended as an exhibit together with the reply. Also exhibited should be the document in which it is contended inadequate particularisation has been made. The application should state the matters in which clarification is sought. Costs should be claimed and subject to summary assessment, so a statement of costs should accompany the application. Normally the application would be listed on notice but if there was no reply to the request, then after 14 days have passed, the court may deal with the application without a hearing (**PD 18, para 5.5**).

An example

Consider a clinical negligence case whereby the claimant alleges that swabs erroneously were left in situ in the surgical wound. A principal allegation is that the defendant had no proper system to guard against this risk. The defendant pleads a bare denial putting the claimant to proof. Given that the claimant has not made an admission, then it must be assumed that that denial represents an assertion that there was a proper system in place. Whilst Further Particulars cannot be raised of a denial, they can of a positive assertion of a system. The claimant needs to know what system, if any was in place, how it was implemented and by whom. Does the hospital have guidelines for clinical instruments as this should be disclosed as part of standard disclosure.

6.3.2 Admissions – CPR 14

6.3.2.1 The philosophy of the CPR is to encourage less adversarial litigation and a climate of openness and co-operation. The extent to which this has been achieved is debatable given that we have adversarial, not inquisitorial advocacy, requiring the parties to prove their assertions. We don't yet have a no fault system in clinical negligence although it has been mooted previously.

So extensive admissions in a defence are rare, presumably for the reason that if the claim was admitted then it would have been likely to settle before issue of proceedings. It may be that breach of duty and causation are admitted but quantum is in dispute.

So it begs the question as to what value limited admissions have and whether the claimant can exploit that admission by obtaining a judgment, even if it is a partial admission. Can a defendant tactically make a limited admission and thereby save costs by alleviating a claimant of the requirement to prove that aspect of the admission. This is a relevant consideration when costs are considered under **Part 44.3(4)** as the court will consider the conduct of the parties.

6.3.2.2 The first opportunity for an admission arises in the protocol letter of response – a pre-action admission. There may be admissions on the facts setting out the background to the incident and there may be some admissions on the applicability of statute pleaded as relevant to the claim.

In a clinical negligence claim, it is more likely that an admission is made to some or all allegations of breach of duty but denying causation. It can happen the other way round but that is more unusual.

6.3.2.3 Responding to an admission

Where there is an admission, whether full or partial in a defence, then the claimant is entitled to enter judgment on that admission – **Rule 14.4** or **Rule 14.5**. This assumes that the defendant accepts that there was some damage. In a clinical negligence claim, it may be that some allegations of breach of duty are admitted but the extent of the injury is disputed as arising from that breach. The defence may be vague on pleading causation in which case a request for further particulars should be sought.

It is important for a claimant to check that the defence is consistent with the letter of response. If an admission is made in the protocol letter but forms a denial in the defence, what has changed? Are they seeking to resile from the admission? Should a notice to admit facts be made?

6.3.2.4 Withdrawing admissions

Pre-issue

A defendant is not able to withdraw a pre-action admission given in a response letter under the pre-action protocol, except with the consent of the claimant or with permission of the court– **rule 14.1A(3)(a)**. He must give notice in writing should he wish to do so. If no consent is given then he must issue an application.

Post issue

Once proceedings have commenced, such withdrawal may be by consent or by court order – **rule 14.1(A)(3)(b)**.

Portal case admissions

This is governed by **rule 14.1B**.

Pre-issue

The defendant may withdraw a pre-action admission of causation unilaterally by giving notice in writing. The time to do that is during the initial consideration period of 15 days after receiving the Stage 2 settlement pack. If the defendant decides to withdraw an admission of causation then the claim will exit the portal (RTA's -**para 7.39(b)** or EL/PL – **para 7.36(b)**).

6.3.2.5 Application to the court

It is assumed in the vast majority of cases that the defendant is the party making the admission and seeking to withdraw it. A claimant is unlikely to consent to a defendant seeking to resile from a pre-action admission so an application to the court is inevitable. It will also be necessary if the admission was made after commencement of proceedings. This applies equally to multi-track claims or those formerly started through the portal and now issued as Part 7 claims.

An application must be made pursuant to **rule 14.(1)(5)** after the commencement of proceedings. The court will consider the circumstances of the case and the criteria in **PD 14, para 7.2**. They are:

(a) the grounds for withdrawing the admission – whether any new evidence has come to light.

(b) conduct of the parties, especially that leading the defendant to make the admission.

(c) Any prejudice to the claimant caused by the withdrawn admission.

(d) The prejudice caused to the defendant if the application is refused.

(e) When the application is made and how close to trial.

(f) The prospects of the entire/partial claim in relation to the proposed withdrawn admission.

(g) The interests of the administration of justice.

6.3.2.6 Let's look at the clinical negligence claim of _Mack v Clarke_ [2017] EWHC 113 (QB) which examined the possibility of making a conditional order for disclosure of earlier expert reports from the neurologist and neurosurgeon on which the terms of the original defence were based. The claim concerned GP delay in referral to hospital following symptoms of a stroke. The defendant wanted to withdraw a paragraph stating the cause of the stroke (not as a result of breach of duty) and replacing with a new paragraph amending the cause. The claimant did not oppose the amendment but sought disclosure of the expert reports as the price for agreeing to the amendment. The court considered the import of **rule 14.1(1)** with respect to '*any part*' and whether the relevant pleading constituted an admission. The judge did not accept that it was an admission as there was no distinct element such as breach of duty, causation or loss. As a result, the defendant did not need permission to withdraw an admission, none being made within the rule. Even if the defendant was seeking to withdraw an unequivocal admission, the judge indicated that he still would not have made a conditional order concerning privileged medical reports. He referred to the case of <u>Jackson v Marley Davenport Ltd</u> [2004] EWCA Civ 1225 where the Court of Appeal refused to order disclosure of earlier draft reports.

This case clearly assists defendants who make admissions on facts which turn out not to be facts following receipt of updated expert evidence. It also makes it difficult for the claimant to obtain some tactical advantage by way of seeking disclosure of the earlier expert report.

A claimant may seek an alternative avenue such as a costs sanction under the court's discretion under **rule 44.2.**

6.3.2.7 A more happy result for the claimant concerning a qualified admission arose in <u>Clark v Braintree Clinical Services Ltd</u> [2015] EWHC 3181 (QB). The court was not prepared to allow for the withdrawal of a qualified admission on breach which was conditional upon the claimant proving the matters contended for. In deciding whether to grant permission, the judge considered <u>Woodland v Stopford</u> [2011] EWCA Civ 266. The judge in that case refused to withdraw the admission, stating that "*pleadings still mean something and must be carefully drafted before service, setting out in clear unambiguous terms the nature of the relevant parties' case.*"

The judge in *Clark* held that the criteria to apply in exercising discretion is the same criteria for relief against sanction as out of time applications. No such application for relief had been made and he considered the criteria set out in *Denton*.

6.328 Where an admission has been made and judgment entered on part of the claim, it is not sufficient to simply withdraw the admission. It is necessary to apply to the court to *vary or revoke* the earlier order in exercise of the court's general powers of management under **Part 3.1(7)**.

The court placed considerable emphasis on the *interests of justice* as one of the criteria in **PD14, 7.2** when analysing an application by the defendant to resile from a pre-action admission of liability in the road traffic case of *Cavell v Transport for London* [2015] EWHC 2283 (QB). The court refused the application to withdraw the admission, holding that there was no evidence to indicate anything other than careful consideration given by competent professional advisors.

6.3.3 Notice to admit facts/documents – CPR 32.18/32.19

6.3.3.1 This is an under used technique to elicit facts from the other side so saving the costs of having to prove them. Certain facts may be implied or seem obvious from a case but have not been addressed or admitted in a statement of case or a witness statement. For example, in a road accident, date, time, parties, occupants, vehicles involved etc. are significant facts that ought to be non-contentious, so capable of agreement but it cannot be assumed. The less facts that have to be proved the better. Therefore a Notice to Admit Facts may be served on the other side to try and tease out an admission. If not forthcoming, then at least you know what you need to prove. The notice and the response are part of the pleadings so would go into the trial bundle.

Following exchange of witness statements, give careful consideration to what still needs to be proved for trial. A notice may then be deployed towards obtaining evidence to establish those facts. Or it may be used to reduce the scope for evasion by a witness under cross-examination.

Following standard disclosure, unless a party objects to or questions the authenticity of a document, then he shall be deemed to admit it. The benefit is to avoid the costs involved in calling a witness to prove an item of evidence, usually a minor part such as an item of special damages or photographic evidence.

6.3.3.2 The procedure is set out in **Parts 32.18 and 32.19.**

There is little in the way of prescribed directions in the CPR. A notice to admit facts must be served at least 21 days before trial. Clearly if the notice is to have some real benefit in saving investigative time and costs then it should be served early on, perhaps shortly after receipt of the particulars of claim or defence. If the opponent fails to address the request on facts that should have been admitted, then this may have significant costs implications with respect to conduct.

A receiving party may object to a notice saying that the matters in issue will be covered in a witness statement. If that is their position, then costs will be incurred in seeking to prove or disprove a fact. Consideration will need to be given whether an application to the court is necessary to flush out the opponent's position on a factual issue. It may be that following standard disclosure, the fact is answered but why wait to that stage if it is capable of being resolved earlier.

A notice to admit or produce documents must be served by the latest date for serving witness statements or within 7 days of disclosure of the document, whichever is the later.

Key points

- Part 18 Requests for further information may be used where clarification of a fact pleaded in the particulars of claim or defence or witness statement is necessary, for example a discrepancy or omission in medical records or a vague pleading or putting the claimant to proof when there should be full particulars.

- Part 18 Requests must not be used as a fishing expedition. An informal request should be made first.

- Distinguish between a request for mere evidence and relevant issues, the former will not be allowed, the latter may be allowed subject to prejudice and proportionality.

- Where admissions are made by the defendant, seek summary judgment on that admission.

- Scrutinise the protocol letter with the pleading to ensure consistency.

- Consider tactical admissions, say where breach of duty is indefensible but a causation defence is stronger, or make partial admissions. This may alter the balance of power and cause the claimant to concentrate on proving quantum on the admission to the detriment of proving the denials.

- Admissions may be withdrawn, typically may arise where the value of the claim exceeds what was first intimated. Prejudice and time of request will be examined and prospects of success.

- A notice to admit facts under Part 32.18 can save costs. Normally served after exchange of witness statements, used in a similar manner as cross-examination. Requires careful review of witness statements to determine evasion or ambiguity.

6.4 Summary judgment/dismissal – CPR 24

6.4.1 This enables the court in exercise of its case management powers to decide an issue or to dismiss a claim or strike out a defence where it has no merit. An application may be made by either party. The procedure is only applicable where oral evidence is not required and where there is no dispute on the facts.

In this section, the tests for establishing summary judgment or dismissal will be considered. The procedure for making an application is covered in chapter 7 on interlocutory applications.

6.4.2 The grounds the court will apply in an application for summary judgment/dismissal are:

CPR 24.2

> "(a) it considers that -
>
> (i) that claimant has no real prospect of succeeding on the claim or issue; or
>
> (j) that defendant has no real prospect of successfully defending the claim or issue: and
>
> (a) there is no other compelling reason why the claim or issue should be disposed of at a trial."

The hearing is not a trial so the requirements for hearing witnesses to make findings of fact do not apply. It might be that where a claimant is contesting an application for dismissal of the claim, that he may wish to adduce evidence, if only to show to the court that there are matters of fact to be determined that are relevant to the case and therefore making it inappropriate for the application to succeed. However a court will not permit oral evidence.

Timing is important as a court generally will not entertain an application for summary judgment until an acknowledgment of service or defence has been filed (**Part 24.1**). Normally it will be filed before filing or at the same time as filing the Directions Questionnaire (**PD 26, para 5.3(1)**).

6.4.3 The test

'*Real prospect of success*' is the same test as that used in applications to set aside default judgment (see <u>E D and F Man Liquid Products Ltd v Patel</u> [2003] EWCA Civ 472). It applies the overriding objective of dealing with the case justly. The test is whether there is a real prospect of success on the case as pleaded in the particulars of claim. It muse not be a 'fanciful' prospect. This was considered (and has since been adopted in other cases) in the above case when Potter LJ said:

> *I regard the distinction between a realistic and fanciful prospect of succcess as appropriately reflecting the observation in the* Saudi Eagle *that the defence sought to be argued must carry some degree of conviction. Both approaches require the defendant to have a case which is better than merely arguable, as was formerly the case under RSC ord 14*

The burden for satisfying a summary judgment claim is on the claimant to show that the defendant has no real prospect of success. The contrary position applies to a defendant in seeking to strike out the claimant's claim. The Court of Appeal in <u>Director of the Assets Recovery Agency v Woodstock</u> [2006] EWCA Civ 741 said that the onus is on the applicant. Where the applicant establishes a prima facie claim against the respondent, there is an evidential burden on the respondent to show a case answering that advanced by the applicant and if they do, they ordinarily they should be allowed to take the matter to trial.

In order for an application for summary judgment to succeed where a strike out application would not, three conditions must be satisfied:

> (1) all substantial facts relevant to the claimant's case that are reasonably capable of being before the court must be before the court;

(2) those facts must be undisputed or there must be no reasonable prospect of successfully disputing them;

(3) there must be no real prospect of oral evidence affecting the court's assessment of the facts (*S v Gloucestershire County Council* [2001] Fam 313).

The facts must be germane to the matters in dispute. If there is no or no real prospect of the defendant establishing facts sufficient to justify the principal elements of the defence then judgment should be entered (*P and S Amusements Ltd v Valley House Leisure Ltd* [2006] EWHC 1510 (Ch).

A defence consisting mainly of denials may cause the court to conclude that the defence has no real prospect of success (*Broderick v Centaur Tipping Services Ltd* (2006) LTL.

The written evidence will assist the court but does not mean invariably that it is accepted, either by the claimant or the defendant. There has to be some basis for disbelieving the evidence but if not, then it is suggested that a statement on behalf of the respondent is likely to carry weight in a finding that there are disputed facts.

Of course an application for summary judgment may turn on strict liability. So if a claim is made under section 41 *Highways Act 1980*, alleging a substantial and dangerous defect in the highway which could be proved and the defendant could not evince a reasonable system of inspection, then in this situation it is ripe for an application for summary judgment. But if there are factual disputes about causation of injuries and whether this was down to any defect in the highway or because of the want of care of a claimant, then such application should fail.

6.4.4 Power to strike out a case – **CPR 3.4**

This has a close relationship with summary judgment as striking out the whole or part of a statement of case will be liable for entry of summary judgment. So where a defence includes bare denials, it may be appropriate to apply to strike out those paragraphs under **rule 3.4(2)(a)** and to grant summary judgment under **rule 24.2** on the parts of the claim denied.

CPR 3.4(2) provides that the court may strike out a statement of case if it appears:

> *'(a) that the statement of case discloses no reasonable grounds for bringing or defending the claim;*
>
> *(b) that the statement of case is an abuse of the court's process or is otherwise likely to obstruct the just disposal of the proceedings; or*
>
> *(c) that there has been a failure to comply with a rule, practice direction or court order.'*

It may be that a joint application under both rule 3.4 and Part 24 could be made where the case is clearly misconceived. Consider the clinical negligence claim of *Smith v University of Leicester NHS Trust* [2016] EWHC 817 (QB) where both parts of the CPR were applied. The claimants had no cause of action against the defendant as they were not owed a duty of care. They were third parties seeking a remedy in connection with treatment provided by the defendant to another. There was insufficient proximity in accordance with the *Caparo* test such that it would not be *fair, just and reasonable to impose a duty of care*. As a result the statement of case was struck out on the basis that it disclosed no reasonable grounds for bringing the claim.

Key points

- Summary judgment is a strong weapon in the litigator's armoury but it won't be appropriate where complex issues are in dispute or where the court has to conduct a mini-trial to resolve conflicts of evidence.

- An application may be appropriate where admissions have been made, or inappropriate non-admissions, or cases of absolute or strict liability or where the burden of proof is reversed but not appreciated by the defendant or in a res ipsa situation.

- A detailed skeleton argument will need to accompany the application, illustrating why the applicant has a real prospect of success and there is no other compelling reason why the case should not proceed to trial.

- If contesting an application, file a detailed witness statement with a skeleton argument setting out the facts in dispute and any points of law that arise, as well as the burden that the applicant has to overcome in order for judgment to be entered.

6.5 Interim payments

6.5.1 An injured claimant is likely to require an interim payment in a claim that is likely to take some time to conclude. The procedure differs in claims above £25,000.00 as they will be allocated to the multi-track and governed by **Part 25** of the CPR.

A claim for less than £25,000 will proceed via the low value protocol through the online portal which has its own defined procedures – paras 7.13 to 7.21 of the protocol for RTA claims or paras 7.12 to 7.20 for EL/PL claims.

6.5.2 Portal claims

As portal claims have their own self-contained rules, an application to the court is not normally necessary. Both protocols governing RTA's, EL and PL claims provide that a claimant may request and receive an interim payment of at least £1,000 in relation to general damages.

The procedure is that the Interim Settlement Pack plus a medical report and evidence of pecuniary losses is uploaded onto the portal (paras 7.13 (RTA) or 7.14 (EL/PL) of the protocol). The interim is payable within 10 days of receiving the Interim Settlement Pack. If more than £1,000 is claimed, the defendant either pays the requested sum, less any deductible amount payable to the CRU, or another amount within 15 days of receiving the Interim Settlement Pack.

If the claim is valued at more than £10,000 then the claimant may request a second interim payment.

6.5.2.1 Disputing an interim - exiting the portal

Should the defendant refuse to pay an interim payment under the portal, then the claimant may start **Part 7** proceedings and apply for an interim in those proceedings (see para 7.28 – RTA or para 7.26 – EL/PL).

Also, if the amount offered by the defendant for an interim is not sufficient, then the claimant may also start Part 7 proceedings. Notice must be given to the defendant that the claim will no longer continue under the protocol. There is an additional period of 10 days from the last date that payment was due from the defendant according to the circumstances (see paras 7.18, 7.19 or 7.25 for RTA or paras 7.17, 7.18 or 7.23 for EL/PL). However the claimant should know that if the court orders no interim payment or one which does not exceed the defendant's offer, then the claimant will only recover stage 2 fixed costs.

The information required for Part 7 proceedings will be similar to that contained in an application under part 25.7 (see below).

6.5.3 Multi-track claims under **Part 25.6**

An order for an interim payment is an order for payment by a defendant on account of any damages, debt or other sum (except costs) which the court may hold the defendant liable to pay (see **25.1(k)**). It forms part of the interim remedies that the court may grant.

Normally a claimant would request the defendant to make a voluntary payment. Where liability is not in dispute and the amount requested is not likely to exceed the damages payable, then the defendant is likely to agree. However where the claim is still being investigated or liability is in dispute or where the amount sought appears to be excessive (perhaps there are allegations of contributory conduct) then an application under **Part 7** is indicated.

6.5.3.1 Objective of the claimant

The main purpose of an interim payment is to avoid or relieve hardship that the claimant may suffer as a result of sustaining injuries. Typically, the claimant may be absent from work as a result so is in financial difficulties or if not employed, may be expending more money than usual on transport, or on medication or other aids to assist recovery. The court will be sympathetic to a claimant who has financial need when otherwise they would have to wait for trial or a final assessment of damages.

6.5.3.2 Time for applying

The earliest time is the expiry date for the defendant filing its acknowledgement of service. The claimant can of course request an interim earlier, perhaps in the letter of claim, but if this is ignored or denied then proceedings will need to be issued.

6.5.3.3 The grounds for an order

The conditions to be satisfied are set out in **Rule 25.7**. The most likely scenario is where liability is in dispute. So the burden will be on the claimant to satisfy the court that if the case went to trial, he would succeed and obtain substantial damages (**25.7(1)(c)**). He must do this on the balance of probabilities.

25.7(1) conditions required for ordering an interim

*(a) the defendant has admitted liability to pay damages or some other sum of money to the claimant (**25.7(1)(a)**); or*

*(b) the claimant has obtained judgment against the defendant for damages or some other sum (other than costs) to be assessed (**25.7(1)(b)**); or*

*(c) the court is satisfied that, if the claim went to trial, the claimant would obtain judgment against the defendant from whom the interim payment is sought for a substantial sum of money (other than costs) whether or not that defendant is the only defendant or one of a number of defendants to the claim (**25.7(1)(c)**); or*

*(d) the claimant is seeking possession of land, and the court is satisfied that if the case went to trial the defendant would be held liable to pay the claimant a sum of money for use and occupation of the land while the claim is pending (**25.7(1)(d)**).*

6.5.3.4 In assessing merits of the claim, the interlocutory judge is effectively putting herself in the position of the trial judge. The claimant should therefore put as much material before the court as possible to show that the claim is likely to succeed. If the claimant satisfies the conditions in **25.7**, then the court should order an interim payment unless there is a specific reason not to do so, applying the overriding objective.

The fact that contributory negligence is alleged is irrelevant so long as the claimant is still able to obtain a substantial award after taking in to account any deduction for contribution. **Rules 25.7(4) and (5)** provide that:

> *(4) The court must not order an interim payment of more than a reasonable proportion of the likely amount of the final judgment.*
>
> *(5) The court must take into account –*
>
> *(a) contributory negligence: and*
> *(b) any relevant set-off or counterclaim*

It is in the arena of high value claims that an application for interims is most likely to be contested. Some are because of denials of breach of duty or causation, others because the amount sought seems excessive.

Regard must also be had to the possibility of an order for periodical payments under **Rule 41** and under **Section 2(1)(a) Damages Act 1996**. If so, the amount of any interim payment must not be so high so as to affect the court's decision on whether to make a PPs order.

6.5.3.5 It is helpful to review some cases to discern judicial thinking and a common approach.

The first case is that of *Eeles v Cobham Hire Services Ltd* [2010] 1 WLR 409 which was heard at the Court of Appeal and was thought to be groundbreaking and somewhat favourable to defendants where the claimant has a periodical payments order. They held that the amount of the final judgment in rule 25.7(4) meant only the capital sum awarded *exclusive* of any periodical payments. The Court formulated a two-stage test when considering a large interim payment to purchase accommodation. Stage 1 examines the likely lump sum award for heads of damage for PSLA, past losses, interest and accommodation costs. Stage 2 only applies if the interim payment requested exceeds a reasonable proportion of the likely award assessed at stage 1. The court may assess the capitalised value of future losses and if this exceeds the value in stage 1 then a larger interim may be justified, provided only that there is a *real need* for the interim payment to purchase the new accommodation now rather than after the trial.

Eeles was reviewed is the case of <u>Grainger v Cooper</u> [2015] EWHC 1132 (QB) which was a serious injury claim following an RTA. Liability was admitted. The claimant had already received an interim payment exceeding £1 million and sought a further interim of £700,000 (subsequently reduced to £425,000) to fund purchase of a suitable property. The parties agreed that the second stage of *Eeles* applied. For stage 1 the parties reached an agreement on value by splitting the difference between the claimant's schedule of loss and the defendant's counter schedule. The court rejected this approach holding that it was not the role of the interim judge to make an assessment but the task of the trial judge after hearing the evidence. If a large interim created an 'unlevel playing field', then the court had a discretion not to consider stage 1 of *Eeles,* and so it did not do so, but went on to order an interim payment of £133,000.

LJ Mckenna in <u>A v Palmer</u> (March 2012) was not concerned about any risk in making an interim payment would prejudge any issue left to the trial judge in deciding the care that a claimant should receive. He did accept that *Eeles* should be followed when it came to periodical payments and capitalisation on heads of future loss. The claimant was treated at a medical clinic and the total cost of care was contested by the defendant. The court held that it was necessary to determine what was a reasonable proportion of an award that might be made, leaving out of account sums of future loss to be considered by the trial judge in dealing with a periodical payment order.

6.536 On allegations of contributory negligence, it is for the defendant to adduce evidence. This was confirmed in the case of <u>Melvyn Smith v Richard Bailey</u> [2014] EWHC 2569 (QB) where an interim payment was awarded for accommodation costs valued according to stage 1 of the *Eeles* test. On appeal, the appellate judge upheld the finding at first instance, holding that in the absence of any evidence to show contributory negligence, the trial judge was justified in treating the likely award of damages to be on the basis of full liability.

For a contrary finding where contributory negligence was alleged in the clinical negligence claim of <u>Zeb v Frimley Health NHS Foundation Trust</u> [2016] EWHC 134 (QB), the court at first instance, and supported on appeal, did not award an interim payment. The claimant suffered a very serious neurological injury from the untreated condition of tuberculosis meningitis. Breach of duty was admitted but causation was defended, alleging a novus actus and contributory negligence. The court noted that the burden of proof in seeking an interim is on the claimant to satisfy the court that judgment would be obtained. Just because those allegations were made does not necessarily disentitle the making of an interim payment. In reality the defendant's case was that the claimant's conduct by failing to disclose her medical history and failing to continue with a prescribed course of treatment, constituted a complete and sufficient cause for the injury. The court was therefore not satisfied that the test set out in **rule 25.7(1)(c)** was met.

An interim payment was granted where breach of duty was admitted but causation disputed in a case where the claimant disclosed its causation report but the defendant did not in <u>Sellar-Elliott v Howling</u> [2016] EWHC 443(QB). The trial judge noted that whilst a claimant must prove his case, there is an evidential burden on the defendant to raise matters beyond the pleadings where it is maintaining a causation defence. The expert evidence need not be fully disclosed but arguments put forward in summary form or in a letter to undermine the claimant's expert's evidence would be sufficient. The defendants appealed which was dismissed, Sweeny J holding that the trial judge had decided the application on the evidence before him and he was right to do so in accordance with the dicta in <u>Smith v Bailey</u> [2014] EWHC 2569 (QB).

Key points

- Claimants should always consider an interim payment to offset losses they incur and to assist in costs of the case.

- Claimants may obtain an interim where judgment on liability has been entered for damages to be assessed, or liability has been admitted, (or at least some admissions), or they can demonstrate a strong case on liability.

- The conditions to be satisfied are set out in CPR 25.7 whilst the procedure is in CPR 25.6. The earliest date for applying is the last date for filing the acknowledgment of service.

- In a portal claim, a claimant is entitled to at least an interim of £1,000 payable after submitting the interim settlement pack.

- For very large interim payments where periodical payments apply, be aware of the *Eeles* criteria and the three-stage test. A 'real need' must be demonstrated.

6.6 Exit from the personal injury portal

There are clear benefits to the claimant's legal advisors if a claim exits the portal as they then stand to receive more costs from the defendant, subject to the proviso that their retainer letter provides for that, otherwise any additional costs goes to the claimant.

But if they exit the portal in circumstances that are not prescribed or because of their non-compliance or unreasonable behaviour, then they face recovering only the fixed portal costs despite undertaking more work. They may even be liable for paying the defendant's costs, which may be fixed or 'open' and assessed on the standard basis. So getting it wrong can prove expensive when the margins are so small. If it goes wrong, then it will be the claimant's legal advisors who will be standing the bill unless any error can be ascribed to the claimant, which is unlikely unless there is some element of dishonesty.

From the defendant's perspective, they will wish to ensure that the claim remains in the portal, thus avoiding any payment of further costs. They too face an adverse costs order if exit from the portal is because of their conduct.

In this section, we shall look at the opportunities that exist for escaping the portal and the benefits to be gained as well as the downsides – depending on your perspective.

6.6.1 Normal Fixed Costs

Fixed costs and fixed disbursements are payable for RTA and EL/PL claims that come within the pre-action protocol for low value personal injury claims, i.e. for all cases where the cause of action started after 31st July 2013 and are valued between £1,000 to £25,000. Those costs are prescribed by **Rule 45.17** and relate to the three stages of the portal procedure. There is an opportunity to obtain further fixed costs under **Rule 45.23A** where the claimant beats the defendant's offer (as made in the Court Proceedings Pack) in which case he will also receive Stage 3 Type A fixed costs.

Where a litigant does not have a legal representative then they are not entitled to payment of fixed costs.

6.6.2 Portal costs

Rule 45.18 prescribes the fixed costs payable in the portal which are set out in Tables 6 and 6A.

They are set out in **Part 45.18** and accessed at: www.justice.gov.uk/courts/procedure-rules/civil/rules/part45-fixed-costs.

The costs payable to the legal representative are set out in Table 6 for the RTA protocol or Table 6A for the EL/PL protocol. They are referred to as Type A fixed costs. If the case goes to a stage 3 Settlement hearing, an advocate's fees are also payable, known as Type B fixed costs. It is likely that the legal representative having conduct will wish to see the case through from start to finish.

The intention behind the protocol is that cases are dealt with simply and efficiently. Thus a claimant's legal advisor has to have a slick system in order to conclude a claim within a maximum of 3 to 5 hours dependent on whether the claim is an RTA or an EL/PL. The temptation is to look for avenues to escape the portal in the hope that costs are payable at an increased tariff. The additional costs are set out in Table 6B (RTA), Table 6C (EL) or Table 6D(PL). These tables provide for different tariffs dependent on whether settlement is achieved before Part 7 proceedings are issued, post issue of proceedings or disposed of at a trial.

There is some limited scope for increasing costs if an interlocutory application is necessary for an interim payment under **Part 45.29H**. If an order for costs is made, then they are payable in the sum of one half of the applicable Type A and Type B costs together with an amount of 12.5% of those costs.

6.6.3 Exited Portal costs

Rules 45.29C (RTA) and **45.29E** (EL/PL) provide for fixed costs for claims no longer proceeding in the portal. These costs are substantially higher than portal costs as they provide for a fixed sum plus a percentage of the damages. Claimants will therefore hope that their claim does exit the portal.

The tables set out recovery of costs where a settlement is achieved pre-action or post issue of Part 7 proceedings and at trial. Table 6B covers RTA claims, Table 6C covers EL claims whilst Table 6D covers PL claims.

We shall review the opportunities for leaving the portal for RTA and EL/PL cases referring to both sets of rules, which are very similar. There are potentially 14 situations when either the claimant or defendant may elect to give notice that the claim will no longer proceed under the protocol or where there is an automatic exit.

We will not consider the excluded cases (see para 4.5 of the RTA Protocol and para 4.3 of the EL/PL Protocol) that should not have been brought in the portal in the first place.

It should be noted that once a claim does exit the portal, it cannot subsequently re-enter the process (para 5.11 both in the RTA and the EL/PL Protocol). So if a claimant gives notice of exit in unreasonable circumstances, then he is bound by that decision and pays the price for it if he issues **Part** 7 proceedings.

6.6.4 Exit points – timing

(a) Any stage

Claimant election. Where the claimant **revalues** the claim above £25,000. (para 4.3 (RTA); para 4.2 (EL/PL)).

(b) Stage 1

(i) <u>Defendant election</u>. Where D notifies C that it considers that **inadequate mandatory information** has been provided in the CNF. (paras 6.8 and 6.15(4)(a) (RTA); paras 6.7 and 6.13(4)(a) (EL/PL).

(ii) <u>Defendant election</u>. Where D alleges **contributory negligence** (other than C's admitted failure to wear a seat belt in an RTA). (para 6.15(1) (RTA); para 6.13(1) (EL/PL).

(iii) <u>Claimant's election</u>. Where D does **not admit liability** in the CNF response in an RTA within **15 days** (para 6.15(3) or in an EL within **30 days** (para 6.13(3) or in a PL within **40 days** (para 6.15(3)).

(iv) <u>Claimant's election.</u> Where D does **not complete and send the CNF response** within **15 days/30 days/40 days** for RTA/EL/PL respectively. (para 6.15(2) (RTA); para 6.13(2) (EL/PL).

(v) <u>Defendant's election.</u> Where value of claim would be on the small claims track (para 6.15(4)(b) (RTA); (para 6.13(4)(b) (EL/PL).

(c) Stage 2

(i) <u>Claimant's election</u>. Where D fails to pay **Stage 1 costs** 10 days after receiving the Stage 2 Settlement Pack <u>and</u> C gives written notice within 10 days thereafter that claim not proceed under the protocol (para 6.19 (RTA); para 6.17 (EL/PL)).

(ii) <u>Claimant's election.</u> Where **no interim payment** (At C's request in the Interim Settlement Pack) is made or it is inadequate or it is paid late, then C must give notice within 10 days of the last date that payment was due (10 days for interim of £1,000 or 15 days for interim exceeding £1,000) (paras 7.28, 7.29 and 7.30 (RTA); (paras 7.26, 7.27 and 7.28 (EL/PL).

(iii) <u>Defendant's election</u>. Where D considers the **small claims track** is the normal track and gives notice to C within 15 days from receiving the Stage 2 Settlement Pack (para 7.39(a) (RTA); 7.36(a) (EL/PL).

(iv) <u>Defendant's election</u>. Where D **withdraws admission of causation**, giving notice within 15 days of receiving the Stage 2 Settlement Pack (para 7.39(b) (RTA); para 7.36(b) (EL/PL).

(v) <u>Claimant's election</u>. Where D **fails to respond/make an offer** within 15 days (or any agreed extension) of receipt of the Stage 2 Settlement Pack (para 7.40 (RTA); para 7.37 (EL/PL).

(vi) <u>Claimant's election</u>. Where either party **withdraws an offer** made in the Stage 2 Settlement pack within the total consideration period of 35 days (plus any extension) (para 7.46 (RTA); para 7.43 (EL/PL).

(vii) <u>Claimant's election</u>. Where D makes **no Stage 2 payment** (D's offer of damages plus Stages 1 and 2 costs and disbursements) within 15 days of receiving the Court proceedings Pack (para 7.75 (RTA); para 7.58 (EL/PL).

(viii) <u>Claimant's election</u>. Where C give notice to D that claim **unsuitable for the protocol** (e.g. complex issues of fact or law), para 7.76 (RTA); para 7.59 (EL/PL - also where C contemplating applying for a GLO).

6.6.6 Getting it wrong

But if a claimant gets it wrong and issues **Part 7** proceedings unnecessarily of his own volition or because of a court order, then he may find that he does not recover additional costs beyond the initial fixed costs, despite undertaking a considerable amount of work.

Consider the case of *Phillips v Willis* [2016] EWCA Civ 401. This was an RTA case which started in the portal. Liability was admitted and general damages together with other losses were agreed. D objected to pay for car hire charges so C commenced Part 8 proceedings. At the stage 3 hearing the District Judge transferred the claim to the Small Claims Track, giving directions that the case should proceed under Part 7. The court was exercising its purported power to do so under para **7.2 PD 8B** (which covers the need for further evidence). C appealed and it went to the Court of Appeal, the court holding that the District Judge had no such power to direct that the case should proceed under **Part 7**, rather than **Part 8**. The only time that that paragraph should apply was in a case involving complex issues of law or fact when a Stage 3 resolution may not be suitable. The Court of Appeal also stated that it would have been wrong in this case for the court to have exercised its power under **CPR 8.1(3)** to transfer the case into Part 7.

The point to derive from this case is that disproportionate costs incurred by the claimant in seeking to recover disputed hire charges would not be recoverable by issuing Part 7 proceedings. The only issue in this case was the claimant's duty to mitigate hire charges and this did not require significant oral evidence. The lesson to learn is that **CPR 8.1(3)** may not be used to subvert the portal process. If small sums are in dispute then the correct procedure is via stage 3 of the protocol. **PD 8B** is designed to deal with portal cases where quantum is in dispute.

As the appellate judges made clear in *Phillips* it is not open for the parties to elect to exit the process as designated steps must be followed. The rules specified when a case must remain in or drop out.

The cost consequences of non-compliance were spelt out in <u>Mulholland v Hughes,</u> No AP20/15, Newcastle upon Tyne County court, 18 September 2015 and in <u>Uppal v Daudia</u> LTLPI 9 July 2012.

The first case concerned recovery of hire charges in an RTA. There were four conjoined appeals which involved issues as to whether a defendant could raise arguments at a Part 8 hearing that had not been raised at stage 2 – it could not, as the intention of the protocol was for the parties to have clarity of what remained in dispute by stage 2. Defendants challenging hire charges need to raise it at stage 2 in order for the claimant to prove need. The court also held that a claimant is bound to repay an overpayment of damages where the court assessed the losses less than earlier offers made by the defendant. So the non-settlement payment was to be regarded as an interim payment, governed by CPR Part 25. The judge rejected an argument that offers made by the defendant at stage 2 should be regarded as admissions as they were tantamount to Part 36 offers. Although the court did not address costs in the appeal, it is likely that the claimants will have been liable to pay the defendant's costs under Part 36.29 for failing to beat the defendant's protocol offer. Such costs would be fixed costs in rule 45.26 and interest.

Mulholland is a good case for a review of the portal procedure.

A salutary lesson for claimants in starting unnecessary **Part** 7 proceedings is that of *Uppal*. The claim exited the portal at the claimant's behest because they erroneously believed that the defendant's failure to make an offer to the claimant's counter offer during the consideration period entitled them to remove the claim. By unreasonably leaving the portal, the defendant was awarded costs on an indemnity basis and they amounted to over £20,000.

> **Key points**
>
> - Portal claims are very procedural and prescriptive so close attention to dates for compliance must be made. Remember it's business days.
>
> - Claimants should take advantage of the escape provisions but notice must be given in certain circumstances. Beware unreasonable exit and costs penalties.
>
> - Defendants may exercise tactical pressure if the claimant has failed to provide mandatory information causing exit from the portal. The claimant will need to do more work but will only receive fixed costs.

6.7 Know your limitation(s)

6.7.1 This is a crucial area for claimants as they must bring their claim before expiry of the limitation period, otherwise the claim is time-barred under the *Limitation Act 1980* (LA 1980) and cannot be pursued, unless there are exceptional circumstances.

We shall consider the usual limitation period of **3 years** and those situations when a different period applies, how to address imminent expiry and what to do if the period has expired.

In a claim on behalf of a child, time does not normally run until the age of 18.

An accident at sea (including injury in an inflatable off the UK coast) or an accident during flight or (possibly) at the airport is **2 years.** Significantly the 2 years' period for air or sea claims also applies to children so time runs from the date of the accident. A claim to the Criminal Injuries' Compensation Authority is also **2 years.**

6.7.2 It might be thought that this topic is really not about tactics at all but I demur. Limitation periods can represent one of the strongest defences open to a defendant, thus putting the claimant on the back foot. Considerations need to be given as to how to plead the claim and the defence and whether a reply is called for. Even in a case where breach of duty is admitted, a limitation defence may still be relied upon. A claimant needs to give careful consideration as to whether her claim is likely to be statute barred and how one seeks the court's discretion, if available, so as to disapply the limitation period.

A review of the provisions in the Limitation Act concerning the date of knowledge under section 11, and the court's discretion under section 33 is necessary, before considering the procedure to ensure an in-time application and how to proceed if the limitation period has expired.

6.7.3 Table of limitation periods in various personal injury cases

Type of claim	Limitation Period	Statute
Personal injury/Clinical negligence	3 years	S.11(4) LA 1980
Fatal accidents Act 1976 claims (from the date of death or knowledge, whichever is later)	3 years	S.12(2) LA 1980
Product liability claims	3 years	S.11A LA 1980
Accidents at sea	2 years	S.190(3) & sch. 6 Merchant Shipping Act 1995
Aircraft accidents	2 years	Sch. 1 The Carriage by Air Act 1961
Child claim, accrual starts at age 18 (unless claim in sea/air then 2 years from accident)	3 years	S. 28 LA 1980
Criminal Injuries' claim	2 years	Criminal Injuries Compensation Act 2012
Motor Insurers' Bureau claim	3 years	Uninsured Drivers' Agreement 2015 or Untraced Drivers' Agreement 2017
Persons lacking capacity – time only runs when capacity is regained (if at all)	3 years	S.28(6) LA 1980
A claim for trespass to the person	6 years	S.2 LA 1980
Contribution proceedings	2 years	S.10(1) Civil Liability (Contribution) Act 1978

6.7.4 The law

6.7.4.1 Section 11(4) Limitation Act 1980 – date of knowledge

Time runs from the date of the cause of action (which typically is the date of the accident or date of the injury) or, if later, the date of the claimant's knowledge. The knowledge may be actual (s.14(1)) or constructive (s.14(3)).

Actual knowledge is when the claimant is positively aware that he has an injury, that is significant and due to negligence.

Constructive knowledge is knowledge that the claimant is reasonably expected to have acquired from facts ascertainable by him, possibly through medical, legal or other expert advice.

A person who is injured in a car accident knows when they are injured so they have actual knowledge of the start date for bringing a negligence claim. However, someone exposed to asbestos many years previously who suffers latent damage, remaining asymptomatic until perhaps decades later needs to establish their date of knowledge. If they are informed that they have mesothelioma but do nothing about investigating a claim and over 3 years later die and the estate brings a claim, it may be said that the deceased was fixed with constructive knowledge when they were informed about their condition. This is the date of presumed knowledge under the Limitation Act.

Limitation is especially significant in clinical negligence, abuse and industrial disease claims because the injury or damage may not be evident for some considerable time. This is latent damage. In abuse cases, there may be many reasons why the abuse is not reported, often because of psychological reasons and shame.

6.7.4.2 The first date of the claimant's knowledge is defined in **section 14(1)** as knowledge of the following facts:

(a) *that the injury in question was significant; and*

(b) *that the injury was attributable in whole or in part to the act or omission which is alleged to constitute negligence, nuisance or breach of duty; and*

(c) *the identity of the defendant; and*

(d) *if it is alleged that the act or omission was that of a person other than the defendant, the identity of that person and the additional facts supporting the bringing of an action against the defendant;*

and knowledge that any acts or omissions did or did not, as a matter of law, involve negligence, nuisance or breach of duty is irrelevant.

Where 3 years has already elapsed from the date of the incident giving rise to the claim, the claimant will wish to argue that the 3 years' period commences from their date of knowledge. Therefore they will largely be concerned with s.11(4)(a) and (b).

'Knowledge' in subsection (b) does not have to be detailed enough for drafting the particulars of claim, but is sufficient if the claimant knows enough to investigate a case. This may mean visiting solicitors to seek advice.

6.7.4.3 The question of the significance of the injury is set out in

Section 14(2):

For the purposes of this section an injury is significant if the person whose date of knowledge is in question would reasonably have considered it sufficiently serious to justify his instituting proceedings for damages against a defendant who did not dispute liability and was able to satisfy a judgment.

Danger: It is dangerous to assume that the date of knowledge is only fixed from the date of receipt of an expert report addressing negligence because the claimant may be fixed with constructive knowledge at an earlier date.

Constructive knowledge is defined in section 14(3). Time will start running before the claimant has actual knowledge when he has constructive knowledge of *facts observable or ascertainable by him* or obtained with the help of expert advice when it was reasonable to obtain.

6.7.4.4 Constructive knowledge is defined under

Section 14(3):

For the purposes of this section a person's knowledge includes knowledge which might be reasonably have been expected to acquire –

(a) from facts observable or ascertainable by him; or

(b) from facts ascertainable by him with the help of medical or other appropriate expert advice which it is reasonable for him to seek;

but a person shall not be fixed under this subsection with knowledge of a fact ascertainable only with the help of expert advice so long as he has taken all reasonable steps to obtain (and, where appropriate, to act on) that advice.

There is some debate on how constructive knowledge is assessed. Is it an objective test of the 'reasonable person' or is it subjective based on the claimant's own characteristics. Most cases indicate it is objective but special characteristics of a particular claimant should not be ignored and may be relevant.

The test of whether constructive knowledge is imputed to the claimant has been held to be *objective* by the House of Lords in <u>Adams v Bracknell Forest Borough Council</u> [2004] 1 AC76 where the Law Lords disavowed consideration of personal characteristics of the claimant. The test was what a reasonable man in the claimant's position should have done. That reasonable person is expected to have a 'heightened degree of curiosity'.

But in *AB v Ministry of Defence* [2013] 1 AC 78, it was held that time starts running from when the claimant believes their injury was attributable to the relevant act or omission shown by submitting a claim to the defendant and obtaining evidence.

There are other authorities supporting the objective test such as *Forbes v Wandsworth Health* Authority [1997] QB 402. The court considered the question of whether it was *reasonable* for a claimant to enquire further into their condition or not. Some will and some won't, but the person who chooses not to at the time of harm but then changes his mind and seeks advice later outside the limitation period will not be acting in accordance with the intention of the Act. It would make the Act unworkable as a claimant could delay indefinitely seeking expert advice.

The reasonableness of the claimant's actions was also supported in the case of *A v Hoare* [2008] UKHL 6 where the test in section 4(2) was said to be entirely impersonal. The correct approach was to ask what the claimant knew about the injury.

6.7.4.5 There is a potential risk that application of the objective test means imputation of constructive knowledge at an earlier date than when the claimant decides to bring a claim. In arguments over the date, claimants may wish to argue the subjective test, whilst defendants are more likely to favour the objective test.

What should be gleaned from this is that legal advisors should not necessarily accept at face value the date of knowledge given by a claimant. Close review of medical records is advised because they may reveal that information was given to the claimant which should have put them on notice about possible grounds for bringing a claim. If they delayed taking legal advice, that is insufficient to argue a later date of knowledge.

A defendant alive to the possibility that the primary limitation period has expired may seek a **Part 18** request for further information of the particulars of claim where the date of knowledge is pleaded.

Where there is nothing to suggest in a clinical negligence claim that post-operative symptoms were caused by any surgical error, and they are consistent with information given by the doctors before the operation, then there is no constructive knowledge. This was the finding in <u>Rogers v East Kent Hospitals NHS Trust</u> [2009] EWHC 54 (QB) where there was nothing to put the claimant on notice that something may have gone wrong.

The date of knowledge is particularly pertinent in a clinical negligence claim involving misdiagnosis or a delayed diagnosis as the breach of duty happens at the time of misdiagnosis or injury. But this information may not come to the claimant's attention for some time until the correct diagnosis is made.

Industrial disease cases are also problematic as frequently the disease is latent and manifests itself at a much later date.

6.7.4.6 Section 33 LA 1980– discretionary exclusion of time limit

If the claimant has concerns that the date of knowledge, actual or constructive, falls outside 3 years, then s/he may seek the court's equitable discretion to extend the limitation period. The court has more latitude under section 33 than under section 14 as all the circumstances of the case are considered, including the respective *prejudice* (**s.33(1)(a) & (b)**) to the parties and the exercise of *proportionality*.

The burden is on the claimant to show to the court that it would be fair to allow the action to proceed.

There are 6 factors that the court will consider:

Section 33(3) (in summary form):

(a) the length and the reasons for the delay by the claimant;

(b) the effect of the delay on the cogency of the evidence;

(c) the conduct of the defendant

(d) the duration of any disability suffered by the claimant since accrual of the cause of action;

(e) whether the claimant acted promptly and reasonably once he knew he had a potential claim;

(f) whether the claimant sought medical, legal or other expert advice.

Essentially **conduct** and the **effect of delay** from expiry of the limitation period to the date that proceedings are issues are at the heart of the section 33 discretion.

One of the main authorities on the section 33 discretion is that of <u>Thompson v Brown</u> [1981] 1 WLR 744 where the House of Lords held that the court has a discretion which is unfettered and is not merely bound by the criteria set out in subsection 3.

6.7.4.7 Delay

In the case of *Adams,* mentioned above, the length of delay and the reasons for it are relevant. The principles set out in *A v Hoare* remain broadly good law. The longer the delay, the more likely, and the greater the prejudice is caused to the defendant. In <u>Sanderson v City of Bradford City Council</u> [2016] EWHC 527(QB), the court stated that delay by the defendant in complying with the pre-action protocol can be a factor in a section 33 application. The court looked at delay before expiry of the limitation period and afterwards in considering prejudice. A period of delay was 10 weeks before issuing proceedings outside the limitation period. This was considered reasonable in the circumstances given Mr Sanderson's condition and treatment.

<u>Cain v Francis</u> [2008] EWCA Civ 1451 confirmed the question to be answered is what is equitable, i.e. fair in all the circumstances of the case and the six factors in subsection 3. The length of the delay is not a deciding factor, but rather the effect of the delay is relevant. In this case the limitation period was disapplied despite a delay of 1 year.

The issue of pre-limitation delay was reviewed in *Collins v Secretary of State for Buisness Innovation and Skills and anor* as there was a long period of time between alleged exposure and bringing the claim (around 45 years). This was a factor which the court would take account of. It recognised that 'delay' under subsections (a) and (b) represented the length of time the claim was statute barred but for the purposes of section 33 as a whole, the court could examine prejudice experienced by the defendants between exposure and bringing the claim. Consequently the court refused to exercise discretion under section 33.

Overall delay as part of all the circumstances of the case was also affirmed in *McDonnell v Walker* [2009] EWCA Civ 1257. The court should consider the cause of the delays, whether excusable, effects of the delay, and whether a fair trial is still possible.

6.7.4.8 Cogency of evidence

This concerns examination of the strength of evidence lost by the delay from the date of the cause of action or date of knowledge.

Invariably this requires an assessment of prejudice to the defendant in its ability to investigate and obtain evidence – whether documentary or witness statements.

The case of *KR v Bryn Alyn Community Ltd* [2003] 1441 is not considered good law any longer as it is not considered an *'exceptional indulgence'*, rather what is *fair* that it is for the court to establish when considering section 33. However some of the principles laid down by the court remain applicable. The relevant prejudice is that which affects the defendant's ability to defend, i.e. an evidential one, not the loss of the limitation defence. The court stated that the longer the delay, the greater the prejudice to the defendant. It also indicated that a preliminary hearing referring to the pleadings, statements and disclosure should be held. It also noted that the more cogent the claimant's evidence, the greater the prejudice to the defendant. This reflected the fact that the court must exercise a balancing exercise.

So once the claimant or his advisors realise that there may be a limitation problem, the options are either to agree a moratorium with the defendant, or issue proceedings as soon as possible. That may involve issuing the claim form and not serving until medical evidence has been obtained. It must be served with the particulars of claim, schedule of loss and medical report within 4 months from the date of issue. Alternatively, the claimant should serve the claim form after issue and then agree a stay of the proceedings with the defendant until ready to the serve the documents.

6.7.5 Case law. We shall review some cases where section 11(4) on date of knowledge and section 33 on equitable discretion have been considered before looking at some unusual situations at sea and in the air where the limitation period is 2 years.

6.7.5.1 Clinical negligence

• *Forbes v Wandsworth Health Authority* – C's individual characteristics not relevant for determining constructive knowledge. It was how a reasonable person with C's condition would have acted. Harsh decision for C as deemed to have constructive knowledge 12 to 18 months after leg amputation despite not receiving medical advice until 10 years post operatively.

• *Rogers v East Kent Hospitals NHS Trust* – C not have constructive knowledge where post operative symptoms consistent with medical advice and nothing to put her on notice.

• *Spargo v North Essex District Health Authority* – C had constructive knowledge where suspected a connection with D's conduct and the injury, despite fact that others may wish to get expect advice. This does seem closer to subjective test.

• *Whiston v London Strategic Health Authority* – Confirmed constructive knowledge test is objective. C has an 'obligation of curiosity' re injury and its cause. Knowledge of significance of injury not determinative of constructive knowledge. Appeal allowed on constructive knowledge and allowed to proceed under s.33.

6.7.5.2 Industrial disease

Noise induced hearing loss

- *Malone v Relyon Heating Engineering Limited* - examination of constructive knowledge when C consulted GP started limitation clock, not when exposure ceases. Further delay required s.33 application. CA denied discretion, arguing significant time lapse from exposure and proportionality given modest value of claim.

- *Johnson v MOD & Hobourn Eaton* [2012] – CA held C entitled to 'thinking time' of 1 year before getting medical advice. Fixed with constructive knowledge as a reasonable man with early onset deafness and knowing employment history of noisy environments would seek medical advice.

6.7.5.3 Asbestosis

- *AB v Ministry of Defence* [2012] UKSC 9 – constructive knowledge imbued when C believes injury attributable to an act or omission giving sufficient confidence to embark on preliminaries such as obtaining advice or submitting a claim. Reasonable belief is sufficient to constitute knowledge.

- *Collins v Secretary of State* [2013] EWHC 1117 (QB) - s.33 refused. Prejudice to D through C's solicitors' delay in issuing resulted in difficulties investigating claim. C's own evidence was poor. Proportionality relevant.

- *Nicholas v Ministry of Defence* [2013] EWHC 2351 (QB) – s.33 discretion allowed No prejudice to D. Delay in issuing proceedings due to debilitating effects of illness.

- *Summers v City & County of Cardiff* [2015] – a finding of actual knowledge based on symptoms and admission from C that believed the symptoms were due to asbestos-related changes. C argued ignorance of cause of symptomatic condition so not a 'significant injury' so as to constitute knowledge under s.14(1)(a). C time barred with knowledge of actual injury.

- *Sanderson v Bradford Metropolitan District Council* [2016] EWHC 527 (QB) - C's delay of 10 weeks post limitation was small, evidence was cogent, not advised to take legal advice. Court was sympathetic to C's illness as being the reason for the delay and critical of D's delay to inform insurers of 3 months. S.33 discretion allowed.

6.7.5.4 Historic abuse claims

- *A v Hoare* – Changed law to permit limitation period extension under s.33 for deliberate assaults (previously fixed at 6 years). The approach on constructive knowledge is to ask what C knew about injury, add any 'objective' knowledge imputed under s.14(3) and then apply reasonable person test as to whether with that information it was serious enough to issue proceedings.

- *B v Nugent Care Society* [2009] EWCA Civ 827 - date of knowledge objective, not C's characteristics. Important case for claimants as greater emphasis on reasons for delay in reviewing s.33.

- *Re v Ge* [2015] EWCA 287 – s.33 discretion refused by CA as no good reason for delay and cogency of evidence considered.

- *Ellam v Ellam* [2015] EWCA Civ 287 – s.33 discretion refused by CA as C could not shelter behind professional advisors' delay of some 5 years before issuing claim after first consultation, C had also delayed in seeking advice.

- *KR v Bryn Alyn Community Holdings Limited* [2003] QB 1441 – the longer the delay, the more likely, and the greater, the prejudice to the defendant.

- *TCD v Harrow* [2008] EWHC 3048 – constructive knowledge fixed at age 18 when raped from age 8. S.33 discretion refused on grounds that public authorities should not be exposed to threat of litigation indefinitely as public interest for finality.

6.7.5.5 RTA

- *Cain v Francis* [2008] EWCA Civ 1451 – S.33 discretion is wide and unfettered. Loss of limitation defence is not a head of prejudice – it is the impact on the ability to defend, i.e. evidential or forensic prejudice. Did D know about claim and have an opportunity to investigate and obtain evidence. Length of delay is not a factor, it is the effect of the delay.

6.7.6 Accidents at sea[1]

6.76.1 *Time limits*

This can be an area to catch out the unwary because the limitation period is **2 years** for accidents at sea. It also covers claims for food poisoning or clinical negligence suffered whilst on an international cruise.

It is important to determine from when time starts to run. The UK law prescribing the limitation period is *section 190 Merchant Shipping Act 1995*. This enacts the provisions of *Article 16* of the *Athens Convention 1974* which covers personal injury claims. So the Limitation Act 1980 does not apply and therefore there is no provision for an extension to the limitation period or disapplication of the Act.

Where a passenger suffers injury on board a ship then time starts to run from *the date of disembarkation*. If death results during carriage, then time runs from the date that the passenger should have disembarked.

If a passenger is injured on a vessel which collides with another vessel, and where it is the fault of the other vessel, then the 2 years runs from *the date that injury was caused*.

One may think that such claims only relate to cases on cruise liners or ferries but they have much wider scope extending even to a pleasure

---

1 Credit is given to Gordon Exall, Barrister for his article in Civil Litigation Brief www.civillitigationbrief.wordpress.com on 'Trouble at sea: limitation periods and water travel' 15.09.2013

craft sailing down the Menai Straits in Anglesey. Such was the case of *Michael v Musgrove* [2011] EWHC 1438 where the claimant was a passenger on a rigid inflatable boat. The claimant took a tumble when the boat hit a wave. Issues were whether the boat was a seagoing ship which it was.

Whilst the Athens convention applies to international voyages, it also applies to domestic voyages around the UK by virtue of the *Carriage of Passengers and their Luggage by Sea (Domestic Carriage) Order* SI 1987/670.

6.7.6.2 Which defendant

This is not intended to be a definitive guide on travel law but care must be taken to ensure that the correct defendant has been identified. Generally a claim arising from a cruise arranged through a Tour Operator entitles the claimant to pursue either the carrier under *Article 3(1) of the Athens convention* or the tour operator that sold the package holiday.

The danger is that if the wrong defendant has been pursued and limitation has expired then the claimant has no cause of action, apart from perhaps against his legal advisor if negligent. If in doubt include all potential defendants, and if any have been included unnecessarily then discontinue against them. Beware the possibility of an adverse costs order so discontinuation should be by consent with no order as to costs.

6.7.6.3 Contribution proceedings

Whilst the 2 years' limitation period applies to an action for damages under *Article 16 Athens Convention*, it does not apply to contribution proceedings.

This was the decision of the Court of Appeal in the case of *South West Strategic Health Authority v Bay Island Voyages* [2015] EWCA Civ 708. A claimant suffered severe injuries on an away day arranged by her employers on a boating trip in the Bristol Channel. The claim was brought against the boat company outside the 2-year period under the

Athens Convention. The claim was time-barred so new solicitors brought a claim against the employers, who brought **Part 20** contribution proceedings against the boat company.

Under *section 1(3) of the Civil Liability (Contribution) Act 1978*, a party may claim a contribution from another potential defendant who is liable for the same damage. The CA held that the Convention was not a complete code but dealt with claims by passengers against carriers and nothing else. Contribution proceedings were autonomous derived under English Law. The time-bar did not extinguish the right as it was not a claim for damages within the meaning of Article 16. The time limit that applied will be 2 years from the date on which the right to a contribution accrued, namely 2 years from the date of settlement or judgment.

The lesson to be learned from this is that the facts in this case were somewhat unusual giving the claimant a second opportunity to bring proceedings within 3 years against her employer. Normally her right of action would have been extinguished by the 2- year time bar. This is a helpful case for defendants who might wish to consider bringing third party proceedings where a claimant issues just before the 2-year limitation period expires, and there is another tortfeasor that should be joined into the proceedings. The defendant may still join the Part 20 defendant into the action.

6.7.7 Accidents in the air[2]

6.7.7.1 *Time limits*

Under *Section 5 Carriage by Air Act 1961* (which incorporates Article 17 of *The Warsaw Convention 1929 (as amended)* and *Article 35* of *the Montreal Convention 1999*), the time limit for bringing claims is **2 years.**

---

2 Credit is given to Gordon Exall, Barrister for his article in Civil Litigation Brief www.civillitigationbrief.wordpress.com on 'Aviation and the really vicious limitation period' 30.07.2013

The 2-year period runs from the date at which the aircraft arrived, or should have arrived at its destination.

The Montreal Convention applies to international flights which means flights between two different countries or a domestic flight which has a stop in another country. The Convention has been ratified by most countries but not Russia or Thailand. Domestic flights in the UK will be covered by the Warsaw Convention. The differences between the two conventions will not be covered in this text but suffice to note the limitation period is 2 years whether it is a domestic or international flight.

6.7.7.2 Article 17 states:

> *The carrier is liable for damage sustained in the event of the death or wounding of a passenger or any other bodily injury suffered by a passenger, if the accident which caused the damage so sustained took place on board the aircraft or in the course of any of the operations of embarking or disembarking.*

The accident must have happened on board an aircraft or in the process of *embarking* or *disembarking*. These are important definitions should an accident occur in an airport as to whether it is caught by the limitation provisions in the *Carriage of Air Act* or *The Limitation* Act.

It has been held that a claimant sustaining injuries in the airport whilst proceeding to an embarkation gate was covered by the convention (*Phillips v Air New Zealand Ltd* [2002] EWHC 800).

The test is whether the passenger is under the control of the carrier. So it could apply once a boarding pass has been issued, thus the Carriage by Air Act applies. It may be best to be cautious from the perspective of identifying the correct defendant and the limitation period to pursue both the airport and the carrier and assume that the limitation period is 2 years. One could say that embarkation only occurs once a passenger has gone through security or even when called to the gate.

Clearly the defendant will be different; establishing liability will be different; and the limitation period will be different dependent on where an accident occurs in an airport.

6.7.8 Problems to look out for

(i) Applications under section 33 are difficult to predict with any certainty. Reasons for delay rather than excuses must be clearly defined in a claimant's witness statement. Medical evidence should be relied upon if there are psychological reasons for the delay. Cogency of evidence and prejudice must be considered. Claimants should notify defendants as soon as possible of a claim so as to reduce risk of prejudice through a lack of investigation. Such notice should be made even if the merits of the claim are not yet known.

(ii) The key to avoiding problems of limitation expiry and falling back on section 33 is by knowing the pitfalls.

> (a) If in doubt, check the limitation period – it could be 2 years. An injury on a plane or on a boat will be 2 years. An injury in an airport, dependent on location could be 2 or 3 years. A claim to the CICA is 2 years. Contribution proceedings will be 2 years.

> (b) Do not assume the date given by the claimant is correct. They may be mistaken, so check medical records and other contemporaneous documentation such as accident report, police report or Root cause analysis investigation report.

> (c) Record limitation date (and other important dates) on the file. Use a diary system and back-up with your secretary and other fee-earners working on the file. Issue reminders to review in good time before limitation expires (say at least 2 months). Review files with impending limitation dates frequently – at least once per week in the last 2 months.

> (d) If inheriting a file from another fee-earner, double-check that the limitation period has been recorded correctly. The same investigations as in (b) are recommended.

(e) Beware the possibility of the claimant not being contactable or moving address or losing interest at a time of impending limitation. What to do? Ideally prior instructions on this will have been obtained on how to proceed. If no instructions to issue, seek extension (as below). Consider a clause in the retainer letter about this eventuality and the risks associated with missing limitation.

(f) Consider, if acting for a claimant, whether the risks are worthwhile in taking on a case where either the primary limitation period may have expired or is shortly to do so.

(g) If in doubt, issue, issue, issue! Don't leave it to the last minute. Don't forget the corresponding directive, serve, serve, serve!

(h) If acting for a defendant, check to see whether the claim has been issued in time. That will involve review of contemporaneous documentation. Fully particularise in the defence expiry of the limitation period, either on date of knowledge or in equity. Consider a Part 18 Request for further information of the Particulars of Claim. Consider an application for summary judgment.

6.7.9 Procedural points

Dealing with imminent limitation expiry

If limitation is coming up, the claimant has various options:

(a) Issue proceedings in time, then seek a stay or an extension by agreement, if required;

(b) Seek agreement with the defendant on suspension or an extension of time – a standstill agreement;

(c) Issue proceedings in time then apply to the court for a stay.

Starting protective proceedings by issuing the claim form may not be ideal if investigations into the merits of the case are ongoing. But it is the safest option. Ultimately the claim may not proceed and a substantial court fee has to be paid reflecting the actual value (to avoid a subsequent strike out). There may then be pressure to obtain medical or other evidence so as to serve the full statement of case within 4 months.

6.7.9.1 A standstill agreement is frequently used but is it safe for claimants? Section 11(3) of the Limitation Act provides that no action shall be brought after the expiry of 3 years. It is open to the defendant to plead expiry if such has occurred. The Act does not act as a procedural bar on the right to bring claims which are statute barred as the cause of action remains unaffected. This has an impact for claimants who should not plead limitation.[3]

But if the limitation period has expired and the defendant chooses deliberately or by omission not to plead it as required under **PD 15, para 13.1** then it is suggested that by acquiescing or by estoppel, they may not rely upon it as part of their defence. However, consider the case of _Holding & Management (Solitaire) Limited v Ideal Homes North West Limited_ [2004] EWHC 2408, where the judge said that establishing estoppel in relation to Limitation Acts can only be accomplished in the most exceptional cases.

So where does that leave standstill agreements? They are contracts between the parties reached before the limitation period has expired, agreeing either to _suspend_ time from running at the date agreed or an _extension_ of time up to a defined date that will count as the new limitation date.

A defendant could agree to a standstill agreement and then change their mind and plead limitation in the defence. They may not be estopped from doing so, especially if they can argue that the standstill agreement is not contractual.

Example of a standstill agreement (in shortened form)

---

[3] Extract from an article by the late Tim Hurst, former Barrister at Parklane Plowden, 'Can the Limitation Act really be suspended?'

1. The parties agree that the period within which this Agreement remains in force ('the Period') shall not be taken into account for the purposes of determining the limitation period prescribed by section 11(4) Limitation Act 1980.

2. Any limitation period running at the date of this agreement shall be deemed to be suspended during the Period, and any limitation period that would (but for this Agreement) have started to run during the Period shall not begin to run until the end of The Period.

3. Any limitation period suspended by operation of clause 2 shall continue once again to run on the day immediately following the date of the termination of this Agreement.

4. This Agreement has no effect upon any Time Defence available to the Defendant which has already accrued at the date of this Agreement.

5. The Defendant undertakes that it will not plead any limitation defence for the Period elapsed under this agreement or any lesser period upon the happening of either event in clause 6.

6. The Period begins on the date of this Agreement and continues unless and until the earlier of the following occurs:

>*6.1 14 days' written notice of termination of this Agreement is served by one party on the other;*
>
>*6.2 the service of proceedings by the claimant on the defendant.*

This represents a more formal agreement than many practitioners will use. Generally it is to the effect that the defendant will agree to an extension of time of 3 months (or whatever date is agreed) from expiry of the limitation period up until [date] and will take no issue or plead any limitation defence for the period accrued by the extension.

But as this must be a contract, there must be consideration or forbearance moving from the claimant to the defendant. It may be implied that in consideration for the defendant agreeing to extend or suspend time, that the claimant agrees not to issue or serve proceedings during the period of the agreement. Will this be enough or does the claimant have to offer something more, perhaps to agree to engage in ADR?

A standstill agreement was considered in *Russell v Stone [2017] EWHC 1555 (TCC)*. There were 3 standstill agreements, the first entered into 3 weeks before the limitation period expired. The claimant issued proceedings 1 day after the standstill agreement ended, arguing that the limitation period had been suspended so still had another 3 weeks to issue. The defendant argued that the agreement was for an extension of time to the last day of the final agreement. The judge was critical of the drafting of the agreement which was unclear but he found for the claimant in that the agreement did refer to time being suspended.

Interestingly the same judge, Coulson J who heard *Holding and Management Limited*, remarked that the safer option might have been for the claimant to issue and then seek a stay for a period of time. He had previously expressed his reservations about finding an estoppel.

The risk is that defendants may change their mind after agreeing to a standstill agreement once the limitation period has expired and plead time-bar in their defence. The claimant could then be in trouble, having to rely on estoppel or equity under section 33 - which may or may not be successful.

6.7.10 Drafting Particulars of claim

If the claimant believes the limitation period may have expired under section 11 LA and considers that a section 33 direction may be required, it is not necessary to plead this in the particulars of claim. It is for the defendant to raise limitation expiry as a defence which they may or may not do. If it is the intention of the defendant to raise a limitation point then this must be pleaded (**PD 16, para 13.1**). That leaves the claimant having to amend his Particulars of claim to address limitation either by asserting the date of knowledge and in the alternative seeking the court's equitable jurisdiction to disapply the provisions of section 11 under section 33. The claimant will need to seek the court's permission to amend the particulars of claim as now the defendant has raised limitation. This would involve **Part 17.4(2)** by seeking to add a new claim, effectively seeking reliance on section 33 should the court find that the claim was begun outside the 3 year period from the date of knowledge.

6.7.11 Issuing interlocutory application to determine limitation issue

Consideration will need to be given whether the limitation issue is tried as a preliminary point during an interim hearing or at the trial. Clearly evidential and costs issues will be uppermost in the parties' minds. Auld LJ in *KR v Bryn Alyn Community (Holdings) Ltd* believed that where feasible to do so, section 33 should be decided by reference to the statements of case, witness statements and documentary evidence. Presumably that would omit expert evidence but a considerable amount of the case will have been prepared. There may be cases when expert evidence is relevant in such considerations, particularly from a psychologist or psychiatrist that may explain reasons for the delay. Once expert evidence has been obtained, then one is really looking at a split trial on the issues by that stage.

6.7.12 **CPR 17** amendments after end of limitation period – available in 3 situations:

(i) To add or substitute a new claim only out of the same facts or substantially the same facts (17.4(2));

(ii) To correct a genuine mistake as to the name of a party (17.4(3));

(iii) To alter the capacity in which a party claims provided such party had capacity when proceedings issued or since acquired (17.4(4)).

Key points

- Ascertain the limitation period at the outset of the case. Don't assume information provided is correct. Consider as part of risk assessment whether the case should be taken on if imminent expiry.

- If in time, issue protective proceedings remembering to serve within 4 months. Pay the correct issue fee.

- Treat standstill agreements with some caution.

- Consider constructive knowledge as well as actual knowledge to determine when enquiries should have been made. It may be earlier than a formal diagnosis or receipt of expert evidence.

- If out of time, issue as soon as possible. If acting for the claimant, consider whether limitation should be pleaded at all or await the defence. Consider an amendment to the Particulars of claim or filing a Reply, pleading section 11(4) and/or section 33.

- Defendants will wish to examine all evidence to check whether limitation is in time. If a section 33 application is made, focus on lack of cogency of evidence caused by delay and prejudice to the defendant in investigating the claim.

CHAPTER SEVEN
INTERLOCUTORY APPLICATIONS

CPR 23 – Governs general rules about applications for court orders

7.0.1 For many lawyers – and certainly those starting out – interim hearings or interlocutory applications provide a great opportunity to hone one's advocacy skills. Use them to ensure that you are best placed to proceed to trial and to earn or save costs that otherwise would be incurred in instructing an agent or counsel. Given the constant bearing down on recoverability of costs and ensuring proportionality, it is a necessity for you to do as much of the work as possible. Not only will this lead to a good deal of satisfaction but should make you a more rounded lawyer. Not a combative one, but one who 'owns the case' and is assertive when required.

The main rules governing interim applications are set out in **CPR 23** that proscribes the procedure for making applications on notice and without notice. There are other rules for specific applications such as **CPR 24** for summary judgment or **CPR 3.9** in seeking relief from sanctions or more generally the court's case management powers under **rule 3**.

This chapter will explore some of the more common scenarios that arise when progressing a claim, including the pitfalls to be wary of in serving documents. Inevitably you will develop your own technique that you are most comfortable with in making or defending applications and to a certain extent be responsive to the style and requirements of the judge hearing the application. In all applications, ensure you know the relevant section of the CPR and have filed evidence supporting the facts. You should also know the significant cases relevant to your application. So, in an application for relief from sanctions, <u>Mitchell v News Group Newspapers Ltd</u> [2013] EWCA Civ 1526 and <u>Charles Graham Denton v TH White</u> [2014] EWCA Civ 906 (i.e. Mitchell and Denton) are currently the most significant cases to rely upon..

7.0.2 Interlocutory applications arise during case management and are used to progress the case when it has faltered. Mostly the application will be made after the issue of proceedings but exceptionally may be required before proceedings, such as in an application for pre-action disclosure. This should not be required if the pre-action protocol has been observed but be prepared to file the application notice if the defendant has failed to comply after giving due warning.

The case may be characterised as a game of chess; we have the opening – commencing proceedings, the middle game in the development of the pieces, by obtaining evidence – documentary, lay, expert and schedules of loss and the end game – culminating in the trial. It is not intended to reduce the case to that of a game, albeit a complex one, but to highlight the need to think tactically; do you have the evidence to prove/disprove the claim? What more is required? Is it obtainable? Have any admissions been made - should a summary judgment or dismissal application be made? Do you have a limitation problem? If so, should this be tested at trial or before? Do you need to change experts? Has there been a material breach of a case management order requiring relief from sanction?

The middle game is where you 'get your ducks in a row' or to follow the chess analogy, ensure your pieces are fully developed and working towards a checkmate. In order to advance your pieces, assistance may be required from the court in seeking an interim order. Don't leave it to the start of the trial – it will be too late. Judges don't like last minute applications and are more likely to refuse them, or exact a costs penalty.

The main rules governing interlocutory applications are contained in **CPR 23** but other rules apply specific to a particular application, such as CPR 3.4 for striking out a claim or summary judgment under CPR 24 as examples.

7.0.3 *General Procedure*

7.0.3.1 Applications are normally on notice (inter partes) served on the opponent. Form N244 may contain supporting evidence or exhibit a separate witness statement. It must state the order being sought and the reasons for seeking the order. A copy of the draft order must be appended to the notice. The notice must state –

(a) what order the applicant is seeking; and
(b) why the applicant is seeking the order.

A without notice, ex parte application will be rare and only where permitted by a rule, practice direction or a court order (**Rule 23.4(2)**). Typically this may be where the defendant is not yet on the court record, such as in an application to extend the time for serving a claim form (**Rule 7.6(4)**) or in an urgent situation where it is not feasible to give the required minimum of **3 clear days**' notice to the other side. There is a duty in ex parte applications to give full and frank disclosure of all matters relevant to the case, including those adverse to the application.

What is frequently forgotten is the requirement to serve an order obtained without notice and the application notice on the opponent together with any evidence in support. The order should state that the person/entity against whom the order has been made has a right to apply to set aside or vary the order within **7 days** of service of the order.

It is not unusual for a defendant to apply without notice for more time for filing and serving its defence (usually after the claimant has already granted an extension). The courts will sometimes make the order without giving the claimant the opportunity to object. This is based on their case management powers to further the overriding objective. The onus would then be on the claimant to apply to set aside (which in reality they are unlikely to do). As a claimant, one therefore has to be careful not to over indulge a defendant who may be delaying unnecessarily simply because they can. In such a situation, consider whether an extension is justified, especially if the defendant has failed to serve its letter of response or has delayed throughout the pre-action process. Clearly the merits must be examined. Good reasons may exist for obtaining expert evidence or arranging a conference with counsel. Much will depend on what efforts have already been made to make arrangements, and the amount of notice the defendant has had about the claim.

Both parties should be reasonable when it comes to extensions of time but if there is a sense of delaying tactics, then the sooner the application is made, the sooner the order is obtained.

7.0.3.2 Evidence

Written evidence is necessary setting out the facts justifying the relief sought (**Rule 25.3(2)**). Evidence may be in the form of a statement of facts in the body of the application notice (question 10), a separate witness statement, correspondence or reliance on the statement of case. It is suggested that where the application may involve complex facts or law or reliance on several cases, that a separate witness statement is preferable. If the application is likely to be agreed then information in the N244 will most likely be sufficient.

Skeleton arguments are often not necessary but they are preferable in interim hearings before High Court Judges or Circuit Judges. In County Court applications it will depend on the level of complexity and nature of the case. So, in an application for a striking out of a claim or seeking relief from sanctions retrospectively, for an extension of time to serve the claim form should rely upon skeleton arguments. Interestingly in the latter example, the application may be made without notice but given the possible consequences it would be wise to file a skeleton argument.

A cost schedule in form N260 must be filed no later than 24 hours before the hearing. If not, the court may take this into account in deciding what order to make about costs – which may be disallowed even if you succeed on the application.

7.0.4 Style of presentation

7.0.4.1 The public are entitled to sit in on most cases (excepting those cases involving children and vulnerable adults). However it is a remote prospect if only because most people will not be interested. Indeed, most hearings – interim applications, allocation hearings and listing hearings will take place by telephone so the occasion does not arise anyway.

In most applications a case summary is not necessary (unless the court has directed that one be filed). But the court will not criticise a party for drafting one and it may help focus your advocacy on the issues as well as assist the judge. A well-drafted application will set out the section of the CPR relied upon and the facts in support.

7.0.4.2 Advocacy before a District Judge on an interim application is different clearly from presenting a case at trial. Firstly, time is short and you will probably be at the end of a telephone. Brevity is key so the judge will be running the show. But don't forget that just because you're on the phone, this is not an informal chat. Remember you are before a judge, so the usual niceties apply – respect, politeness and deference. Even if you disagree with the judge, maintain control and respect. You will appear before the judge again. It is never personal. Don't ever pass comment on the judge's decision if you disagree. By all means use the time honoured phrase 'I'm obliged' or 'I'm grateful' or just thank you. If you consider the judge is against you but no judgment has yet been given, then you may be able to salvage the situation. This does not mean repeating what you have already said but addressing the judge's reservations about a particular point. You could say something like: 'If I may judge, can I address you on that particular point to suggest why my argument is valid...' or 'I can help you with that point Sir if I may respond.'

It may be that the judge has missed a particular fact or an aspect of the law that you deem is crucial or needs correcting. Apologise to the judge and suggest there are other matters that should be taken into account. Say it calmly and authoritatively.

7.0.4.3 At all times try and anticipate what the judge needs to know to pass judgment. So facts, grounds of application (why necessary) and power conferred by the CPR. It is expected that you have got the procedure right and the evidence necessary to substantiate the application.

On occasion you may find that you are getting a hard time from the judge but in fact she is testing your case and may be supportive of it. So don't assume you're a dead duck. Of course if the judge says she's against you then clearly there is work to be done to convince her. Try saying 'well let me put it this way' and having another go. Or 'that is a helpful point…' (even if it isn't) '…but here the issue may be distinguished because…and therefore I submit…'

Having read the application, the judge is unlikely to require you to rehearse your application. Be prepared to know the basis upon which the judge has power to make the order. So know your CPR, test of negligence and relevant authorities.

You must be prepared for the judge to say, 'Your application, Miss X….' and then you're given the floor to make your case. Check the judge has read the application and has the exhibits. Explain why the application is necessary. Give a brief summary if the judge has not read the application and then proceed to the detail if necessary.

7.0.4.4 The judge may open the hearing by saying she has read the application and turn to the opponent by asking why it is opposed. If you are the opponent, be ready with your reasons. The applicant has had the benefit of putting all their evidence before the court. You may have issued a cross-application returnable at the same hearing in which case your evidence is also before the court. This is most likely in a case where a possible sanction is strike-out of the case. If you have put no evidence before the court, then your submissions will concentrate on examining the opponent's chronology. Has there been inexcusable delay and prejudice to your client that cannot be resolved or should not be resolved? In many cases, the court's overriding objective will be the starting point in exercising its case management powers.

If you are pushing against an open door, stop pushing! To use another well worn cliché, don't snatch defeat from the jaws of victory. Let the other side do the work. But if they make a good fist of it, then you may need a right of reply. Naturally your tendency will be to repeat the points the judge has made in clarifying the issues by agreeing with her. Normally if the opponent makes a good point, the judge might invite you to comment. This typically will be some new ground not covered in the papers so a reasoned reply is called for as the judge has given it credence. This is the most dangerous time for you because the judge may be having his head turned. Presumably your opponent's point is a good one, as otherwise it would have been given short shrift. Your reply should be succinct so as not to give your opponent's argument much credit. 'I can answer that simply by saying…' or in an older style, 'my friend's point is misconceived because…' Caution must be adopted in this strategy if indeed your opponent has made a detailed and strong argument. Your brief reposte won't then work and may be viewed as you having no real answer to their argument.

7.0.4.5 If your opponent comes up with some devastating legal argument or appears so, whereby you have not had advance notice, then you should object for their failure to disclose the evidence or case authority in advance of the hearing. You are entitled to 3 days. Either you ask the court to stand down the case whilst you consider the authority or seek an adjournment. The court will not be impressed by one party attempting to obtain an unfair advantage over the other by ambushing them with undisclosed authorities and should be receptive to calls for an adjournment.

In the courtroom, you may be passed case reports from your opponent. If these are well known, then objecting for no good reason is pointless and may irk the judge. A more likely scenario may arise whereby you receive a skeleton argument emailed to you 1 hour (or less) before the telephone conference. If this presents no problems, then you can try and turn this to your advantage before the court. 'Whilst I have only received the claimant's skeleton submission 1 hour ago Ma'am, I am happy to proceed with the hearing and can address the points raised in it quite succinctly…'

You may find your opposing advocate is taking up a lot of the hearing time with his loquacious arguments, leaving you with little time for reply or to develop your points. Remember brevity is preferred - cases aren't won on the length of advocacy. Politely interject if the judge is reluctant to do so once over half the hearing time has elapsed. Obviously if you think your opponent is not making any headway, then you may want him to continue, but one would think the judge would intervene if the issues are not being addressed.

7.0.5 The Judge

Before a Master in the High Court or District Registry or County Court hearing Centre in London.

A District Judge or Deputy District Judge usually presides at a provincial District Registry of the High Court or County Court hearing Centre, or at the County Court Money Claims Centre.

Exceptionally a Circuit Judge may hear an interlocutory application - but must do so in an application for an injunction or where a committal order or attachment of a power of arrest are necessary. This is unlikely to concern most practitioners but whosoever hears the application, the preparation is the same. Knowledge and persuasion are crucial, perhaps more so before a circuit judge who may be expecting more detail.

7.0.5.1 Addressing the judge.

A (Deputy) District judge is: Sir, Madam (or Ma'am) or just judge. A Circuit judge or Recorder should be referred to as Your Honour (indirect speech – Your Honour), whilst a (Deputy) High Court Judge is My Lord/Lady (indirectly – Your Lordship/Your Ladyship).

7.0.5.2 *Defects (or What if's)*

Do not make excuses if you are in error. Apologise and ask the court to waive the defect, by its exercise of discretion, if it has power to do so. Indicate, where applicable, that the other side is not prejudiced. Ultimately can a fair trial take place if the defect is cured? If the opponent is prejudiced, eg by incurring more costs in responding to a revised statement of case, then this may be addressed by making a costs order in their client's favour.

If the court does not have an exhibit, or witness statement, will the judge proceed to hear the case based on your oral evidence, or is a statement from the claimant/defendant required? If so, then an adjournment is indicated and you are likely to have to pay those costs thrown away, assessed summarily. It will be difficult to argue otherwise unless the court is at fault (which it is unlikely to admit). You could invite the court to reserve the costs or order costs in the case, but if you are at fault this is a forlorn hope.

7.1 Specific Disclosure – CPR 31.12

7.1.1 Unusual as discovery is normally provided by pre-action protocol disclosure or standard disclosure. If say, risk assessments are missing or some medical records have not been disclosed for example, then the court may order that the documents specified in the draft order are disclosed or for a designated person to carry out a search to the extent specified in the order. It is important to seek an order that an appropriate witness gives a statement in the event of a missing document. They must explain what documents they did have in their possession, how the missing document went astray and when. It is not sufficient to rely upon a statement from the defendant's solicitor or in correspondence. The applicant will require the respondent to specify the time and place for disclosure and inspection (most likely through correspondence to the acting solicitors).

7.1.2 Which Court?

If pre-action then issue in the court where the proceedings are likely to be brought. This will probably be the claimant's home court.

Post issue – Either the County Court Money Claims Centre before transfer or to the County Court Hearing Centre

Method of hearing

By telephone hearing unless the time estimate will exceed 1 hour.

The hearing will be in person at the court where there are multiple parties wishing to make representations at the hearing. Exceptionally the court will list in chambers if a party makes a request that the hearing should not be conducted by telephone.

7.1.3 *The application*

[The claimant/defendant] seeks an order that the claimant/defendant do give specific disclosure of documents because [the claimant/defendant] [has failed to give full standard disclosure][further disclosure is necessary in order to investigate this claim fully].

7.1.3.1 Draft order

(1) The [claimant/defendant] do give specific disclosure of documents by filing and serving a (supplementary) list of documents (in form N265) by 4pm on [date] specifying whether each of the [documents] and/or [classes of documents] specified in the schedule to this order are presently in its control, and if not, specifying which of those [documents] and/or [classes of documents] are no longer in its control (and indicating what has happened to such documents), and also specifying which of those [documents] and/or [classes of documents] it claims a right or duty to withhold inspection of.

(2) The [claimant/defendant] do make any request for inspection in writing within 7 days after service of the list of documents.

(3) The [claimant/defendant] do provide the [claimant/defendant] with copies of the requested documents within 7 days of receipt of the request.

(4) The [claimant/defendant] do pay the costs of this application summarily assessed in the sum of £X within 28 days.

In the case of a claimant seeking a witness statement about missing scans:

(1) The defendant's records manager do provide a witness statement within 14 days stating when they last had in their possession x-rays taken on [date] and what has become of them.

(2) (costs order as before).

And possibly an order for inspection of the original records:

(3) The defendant do provide facilities for the claimant's solicitor to attend [address] on the giving of 7 days' notice for the purposes of viewing the claimant's original medical records and scans.

7.1.3.2 Supporting evidence

Either as a statement as part of the application notice N244 or in a separate witness statement stating:

(a) Why the document is believed to be in the control of the other side; and

(b) Why it should be disclosed (because it is relevant to an issue in the case) and should have been disclosed in accordance with the relevant pre-action protocol/ or under standard disclosure (as appropriate).

Exhibits: Correspondence on the issue and schedule of documents sought. Any list of documents already disclosed.

7.1.3.3 Service of application notice

The Application notice, witness statement and draft order must be served at least **3 clear days** before the return day. If the defendant is on the record then the court will serve the documents unless requested not to do so.

7.2 Service of claim form – CPR 7.5

7.2.1 Under **CPR 7.5**, the claim form must be served before midnight on the calendar day **4 months** after the date of issue of the claim form.

A failure to serve on the correct party or on time can have serious consequences and possibly cause the claim to be struck out. If the limitation period has expired then the cause of action will be time-barred. So the rules on service in **CPR 6 and** 7 must be followed. This section will cover service within the jurisdiction of the United Kingdom as set out in **Practice Direction 6A**.

7.2.2 On whom

Service of the claim form must either be on the defendant or his solicitors. If it is to be on the solicitors, either they must have been nominated by the defendant/insurers or the solicitors must have stated in writing that they have been instructed to accept service - see **CPR 6.7**.

The most common forms of service are by first class post or document exchange (DX) providing that delivery is on the next business day. Caution must be exercised to ensure that the defendant's solicitors have not stated on their letterhead that they are unwilling to accept service by DX. Service by both methods is effected by placing the claim form in a post box.

All forms of service are set out in **Part 6.3(1)**. In addition to those mentioned above, there is also personal service; fax or other electronic communication (email) and leaving at a place specified in the rules which are:

- **Part 6.7** – nominated solicitor,
- **Part 6.8** – defendant at residence or business address;
- **Part 6.9** – this applies where the defendant does not give an address for service. On an individual – the usual or last known address; On an LLP – the Prinicpal office; on a Company registered in England and Wales – the Principal office;
- **Part 6.10** – Crown. Service on the Attorney General must be effected on the Treasury Solicitor. Service on a government department must be effected on the solicitor acting for that department.

Service on a company or Limited Liability Partnership may be effected as in **Part 6.9** or under the Companies Act 2006 at its registered office.

7.2.3 Time for service

In calculating the time for <u>expiry of service of a claim form</u>, it is the date at which the **relevant step** is completed under **Part 7.5(1)**. This is the date of posting or sending by email or completing the transmission of the fax or personal service or delivery at the defendant's address. Once the relevant step has been completed, this constitutes actual service.

In determining the period of validity, the relevant step may be taken on any day, including Saturdays, Sundays and bank holidays and at any time of day or night.

So whilst deemed service under rule 6.14 for all these methods is the second business day after the relevant step, this is not the crucial date for effecting service.

It cannot be presumed that the other party will accept service by email unless they have previously indicated in writing that they do accept service. Even though an email address will usually be given on a solicitors' letterhead, this is inadequate, as it must also state that it may be used for service. This is rarely the case.

So, if you are against the wire, it is the eleventh hour before midnight, and the other party has indicated that they do not accept service by email, what can you do? If a fax address is displayed on the letterhead, then fax the claim form but do ensure that the transmission is not interrupted otherwise you will need to resend. Alternatively, arrange for personal delivery by courier ensuring that the claim form is served before midnight. Or you could just post the claim form as you will have complied with the relevant step. It does not need to arrive before expiry of the 4 months' period, provided it has been sent.

But why put yourself under stress? Diarise service at least 2 to 3 weeks before the 4 months elapses so that if there are any issues arising you will be able to deal with them in good time.

7.3 Service of particulars of claim – CPR 7.4

7.3.1 Once the claim form has been served, the Particulars of claim must be served within 14 days after service of the claim form (**CPR 7.4(1)(b)**). But the last date for service of the Particulars of claim is also the last date for serving the claim form, i.e. 4 months (**CPR 7.4(2)**).

In *Venulum Property Investments Ltd v Space Architecture Ltd* [2013] EWHC 1242 (TCC), the claimant's solicitors served the claim form on the last day but did not serve the Particulars of Claim thinking they had a further 14 days. This was a mistaken reading of **CPR 7.4(1)** and **(2)**. They applied for an extension of time for service of the Particulars of Claim under **CPR 3.1(2)(a)** and **CPR 3.9**. The application was not successful. The judge found that even though the defendants were aware of the claim and it would not otherwise be just and proportionate to refuse the application where there was a few days delay in service, and the application was made promptly, other circumstances were more important. Significantly the claimant delayed for over 5 years before instructing solicitors; the claim was not a strong one; and the claim was pleaded in vague terms alleging bad faith.

7.3.2 Difficulties may arise because the claimant has issued protective proceedings because of the impending expiry of the limitation period but is not in a position to serve the statement of case within 4 months of issue. This may be because a medical report has not yet been obtained. Under **PD 4.2** the medical report and schedule of loss must be served with the particulars of claim. In clinical negligence claims, normally breach of duty and causation reports are obtained before condition and prognosis reports, but one would not normally serve liability reports until after exchange of witness statements.

But unfortunately these difficulties are unlikely to wash with the judge in determining whether there is a good reason to grant an extension of time within **CPR 7.5(2)**.

To underline this, consider the case of *Foran v Secret Surgery Ltd* [2016] EWHC 1029 (QB).

In *Foran,* service was out of the UK jurisdiction so the period of time for service of the claim form is 6 months, not 4 months. The solicitors realized that they would not have sufficient time to effect service by the deadline under **CPR 7.5(2)** so made an ex parte application for an extension of time. The original application was successful but dismissed on appeal. Mrs Justice Cox held that the CPR time limits had to be met unless there was good reason. Limitation had expired before the application was made and there was an inadequate explanation for the delay. Delaying service of the claim form until medical evidence was available would not be a good reason, nor would waiting until detailed particulars and supporting documents were available. To avoid such difficulties, the claim form must be served in time and thereafter an application to vary the case management directions be made.

7.4 Extending time for serving a claim form – CPR 7.6

This may be achieved by agreement between the parties or by making an application either on notice or ex parte.

7.4.1 By agreement

Under **CPR 2.11** the parties may reach a written agreement agreeing to an extension of time for service of the claim form. Generally this would be via an exchange of correspondence. Caution should be exercised so that both parties specify the same date by which the claim form and particulars are to be served.

In *Abbott v Econowall UK Limited* [2016] EWHC 660 the claimant's solicitors sent an unsigned copy of the claim form to the defendant's solicitors and sought an extension of one month for service of the claim form and particulars of claim. However they indicated a deadline that exceeded one month. In reply, the defendant's solicitors stated one month should be sufficient to consider the documentation provided. This was taken as an agreement to the extended deadline and the claim form and particulars of claim were served on a date exceeding one month. The defendant then applied to strike out and the claimant applied for an order that service be deemed good under **CPR 6.15**, namely service of the claim form by an alternative method. The judge found that there was a genuine misunderstanding between the parties and the defendant's conduct did not comply with the overriding objective and so applied **rule 6.15(2)**. In making this determination, knowledge that the claim form had come to the attention of the defendant was significant in that it had previously been served. In the alternative the claimant placed reliance on **Part 3.9** but the judge ruled that relief from sanctions could not be given where the terms of **Part 7.6(3)** applied.

The lesson to be learned from this case is that an early agreement should be reached in good time before the claim form is due to be served. If there is disagreement or a lack of clarity, either serve the claim form and particulars of claim immediately or apply in good time for an extension.

7.4.2 On application

7.4.2.1 Where an application for an extension of time for service of the claim form and particulars of claim is made <u>before the period for service has expired</u>, this is covered in **Part 7.6(2)**. It is not necessary to consider **rule 3.9** for relief from sanction as the court is being invited to apply its discretion generally under the court's case management powers under **rule 3.1(2)(a)** to extend time.

Such an application should really be on notice and be made under **rule 7.6**, seeking an order extending the period for compliance with **rule 7.5**. Whilst **rule 7.6(4)** provides that it may be made without notice, it depends on the circumstances. The court has power to dispense with a hearing where it is not appropriate (**CPR 23.8(c)**) such as where there are clear grounds for granting an extension. But if the limitation period has expired before making the application or it is made close to expiry of the date of service, then according to the appellate judge in *Foran* it must be made on notice.

The danger of obtaining an extension of time for serving the claim form, without giving notice to the defendant is that the order may subsequently be set aside.

7.4.2.2 **PD 7A** at **paragraphs 8.1 and 8.2** sets out the requirements for the application notice and the evidence to include:

(1) all the circumstances relied on,

(2) the date of issue of the claim,

(3) the expiry date of any rule 7.6 extension, and

(4) a full explanation as to why the claim has not been served.

The rule is silent as to the criteria to be applied but the overriding objective is most likely to be uppermost in the court's mind by considering the list of factors in **rule 1.1(2)** - to deal with the case justly and at proportionate expense. It is suggested that where the delay is short, the limitation period has not expired, there is no prejudice to the defendant and the case has merit and general significance are factors that will assist the claimant in securing an extension.

7.4.2.3 What is a good reason for the delay? Taking all reasonable steps to locate and serve the defendant may be one example. Incompetence of the legal advisor will not be, nor will more time sought for preparation. The absence of having expert evidence is less clear based on conflicting authorities. In clinical negligence if you have breach of duty/causation reports but not a condition & prognosis report, you may struggle to justify this as a reason to seek an extension because there may be sufficient evidence to establish whether the claim is viable. But if you have no expert evidence because of late instructions then this should be viewed with more leniency, applying _Imperial Cancer Research Fund and Anor v Ove Arup & Partners Ltd and Ors_ [2009] EWHC 1453 (TCC).

If you don't have a medical report on condition & prognosis, or you don't have a schedule of loss, or the particulars of claim are not yet finalised, then what should you do? The appropriate procedure is to serve the proceedings and then either reach agreement with the defendant or apply for a stay or an extension of time for completion of the next steps, rather than applying for an extension of time to serve the claim form.

7.4.2.4 What is the procedure if you need to apply for a <u>retrospective extension of time</u> for service after the 4 months' period has elapsed? This is covered in **Part 7.6(3)**.

CPR 7.6(3) requires that the court may make such an order only if (a) it is the court's fault in serving the claim form; or (b) the claimant has taken all reasonable steps to serve in time but has been unable to do so <u>and</u> (c) in either case the claimant has acted promptly in making the application.

The issue here is what constitutes 'all reasonable steps', so there is less scope for discretion. It only relates to steps taken during the four month period allowed and is an objective test at the time the circumstances prevailed (see <u>*Carnegie v Drury*</u> [2007] EWCA Civ 497).

The range of circumstances in which the court will be sympathetic to the claimant will be narrow and restricted to situations where the court has failed to serve the claim form or where the claimant has used the 4 month period for service in trying to locate the defendant who has been evading service. It will still be necessary for the claimant to act promptly in making the application.

7.4.2.5 Where the limitation period has expired in situations either where **Parts 7.6(2)** or **7.6(3)** are invoked, it has been held in <u>*Cecil v Bayat*</u> [2011] 1 WLR 3086 that a defendant should not be deprived of a limitation defence by the court allowing the claimant an extension of time for serving a claim form, save in exceptional circumstances. The good reason that the claimant must establish will be a difficulty in serving the claim form on the defendant, not other problems which the claimant might have. The Court of Appeal said in *Cecil* that in applications to extend time within the 4 months' period under **Part 7.6(2)**, where the limitation period has expired should be similar to the criteria under **Part 7.6(3)**, and a need to establish if not all reasonable steps, then reasonable steps.

In most cases it is suggested that where limitation has expired, an extension will only be granted in exceptional circumstances, such as where a good reason in failing to serve the claim form in time directly impacts on the limitation problem.

7.5 Variation of Case Management timetable – CPR 3.1(7)

7.5.1 Compliance with court orders and the timetable is crucial if sanctions are not to apply which might lead to striking out of a claim or defence. If difficulties arise making it difficult to comply with a particular order, for example filing a costs budget by the due date or giving disclosure or exchanging witness statements or an expert report or schedule of loss, then an application in time to the court should be made.

The court's intention in making and enforcing case management orders is to further the overriding objective and ensure cases are dealt with expeditiously and at proportionate cost. Case management directions should also be proportionate and therefore capable of compliance. The court does have the power to vary or revoke an order under **Part 3.1(7)**.

7.5.2 The starting point is **Part 3.8(4)**. This provides that the parties my reach an agreement to extend the time for a maximum of **28** days for complying with a direction provided that the procedural step has a deadline. These so called 'buffer agreements' must be in writing.

The issues will be whether the opponent agrees or not and whether more than 28 days are needed or if a further extension is required.

If agreement is not forthcoming then an application to the court will be necessary. It is not an application for relief from sanctions if the time for complying with the order has not expired. As held by LJ Jackson in *Hallam Estates v Baker* [2014] EWCA Civ 661, the requirement for the application to be made in time requires the application and court fee to have been paid in time. Even if the application notice is stamped out of time, it will be classified as being made in time. If the hearing occurs after the date for complying with the court order, it will still be treated as in time if the application notice was submitted in time.

7.5.3 If the provisions under **Part 3.8(4)** cannot be complied with, then consider an agreement with the other side to extend time under **Part 2.11**. However in most situations there is a sanction for non-compliance so **Part 2.11** will not be helpful. **Part 3.8(4)** would not apply for a retrospective application for an extension of time or where there is no specific sanction for default.

Part 3.1(2)(a) provides that the court may extend or shorten the time for compliance with any rule, practice direction or court order. The overriding objective will be considered as in the case of <u>Robert v Momentum Services Ltd</u> [2003] Civ 299 where the claimant made an in-time application to serve the Particulars of Claim after 4 months from issue of the claim form. The Court of Appeal were involved as the application was refused. The CA held that applications for extensions of time made prospectively under rule 3.1(2)(a) should be simple and straightforward affairs and allowed the appeal. The lower judge was wrong to apply the test under rule 3.9 for relief from sanctions. The discretion was to be applied having regard to the overriding objective.

When applying the overriding objective, the court will take into account all the circumstances of the case. Various factors were considered in <u>James Wiemer v Nigel Zone</u> [2012] EWHC 107 (QB). This was another case seeking an extension of time for service of the Particulars of claim. The claimant was a litigant in person so some indulgence may have been granted where there had been a failure to comply with the pre-action protocol. The defendant claimed prejudice if the extension were granted but adduced no evidence in support. On appeal the application was allowed having regard to the overriding objective and rule 1.1(2) and the fact that a refusal would have meant the claimant not being able to pursue the claim.

7.5.4 The application

Consider an application to vary the date for exchange of expert reports from 35 days to a period of 70 days, made in time. It cannot be agreed with the other side so the court's permission is necessary.

An application for permission is made in accordance with **Part 3.1(7)** and **Part 3.1(2)(a)**.

The test

The court will apply the overriding objective, taking into account all the circumstances of the case. Reasons for delaying simultaneous exchange must be given, emphasising that it will not affect the trial date. A delay in instructing the expert will not suffice but illness of the expert or unexpected commitments may do so.

If acting for the defendant and opposing the application, set out any prejudice with supporting evidence.

In reality such an application will be successful provided there is no danger that the trial date will be imperiled because of the knock-on effect of other directions, joint experts' meeting, service of schedules etc. If the trial date needs to be put back, then the application will need to ask for a vacation of the trial. The court will only grant vacation in exceptional circumstances – perhaps owing to serious illness of a significant witness supported by sufficient medical evidence. If allowed, expect an adverse costs order..

7.6 Relief from sanctions – CPR 3.9

Relief may be required if the case management timetable has not been complied with and no application to vary (see above) has not been made.

7.6.1 When they apply

This is the bête noir for practitioners as failures in procedure can prove costly and lead to negligence for the defaulting party if automatic sanctions apply, unless relief is obtained. Appendix I sets out the areas where sanctions apply and it's worth getting to know them and ensuring all dates are diarised with a back-up system.

WARNING!

CPR 3.8 provides that a failure to comply with a rule, practice direction or court order may cause a sanction to take effect automatically. But only if it specifies the consequences of failure to comply – see **rule 3.8(3)(b)**. If no consequences then no relief need be applied for.

Often the sanction applies if a time limit for compliance is breached – **rule 3.8(3)(a)**. So if it appears that an order for directions, say for exchange of witness statements by a certain date is not achievable, then the parties may agree to extend the time for exchange by up to a maximum of **28 days**, provided such extension does not risk the hearing date (**rule 3.8(4)**).

The most draconian sanction that could be imposed is striking out. **Rule 3.4(2)(c)** provides that the court may strike out a statement of case if it appears that there has been a failure to comply with a rule, practice direction or court order.

Other sanctions that are less severe but could have a significant impact on the outcome of the case at trial include: debarring a party from calling a witness or expert witness; debarring a party from amending or updating its statement of case or a schedule of future loss; making an adverse costs order (where otherwise QUOCS would apply), possibly on an indemnity basis; or staying the proceedings in the event of non-compliance.

Pre-action protocol failures

One area that is often ignored but where sanctions may be applied (but not automatically) following a breach is the time limits in the Pre-action protocols. In particular there should be a letter of response served within 4 months of the acknowledgment letter responding to the letter of claim in clinical negligence claims and 3 months in both personal injury claims and Disease claims.

Sanctions may also be applied for other breaches of the protocol such as a failure to provide disclosure of documents material to the issues in a denial of liability.

A failure to comply with a pre-action protocol may attract a sanction. It could arise if the innocent party applies to the court requesting a sanction be applied or the court may consider any breach at the case management conference. The extent of the breach and the overall effect of the non-compliance on the other party will determine if a sanction is imposed. So a minor infringement, say 1 week's delay in serving the response letter is unlikely to result in sanctions. If they do apply, the court has a variety of orders at its disposal, including:

(a) staying the proceedings until the required steps are undertaken;

(b) requiring the defaulting party to pay the costs of the proceedings or part of them;

(c) a defaulting claimant being deprived of interest on some or all of the damages awarded;

(d) a defaulting defendant paying interest up to 10% above base rate on some or all damages due to the claimant.

Automatic sanctions

Where sanctions apply automatically, they are more significant and include as follows:

- Striking out the entire claim or defence
- Striking out part of the statement of case
- Debarring a party from calling a witness or expert witness
- Debarring a party from amending part of its statement of case or schedule of loss
- Paying the other party's costs of the proceedings

The full list of possible areas for default and the imposition of sanctions appear in Appendix I.

7.6.2 How to obtain relief

• **Resolving a breach by consent**

CPR 2.11 provides that certain time limits may be varied by the parties, unless the rules or a practice direction provide otherwise or the court orders otherwise.

So 'milestone dates' such as the date for returning a Directions Questionnaire or the trial date or trial window may not be altered by the parties and will require an application. Even then, the court will be slow to vary the dates unless there are exceptional circumstances.

If, for example, you cannot comply with a date for exchange of expert reports then seek agreement with the other side for a new date up to **28 days**.

The architect and proponent of sanctions, Jackson LJ has expressly approved of the parties reaching agreement on extending time limits. This is subject to the caveat that the proceedings are not disrupted nor the trial dates imperilled (see paragraphs 30 and 31 in *Hallam Estates v Baker* [2014] EWCA Civ 661).

If a deadline cannot be met and the other party will not consent to an extension, then apply in advance of its expiry. Provided it is made in time (prospectively, not retrospectively), then the application will be considered as part of the court's case management powers under **Part 3.1(2)(a)**.

- **Applying to the court**

Once a sanction has come into effect automatically, then an application to the court will be necessary either to set aside a judgment striking out a statement of case under **rule 3.6** or to seek relief for any other breach imposed under **rule 3.8**.

Application in time

Where a sanction has not yet taken effect but a party fears that it may not be able to comply with a court order or rule, then the proper course is to make an application in time. The court will then exercise its discretion by applying the overriding objective. This situation applies even if the court hears the application when the sanction takes effect. The result is that rule 3.9 does not apply.

Applications out of time but no sanction applies

Where there is no sanction for breach, then an application to extend time outside the time for compliance is not made under **rule 3.9**. The court will apply the overriding objective and may reach a similar decision under its case management powers.

The principles that the court will consider are set out in **rule 3.9**.

> *CPR 3.9 (1) ...the court will consider all the circumstances of the case, so as to enable it to deal justly with the application, including the need –*
>
> *(a) for litigation to be conducted efficiently and at proportionate cost; and*
>
> *(b) to enforce compliance with rules, practice directions and orders.*
>
> *(1) An application for relief must be supported by evidence.*

Consider an application for relief where the defence has been struck out for breach of an unless order.

N244 application notice:

Para 3 *What order are you asking the court to make and why?*

The defendant seeks an order for relief from sanctions under CPR 3.9 whereby judgment was entered for the claimant after the defence was struck out following an Unless order made on [date]. The circumstances arose because the claimant made an application requiring service of the defendant's list of documents by [date] culminating in an Unless order which was not complied with. The defendant seeks an order setting aside judgment and that the time for delivery of the list of documents be extended to [date].

The order is sought on the following grounds:

(i) In accordance with the overriding principle and on grounds of proportionality.

(ii) The defendant has a good defence to the claim with a real prospect of success.

(iii) The circumstances of the failure were not due to any omission by the defendant but rather his legal advisors, which was not intentional.

(iv) The list of documents was served on the day fixed by the order but served late after 4pm. This was an oversight that does not affect the conduct of litigation nor does it prejudice the claimant.

Para 10 *What information will you be relying on, in support of your application?*

  ☑ *the attached witness statement*
  ☐ the statement of case
  ☑ the evidence set out in the box below

(1) The defendant had failed to serve his list of documents prior to the date of the Unless order because much of the documentation concerning risk assessments and training records was within the possession of a third party Consultancy agency. They were slow to provide it despite reminders to do so. Copies of correspondence are annexed to this application as exhibit 'A'.

(2) The Unless order was not proportionate because if it became operative (as it did), then it would be contrary to the overriding objective in seeking to do justice between the parties.

(3) The defendant did make real efforts to comply with the order and actually did serve the list but after 4pm on the last day.

(4) Overtures were made to the claimant's solicitors to agree a short extension of time and not to enter judgment, as the list of documents was in the process of being drafted but they refused. Copies of the exchange of correspondence are annexed as exhibit 'B'

(5) The court is invited to find that the defendant has a real prospect of defending this case based on the defence of 'reasonable practicability'. It is submitted that the claimant should not be granted a 'windfall' in circumstances when they have not been prejudiced and where the sanction exceeds the seriousness of the default. The court is referred to the principal cases on relief, particularly that of *Denton v TH White Ltd*. In applying the three stage test, this is a situation where the breach was neither serious nor significant. There are good reasons for missing the deadline because of circumstances outside the control of the defendant.

Statement of Truth etc.

Draft order

Before District Judge Wilson sitting in Chambers at Blackheath County Court.

On hearing [the legal representatives] for the parties and on reading the application notice and the evidence filed

IT IS ORDERED THAT:

1. The order [date] be and is hereby set aside.
2. The defence thereby stuck out is reinstated.
3. The defendant's list of documents shall be deemed to have been served.
4. The defendant do pay the claimant's costs of this application summarily assessed in the sum of £ .

Signed .... Dated ....

7.6.3 The main cases

The underlying concept by Woolf LJ and Jackson LJ was to equip the courts with teeth to ensure that litigation is conducted efficiently and at proportionate cost by complying with the timetable. Therefore the court's willingness to grant relief will be restrictive. It does not follow that simply because the interests of justice demand that a case be reinstated that that will apply. The wider public interest may trump the achievement of justice in an individual case.

There are two main cases at the heart of seeking relief – *Mitchell* and *Denton*. The former concerned itself with triviality and good reasons principles, whilst the latter (considered to be a more generous interpretation for the defaulting party) introduced a 3-stage test examining seriousness and significance of the breach, why, and all the circumstances so as to obtain a just result.

Both cases are good law and are likely to be cited by the parties in an application. They are referred to in more detail in the case law toolkit in Chapter 10. The principles to be derived from these cases must be considered.

Mitchell

7.6.3.1 The Mitchell principles

The case – *Mitchell v News Group Newspapers Ltd* EWCA Civ 1537

The Claimant's solicitors did not file the costs budget within 7 clear days before the case and costs management hearing, The reason given was pressure of work. The sanction imposed under **rule 3.14** provides that only court fees are recoverable in a successful claim. This was the order made by the Master and upheld on appeal. Lord Dyson stated that a tough approach was needed to address the problem of non-compliance, with a view to increasing discipline and reducing the need for satellite litigation. He established the following propositions:

1) The court must consider 'all the circumstances of the case, so as to enable it to deal justly with the application' as required by **rule 3.9**, namely:

   (a) apply the overriding objective; and
   (b) perform a balancing exercise taking into account the factors relevant to the application.

2) The two most important factors, with other circumstances being given less weight are:

   (a) the need for litigation to be conducted efficiently and at proportionate cost; and
   (b) the need to enforce compliance with rules, practice directions and orders.

3) Relief from sanctions is unlikely to be granted unless either:

   (a) the breach is trivial; or
   (b) there is a good reason for the non-compliance, the burden being on the defaulting party to persuade the court to grant relief; and
   (c) the application for relief is made promptly.

4) While relief from sanctions is unlikely unless the breach is trivial or there is a good reason, other factors may on occasion justify granting relief.

The court will want to establish why the default occurred. If there is a good reason and the breach is not substantial or cause serious prejudice to the other party, then relief is likely to be granted. If the solicitors overlooked a deadline then this is unlikely to be a good reason, and relief refused.

Lord Dyson specifically addressed applications for extensions of time. Those made before time has expired will be looked upon more favourably than those requiring relief from sanction made after the event (see paragraph 41). As mentioned earlier, a prospective application made in-time will be considered under the court's case management powers under **rule 3.1(2)(a)** and not **rule 3.9**. It is considered that relief for sanction is unlikely to be granted under the Mitchell principles unless there are exceptional circumstances, perhaps where the period for compliance was unreasonable and could not have been appealed.

Ultimately the court must focus exclusively on doing justice between the parties.

One interesting revelation from *Mitchell* appeared at paragraph 44. If there was a legitimate complaint about the seriousness of the sanction (such as applied to an unless order), then the proper course was to appeal it or exceptionally by making an application under **rule 3.1(7)**. If the application for relief is combined with an application to vary or revoke under **rule 3.1(7)**, then it should be considered first and the *Tibbles* criteria applied (see section on varying case management orders). If no application is made, then a party may not complain that the order should not have been made.

Much satellite litigation resulted from subsequent cases interpreting *Mitchell*, which was the express intention that *Mitchell* sought to avoid. The Court of Appeal therefore heard three appeals in *Denton* to provide further guidance on the correct approach.

Denton

7.6.3.2 The Denton principles

The case – *Denton v T.H. White Ltd* [2014] EWCA Civ 906

Three appeals were heard together by the Court of Appeal. The various breaches were late reliance on witness statements, late payment of courts fees in breach of an unless order, late filing of a costs budget and a substantial delay in notifying the court of the outcome of negotiations.

The Court of Appeal applied a 3-stage test in place of the triviality and good reasons approach adopted in *Mitchell*. However the justices emphasised that the decision in *Mitchell* was sound but needed to be clarified and amplified.

The test:

(1) Identify and assess <u>seriousness and significance</u> of the relevant failure. If the breach is neither serious nor significant, the court is unlikely to spend much time on the second and third stages.

> Whether the breach is material may be relevant if a hearing date may be imperilled or the impact on litigation generally as opposed to the specific case. A failure to pay court fees would be deemed serious even though it did not cause disruption. Where a deadline has been narrowly missed such as service of particulars of claim has led to contrary decisions. Relief was granted in *Kesabo v African Barrick Gold plc* [2013] EWHC 3198 (QB) but not in *Venulum Property Investments Ltd v Space Architecture ltd* [2013] EWHC 1242 (TCC). It has been said that where there has been a failure of form rather than substance, then relief is likely to be granted.

(2) <u>Why the default occurred</u>.

This stage is important where the breach is serious or significant. No good or bad reasons were cited, though those mentioned in *Mitchell* were simply examples.

Good reasons:
In *Mitchell* it was found that a good reason for non-compliance was most likely to arise outside of the control of the defaulting party, such as the solicitor suffering a debilitating illness or if the original time period for compliance was unreasonable. Other good reasons include difficulties in contacting the client to compile the witness statement or difficulties in obtaining disclosure from a third party.

Bad reasons:
Bad reasons identified by the Master of the Rolls in *Mitchell* included overlooking a deadline and failing to meet a deadline through other pressures of work. In <u>Durrant v Chief Constable of Avon and Somerset</u> [2013] EWCA Civ 1624, the defendant failed to comply with an unless order for exchange of witness statements and made a very late application for relief from sanction which debarred reliance upon those witnesses. Relief was granted and the trial was adjourned as a result. The appeal was allowed as the appellate judges refused relief as *Mitchell* required a more robust approach to compliance. This case may be the authority for refusing relief for breach of any unless order.

(3) Consider <u>all the circumstances of the case</u>, so as to enable the court to deal <u>justly</u> with the application including the factors in rule 3.9(1)(a) and (b).

The third stage of the test was frequently ignored by judges in applying *Mitchell*. Even if there had been a serious breach and no good reason for the default, the court then had to consider all the circumstances. Factor (a) requires the court to consider the effect of the breach in every case. If the impact of the breach were to prevent efficient or cost proportionate litigation, then this would militate against granting relief. Factor (b) underlined the position that non-compliance would no longer be tolerated. Also relevant at this stage is whether the application for relief has been made promptly and whether there is any history of past breaches of other orders.

The court should also consider whether the sanction was proportionate to the breach. So, in *Decadent Vapours Ltd v Bevan* (one of the appeal cases heard in *Denton*), the failure to pay the court hearing fee would lead to the case being struck out - and this was not considered proportionate. The breach was considered serious at stage 1 and there was no good reason at stage 2 since the solicitor knew that his method of payment would inevitably give rise to a breach of the court order. But relief was granted at stage 3 as late payment of the fee did not prevent the litigation being conducted efficiently and at proportionate cost.

Where both parties are at fault in failing to serve witness statements, relief was granted in *Chartwell Estate Agents Ltd v Fergies Properties SA* [2014] EWCA Civ 506 despite the application being made two months after the deadline and the defendant opposing the application. It was found that the breach was not trivial and there was no good reason for the default. Those factors were outweighed because the granting of relief did not put the trial date at risk, no extra significant cost would be occasioned and refusal of relief would mean the end of the claim.

7.6.4 Examples on relief

Application of CPR Part 3.1(7)

Court's case management powers to make/revoke order apply where relief had already been refused – *Thevarajah v Riordan & others* [2015] UKSC 78.

Failure to file a costs budget

Recoverable costs limited to court fees under CPR 3.14.

Relief refused, *Denton* test applied – *Jamadar v Bradford Teaching Hospitals NHS Foundation Trust* [2016] EWCA Civ 1001.

Failure to file a Pre-trial checklist

after making an Unless order combined with delay in applying for relief resulted in the refusal of relief. *Denton* applied – *British Gas Trading v Oak Cash and Carry Ltd* [2016] EWCA Civ 153

Failure to serve notice of funding (CFA & ATE cover)

Required under para 9.3 of the PD on pre-action conduct. Relief granted under *Denton* despite significant and inexcusable breach as no adverse effect on conduct of litigation. The third stage of the *Denton* test and the approach under rule 3.9(1) required a focus on the effect of the breach, not the consequence of granting relief. So satellite litigation against solicitors would be avoided - *Caliendo v Mischon de Reya* [2015] EWCA Civ 1029

Failure to file notice of appeal in time

No express sanction applies but an implied one as without an extension of time for service, the Respondent could not rely on matters in their appeal notice. A late application for permission to appeal was analogous to seeking relief under rule 3.9, requiring consideration of the *Mitchell* and *Denton* principles – *Altomart Ltd v Salford Estates (No 2) Ltd* [2014] EWCA Civ 1408

Failure to make specific disclosure

In breach of an unless order to make specific disclosure resulting in strike-out of the Defence, the Court of Appeal refused to grant relief – *Fred Perry v Brands Plaza and Others* [2012] EWCA Civ 224

7.7 Setting aside judgment – CPR 13

7.7.1 Such applications may seem straightforward but there are difficulties, as there is an overlap with applications for relief from sanctions or setting aside the striking out of a claim. Consideration of the guidelines laid down in *Mitchell* and *Denton* must be considered in applications to set aside a regular judgment.

As Christopher Clarke LJ sitting in the Court of Appeal in the case of *Dexia Crediop SpA v Regione Piemonte* [2014] EWCA Civ 1298 said at paragraph 40:

> *CPR 13.3 requires an applicant to show that he has real prospects of a successful defence or some other good reason to set the judgment aside. If he does, the court's discretion is to be exercised in the light of all the circumstances and the overriding objective. The court must have regard to all the factors it considers relevant of which promptness is both a mandatory and an important consideration. Since the overriding objective of the Rules is to enable the court to deal with cases justly and at proportionate cost, and since under the new **CPR 1.1(2)(f)** the latter includes enforcing compliance with rules, Practice Directions and orders, the considerations set out in **CPR 3.9** are to be taken into account.*

If a defendant fails to file an acknowledgment of service or a defence within the time for doing so then the claimant may obtain default judgment. Likewise, a defendant may also obtain default judgment if no defence is filed to a counterclaim. It arises out of procedural error.

If a claimant fails to comply with an unless order and judgment is entered against her, then the procedure for obtaining relief from that sanction is to apply under **rule 3.9** (see earlier).

7.7.2 *An irregular judgment*

The court *must* set aside a judgment entered wrongly (an irregular judgment) in three defined situations under **rule 13.2**:

(a) the time for acknowledging service, or for serving a defence had not expired by the time default judgment was entered;

(b) a summary judgment or application to strike out by the defendant was pending when the default judgment was entered; or

(c) the whole of the claim was satisfied before judgment was entered.

The court may not impose conditions, even if the defendant does not have a real prospect of successfully defending the claim, so the court must set aside as of right.

If the claim form has not been served then **rule 13.2(a)** will not apply and the conditions of **rule 12.3(1)** concerning filing of the acknowledgment of service or the defence will not be satisfied. So judgment must be set aside absolutely.

This must be distinguished from the situation where the defendant may argue that she has not received the claim form. It will depend on whether there has been regular service. So if the defendant has moved on without giving notice and is served in compliance with the rules for service under part 6.9, usually at the last known business address, then this will deemed good service. Therefore it is a regular judgment and whether it should be set aside will be governed by the court's discretion under **rule 13.3**.

There is case law that appears to undermine the position on non-receipt. In _Norcross v Constantine_ (2014) LTL 21/5/2014, it was held that service of the claim form at the defendant's usual or last known address was not good service under rule 6.9 where the claimant had reason to believe that the defendant no longer lived there. Judgment was set aside as of right under **rule 13.2**. In that situation personal service instead of postal service is indicated or enquiry agents may need to be employed to ascertain the current whereabouts of the defendant.

7.7.3 A regular judgment

The court has discretion to set aside a default judgment that was entered correctly under

Rule 13.3(1) if:

(a) the defendant has a real prospect of successfully defending the claim; or
(b) it appears to the court that there is some other good reason why –
  (i) the judgment should be set aside or varied; or
  (ii) the defendant should be allowed to defend the claim.

*(2) In considering whether to set aside or vary a judgment entered under **Part 12**, the matters to which the court must consider include whether the person seeking to set aside the judgment made an application to do so promptly.*

In many cases in a contested application, the parties concentrate on the merits of the proposed defence and ignore the alternative ground under (b) as to whether there is *some other good reason*. It is suggested that even where a defendant may have a good defence, a submission should also include the second limb to increase the prospects of succeeding.

7.7.4 Court's discretion

7.7.4.1 The court has to consider: the *nature of the defence, the period of delay* (i.e. delay after issue of proceedings), *prejudice to the claimant if the judgment was set aside*, and the *overriding objective*.

Some cases have referred to a so-called *implied sanction doctrine* starting with the case of <u>Sayers v Clarke Walker</u> [2002] EWCA Civ 645. This provides that where a party has not complied with a rule or order and the court is not willing to grant an extension of time, the consequence will be that the default provisions of the rule or order will stand. In such circumstances there is an implied sanction imposed by the rule or order that engages **rule 3.9** requiring relief to be sought. This doctrine was disapproved of by Lord Dyson in the case of <u>Attorney-General of</u>

Trinidad and Tobago v Matthews [2011] UKPC 38 who held that it cannot have been the intention of the Civil Procedure Rule Committee that two sets of rules would have to be satisfied, i.e. **rules 13.3** and **3.9**.

7.7.4.2 It has been suggested that it should be a two-stage process.

The first stage involves consideration of **rule 13.3** for setting aside.

The second stage for relief from sanction under **rule 3.9** should only arise if the court refuses to set aside, because only then does an implied sanction arise.

This is contentious because more recent cases have not applied a two-stage process, but considered the criteria in **rule 3.9** and the *Mitchell/Denton* principles as part of the overall process. For example consider the cases of *Sharon Hockley v North Lincolnshire & Goole NHS Foundation Trust* HC 19 September 2014 and *Dexia Crediop SpA*, mentioned earlier.

In exercising discretion, it is necessary to examine the three criteria under **rule 13.3**, namely:

- real prospects of success
- some other good reason
- promptness

7.7.4.3 'a real prospect of successful defending the claim'

The burden is on the defendant to satisfy the court that there is a good reason why a regular judgment should be set aside. In *International Finance Corporation v Utexafrica Sprl [2001] CLC 1361,* Moore-Bick J said that it is not enough to show a merely arguable defence. 'Realistic prospect of success' means a case that carries a degree of conviction.

In *E.D. and F Man Liquid Products Ltd v Patel* [2003] EWCA Civ 472, the Court Of Appeal confirmed that the test is the same as the test for summary judgment under **rule 24.2** (although the burden of proof is reversed as the claimant must show that the defendant has no real prospect of success in an application for summary judgment).

Interestingly, it has been held that where an allegation of dishonesty (or at least inaccuracy) is made in a defendant's witness statement, that would not act as a bar to a successful application to set aside judgment (*Pasena Ltd v Lextrex Holdings Ltd & Ors* [2010] EWCA Civ 1539. Perhaps it is more the fact that the court should not make findings concerning disputed facts - as that should be left for trial - that is the relevant point (*CPL Industrial Services Holding Limited v R & L Freeman & Sons* [2005] EWCA Civ 539.

But then in *Shandong Chenming Paper Holding Ltd v Saga Forest Carriers Intl AS* [2008] EWHC 1055 (Comm) LTL, there was a real prospect of success in establishing a time-bar defence where there was some documentary evidence in support of an argument that the cause of action accrued just outside the relevant time limit.

Perhaps the point is that whilst the court will not make findings of fact, provided there is some documentary evidence to show a reasonable prospect of success, then this element of the application should be satisfied.

Alternatively, it is for the applicant to show some other good reason as to why the judgment should be set aside or varied under **rule 13.3(1)(b)**.

7.7.4.4 'some other good reason'

This is not defined under the rule but is similar to the provisions under **rule 24.2(b)** which stipulates that when dealing with an application for summary judgment, the court must also consider whether there is any compelling reason why the case or issue should be disposed of at trial. The overriding objective will also be relevant.

It has been held that the parties' *conduct* may be relevant (*Hart Investments Ltd v Fidler* [2006] EWHC 2857 (TCC) whilst in *Roundstone Nurseries Ltd v Stephenson Holdings Ltd* [2009] EWHC 1431 (TCC), the claimant's unreasonable conduct by failing to extend a stay and entering default judgment was deemed a good reason for judgment to be set aside. The judge also commented that a claimant should not enter judgment in default simply because he is technically entitled to, where he knows that the defendant has a good defence and would be entitled to set judgment aside.

The danger is that a claimant taking advantage of inadvertence will be faced with an adverse costs order on the application to set aside.

An example of a case when setting aside was granted for *some other good reason* even though the defendants did not reach the threshold required to show a defence with *a realistic prospect of success* was in <u>Latmar Holdings Corp v Media Focus Ltd</u> [2012] EWHC 262 (Comm) where there were serious allegations of fraud, it was a large claim and the period of delay was not inordinate.

A failure to serve a response pack with the particulars of claim has been a ground for setting aside even where the defendant has not shown they have a reasonable prospect of defending the claim – see <u>Rajval Construction Ltd v Bestville Properties Ltd</u> [2010] EWCA Civ 1621.

7.7.4.5 'promptness'

This is required under **rule 13.3(2)**.

Guidance on making the application promptly is found in **PD 23A** para 2.7 (applications generally) and **rule 3.9(1)(b)** (applications for relief from sanctions).

Although not an absolute requirement under the rule, applications do fail where there has been significant delay in making the application to set aside.

The authorities vary as to what constitutes 'promptness':

26 days has been held too long before filing the application (*Regency Rolls Ltd & anor v Carnall* (2000) Lawtel, 16 October, CA – '*promptly*' means '*acting with alacrity*').

However, an application made 37 days after default judgment, was deemed to be sufficiently prompt (*BCCI v Zafar* (2001) Lawtel, 2 November, ChD). In this case, the applicant blamed his solicitors for not receiving correspondence.

There is a real distinction on visiting errors made by solicitors on the client for applications to set aside - where the duty is personal to the defendant, and applications for relief from sanctions. Under **rule 3.9(1)(f)**, in a relief application, the court may take into account default caused by the party's legal representative. That may explain the difference in the two cases mentioned above.

But *Mitchell* will rear its head where there has been a considerable delay of 15 months, where the application was refused (*Samara v MBI Partners UL Ltd* [2014] EWHC 563 (QB)). This is an example of the implied sanction doctrine.

7.7.5 The application – documents

- **Application notice, N244**
- **Evidence in support** – either in the body of the application notice or a witness statement
- **Draft defence**
- **Draft order**- see below
- **Schedule of costs**
- **Case summary (with chronology)**
- **Skeleton argument** – desirable (especially if applicant), but not essential
- **Case authorities**

Application notice

Paragraph 3 *What order are you asking the court to make and why?*

(1) The judgment obtained on [date] be set aside under CPR 13.3 on the grounds that the defendant has a real prospect of successfully defending the claim.

(2) The claimant do pay the defendant's costs of this application summarily assessed in the sum of £x. Because the claimant has known that liability is disputed.

Paragraph 10 *What information will you be relying on, in support of your application?*

- ☐ *the attached witness statement*
- ☐ *the statement of case*
- ☑ *the evidence set out in the box below*

1. The defendant seeks the court's discretion to set aside a regular judgment obtained in a clinical negligence claim where damages are claimed in excess of £50,000.00 up to £100,000.00.

2. The letter of response served on the claimant 6 months ago denies breach of duty and causation so there is no prejudice caused to the claimant if the court sets aside judgment.

3. It is contended that there is a substantial defence, exhibit 'A' to this application.

4. The grounds of the application are contained within CPR 13.3.

5. The defendant seeks the court's discretion be exercised in its favour as there is a real prospect that it will successfully defend the claim, or in the alternative, that there is some other good reason why judgment should be set aside, namely the significant value of the claim and its complexity.

6. The reasons for missing the date in submitting the defence are attributed to the trust's omission in failing to instruct its solicitors through an oversight caused by shortage of staff through illness. The court is referred to the attached witness statement of James Bond at exhibit 'B'.

7. The actual delay from the last date for serving the defence to the date of this application is 14 days. We would argue that the application was made promptly.

8. The defendant refers to the case summary at exhibit 'C' and skeleton submission at exhibit 'D'.

7.7.6 Preliminaries at the hearing

Example of a contested application to set aside a regular default judgment, taking place in a telephone hearing.

If a party objects to a telephone hearing because of the complexity of the facts/law and the importance to the client, then they must write to the court at least 7 days before the hearing or such shorter time as the court permits (**PD 23A, para 6.4**).

Service of the above documents (where appropriate) at least 2 clear days before the hearing.

Speak to your opponent, establish if she has any cases for you. They should have been served in advance but this is a point you may wish to raise with the judge, not to seek an adjournment, as you should have the main cases anyway, but a point in your favour if you can accept late service with good grace.

7.7.7 **The hearing**

7.7.7.1 Before a Master/District Judge

The party applying to set aside (usually the defendant) starts the hearing.

Introduce your opponent and yourself.

Check the District Judge has the papers and whether he has read the application notice. Be guided by the judge's response so if he is familiar with the application, do not repeat it.

7.7.7.2 Proceed with your opening, explaining the circumstances as to how the time limits were missed before referring to your evidence – witness statements, exhibits to the application notice (letter of claim and letter of response) and draft defence.

> Sir, I appear on behalf of the defendant trust. This is my application to set aside judgment entered in default and for damages to be assessed ordered on [date]. You will see from the particulars of claim that in this clinical negligence claim, the claimant seeks damages between £50,000.00 to £100,000.00 alleging that the claimant's gallbladder was damaged during keyhole surgery and that this went unnoticed for a period of 4 months, before he had revision surgery. He claims to suffer ongoing problems which are set out in a condition & prognosis report from his expert, Miss X attached to the particulars of claim.
>
> Sir, my client defends this claim, in short, because whilst it is accepted that the gallbladder was damaged (although the extent is denied), it did not constitute a breach of duty in accordance with the Bolam test. Furthermore we deny causation based on expert evidence obtained on behalf of the trust.
>
> The claimant is aware that the claim is defended and has been aware since receiving the letter of response some 6 months ago. The error in failing to respond to the claim by [date] is unfortunately due to an oversight. By their own admission, the trust's legal department failed to pass on the court papers to the instructed solicitors. I refer you to the witness statement of Mr B setting out the circumstances for the oversight.
>
> This has led to a delay of 14 days from when judgment was entered before I submitted my application to the court.

> *May I refer you to my case summary, as this sets out a chronology which I hope is helpful in putting into context the timings in this case.*

This covers an abridged version of an introduction before you proceed to refer the judge to the draft defence (the 'money shot' of your application).

Once you have covered the merits of your case, then address the court about any errors in the claimant's chronology as stated in their case summary (as relevant). Essentially your task is to disabuse the court of any suggestion that the claimant has been prejudiced. Perhaps also to instil in the mind of the judge that the claimant's request was self-indulgent and inconsistent with mutual co-operation.

Invite the judge to ask any questions if he has not already done so.

7.7.7.3 Next step is to make submissions. Don't slavishly read out your skeleton submission.

> *Sir, I have prepared a skeleton submission which addresses some authorities in detail, should you need to consider those.* (Take the judge through those cases, if so invited).

> *You have discretion to set aside a regular judgment where there is a reasonable defence on the merits. The actual wording in part 13.3(a) is '.. a real prospect of successfully defending the claim'. I would invite you to conclude that having read the letter of response and the draft defence that there are strong and persuasive arguments for defeating this claim on breach of duty and causation.*

> *I would also invite you to conclude that the alternative ground under sub-paragraph (b) is also satisfied, namely that there are other good reasons why the judgment should be set aside. The claimant knew that the trust was defending the claim, yet failed to warn the defendant that they intended to apply for default judgment. Their*

behaviour offends the overriding objective as the parties must cooperate to facilitate efficient litigation.

There has been no undue delay because as soon as the trust became aware of the judgment, they instructed me. I did invite the claimant to consent to the application but they refused. In my submission, there is no prejudice to the claimant if you permitted the defence to proceed by setting aside the judgment.

Do you want me to address you on the very well known Mitchell and Denton principles. If not, then those are my submissions, Sir.

Be prepared to address the court on relief from sanctions under **rule 3.9**. This may arise because the court may be against you on your substantive application for setting aside the order, in which case a relief application must proceed. Alternatively, the court may wish to hear you on these principles as part of your initial application. So this will involve: seriousness of the breach, the reasons and all the circumstances. It is the third tranche that must be emphasised, and the effect of the delay in making the application, and its impact on the progress of the litigation. It would be argued here that the delay is minimal, and had the claimants consented, then little time would have been lost.

If the application is successful the court may decide to give case management directions concerning service of the defence.

7.7.7.4 Costs

The court may be prepared to make a summary assessment. So if you are successful, invite the court to award costs against the claimant. If unsuccessful, you will have little or no argument to object to an order for costs but may seek to mitigate them if excessive. The court may decide to reserve costs.

7.7.7.5 **Draft Order**

1. Judgment be set aside.

2. The defendant do file and serve its defence by 4pm on [date]

3. Allocation questionnaires are hereby dispensed with.

4. A Costs and Case Management conference will be listed on [date]

Alternatively, directions may be given in accordance with the model order directions for clinical negligence claims (in this example) or for personal injury claims – see Appendix II.

7.8 Application for an interim payment – CPR 25.6

The grounds for seeking an interim payment are set out in Chapter 6 on tactics.

7.8.1 The procedure

- Application notice, N244

Evidence in support (see **PD 25B**)
- sum of money sought
- reasons for an interim
- the likely award of damages achieved through a settlement or at trial
- that the conditions in **Part 25.7** have been satisfied
- A schedule of loss (exhibit)
- Medical report(s) (exhibit)
- Possibly a witness statement of the claimant (exhibit)

- Application must be served on D at least 14 days before hearing

- Defendant should file evidence in reply at least 7 days before hearing

- Claimant's evidence in reply to be served 3 days before hearing

7.8.2 The application

Paragraph 3 *What order are you asking the court to make and why?*

We intend to apply for an order (a draft of which is attached) that:

> (i) the defendant do make an interim payment of £50,000 or such other sum as the Court shall deem appropriate on account of damages in respect of the claimant's personal injury claim that happened on [date].
>
> (ii) The application is made pursuant to CPR 25.6. It is submitted that the Claimant will secure substantial damages at trial, exceeding £400,000.
>
> (iii) The reason why an interim payment is required is because the claimant has not worked for the last 4 months whilst he has been undergoing further medical treatment, including skin grafts and intensive physiotherapy treatment. He needs to support his family and is now only in receipt of statutory sick pay.

Paragraph 10 *What information will you be relying on, in support of your application?*

> ☑ *the attached witness statement*
> ☐ *the statement of case*
> ☑ *the evidence set out in the box below*
>
> 1. The claimant sustained very serious injuries in the course of his employment while working as a farm hand at the defendant's farm on [date]. The court is referred to the statement of case and the defence. Whilst liability is denied by the defendant, arguing that the claimant was the author of his own misfortune, it is contended that negligence and breach of statutory duty will be established.
>
> 2. The claimant lost his left hand in a Round baler that he was operating when it malfunctioned. It was in a manifestly dangerous

condition and the subject of an investigation by the Health and Safety Executive. A copy of their report is annexed as exhibit 'A'.

3. Whilst the defendant pleads in the alternative that the claimant should be held contributorily negligent, any contribution, which is denied, would still allow for the substantial recovery of damages and far in excess of the interim payment requested. In this regard, the court is referred to the provisional schedule of loss at exhibit 'B' which pleads special damages of £320,000. Of that sum, £80,000 concerns past financial losses, which we contend, is bound to be recoverable in full or a substantial majority. The rest of the claim represents future costs, of which only the claim for future care at £150,000 is anticipated to be contentious. We submit that even with some discount, the claim is still valued comfortably in excess of £450,000.

4. The medical report of Mr Bones, Consultant Orthopaedic Surgeon appears at exhibit 'C'.

5. The court is referred to the conditions to be satisfied by the claimant in **Part 25.7**. The principal issue which the court must determine is that set out in sub-section 1(C), namely that if the claim went to trial the claimant would obtain judgment for a substantial sum of money. A skeleton submission on the issue of liability is appended as exhibit 'D'.

6. Aside from real financial need, the other compelling reason why an interim payment should be paid now is because of the period of time before the case will be heard. The nature of the injuries are such that the claimant will need to see numerous medical specialists, including a Neurologist, Physiotherapist, Pain Management Consultant and a Clinical Psychologist. The claimant has obtained expert evidence from a Consulting engineer on the condition of the baler but does not wish to unilaterally disclose the report. In all likelihood the case will not be ready for trial for at least another 18 months.

7. The claimant claims his costs to be summarily assessed in accordance with the attached statement of costs.

7.8.3 Draft Order

Before District Judge Swan

Upon hearing [the legal representatives} for the parties and on reading the evidence filed

IT IS ORDERED THAT

1. The defendant do make an interim payment of £50,000 to be paid within 14 days by [date].

2. Defendant do pay claimant's cost summarily assessed at £x payable by [date].

Dated the …day of …..

7.9 Application for summary judgment – CPR 24

7.9.1 The procedure

Set out in **Part 24.4.** The earliest opportunity for filing an application is after the acknowledgment of service is filed.

• Application notice, N244

  - Evidence in support (**PD24, para 2**) stating:

    1. That it is an application for summary judgment under Part 24.

    2. The evidence either in the body of the application or in an attached statement, identifying the point of law or provision in a document on which the applicant relies and/or

    3. State the order sought, i.e. on the evidence that the respondent has no real prospect of succeeding on the claim or issue or (as the case may be), of successfully defending the claim or issue, and in

either case state that the applicant knows of no other reason why the disposal of the claim or issue should await trial.

4. Draw the respondent's attention to the time limit for filing its own written evidence, i.e. at least 7 days before the hearing.

- Witness statement of claimant
- Skeleton submission
- Draft court order
- Statement of costs

• Application must be served at least 14 days before the hearing.

• Respondent must serve his statement at least 7 days of the hearing.

• The applicant must serve any evidence in reply at least 3 days before the hearing.

7.9.2 The Application

Paragraph 3 *What order are you asking the court to make and why?*

(i) Summary judgment be entered against the claimant under CPR 24.2 on the ground that the claim has no real prospect of success and there is no other compelling reason why the case should be disposed of at a trial, or alternatively

(ii) The claim be struck out on the ground that it discloses no reasonable grounds for being brought and/or is an abuse of the court's process

because the claimant's claim discloses no cause of action as no duty of care was owed to him.

Paragraph 10 *What information will you be relying on, in support of your application?*

☑ *the attached witness statement*
☑ *the statement of case*
☑ *the evidence set out in the box below*

1. The claimant brings a claim for damages for personal injuries arising from an incident when he tripped in a car park situated at anyplace village, County Durham on 5th June 2017 sustaining a fracture to his right femur. He claims to have tripped in a large pot hole as he was leaving the Fighting Cocks Public House.

2. The claimant alleges negligence and breach of the Occupiers' Liability Act 1957 against the defendant as the supposed proprietor of the Fighting Cocks Public House and owner of the car park, for failing to repair and adequately maintain it.

3. The defendant is not the owner of the Fighting Cocks but is a licensee. A copy of the Licence with Happy Days Brewery is exhibit 'A'.

4. Happy Days Brewery is not the owner nor has any legal interest in the car park which is land believed to be in the ownership of the local council.

5. The claimant has no cause of action against the defendant who owes no common law duty or statutory duty to him. It is submitted that the claim should be struck out under rule 3.4(2) as disclosing no reasonable grounds for bringing a claim.

6. The claimant should pay the defendant's costs of these proceedings, to be assessed at £x in accordance with the statement of costs annexed.

Statement of Truth

I believe that the facts stated in this section are true.

Signed ………….. ……….   Dated ……………...

Key points

- If the end limitation period is looming, seek an agreed extension or amnesty if you are not ready to issue.

- Don't leave service to the last minute (or even the last few days).

- Diarise key dates and have a back-up, so that in the event of illness and holidays, someone else can ensure continuity and knows at a glance the status of a claim.

- Agree all extensions in writing. CPR 2.11 provides for agreement unless a rule or PD states otherwise. A maximum of 28 days is permissible provided it does not affect the trial timetable.

- Make an in-time application if a deadline cannot be met and no agreement with the other side. The court may extend the time for compliance under its case management powers - CPR 3.1(2)(a).

- If a sanction applies, apply on notice promptly for relief. Try and get agreement with your opponent but you will still need the court to grant relief. If breach of an unless order or other serious breach, concentrate your argument on stage 3 of the *Denton* test – the circumstances. Explain how and why the failure occurred and that it will not affect progress of the litigation (or how this may be addressed). Emphasise prior compliance.

CHAPTER EIGHT
THE TRIAL

Judgment does not come suddenly; the proceedings gradually merge into the judgment.
– Franz Kafka, The Trial

8.1 <u>What does the judge need to know</u>

Elementary my dear Watson: evidence and persuasion. Or putting it another way - the facts, the law, standard of proof and closing submissions. Remember, the case is proved through witness evidence, not the advocate's style of delivery. Your role is to apply the facts to the law.

The trial is not the arena to turn around a weak case or to fill in the gaps of inadequate preparation as that surely is the method to lose the case. The best chance of success is being prepared. One assumes you have at least a half decent case. So that means careful drafting of pleadings (check your expert supports them), conferences with your experts and factual witnesses, schedules of loss supported by quantum evidence and a well honed skeleton submission and concise case summary.

If representing the claimant, it is good practice to have prepared a working skeleton early in the case as that helps to define the issues. Sure, it may undergo some refinement as the case progresses, but at trial, you must know how to get your witnesses to confirm the issues you need to prove.

Advocacy should be fluid, articulate and concentrate on the issues. You will have prepared the questions for cross-examination and will know the grounds upon which you hope to win, so you should feel and appear confident and interested in your case.

In terms of style, the advocate will develop with experience what suits them. But if starting out, use simple language and short sentences in a controlled but interesting way. You must appear dispassionate so as not to reveal your own opinions but at the same time must have confidence in your case. Sometimes the distinction between the two can become blurred. Try and present your case in a calm and collected way, but not monotone (vary your pitch). The idea is to enthuse the judge and hold their interest. You need to tell a good story and if needs be, rely upon photographs, diagrams or models to demonstrate technical issues. Of course they may already be in the trial bundle as exhibits, but if not a notice should have been filed with the court alerting it to the additions.

8.2 The trial bundles

Before we start with advocacy, let's look at the trial bundles as poorly presented ones can undermine much good work. It may irritate the judge and may make it difficult for you to find your way around them. They should be clear and be set out in a logical format with no duplicate documents. These can arise because medical reports and schedules of loss will be enclosed with the pleadings and may be attached to an application notice or also exhibited to a witness statement. It is suggested that you only need the medical report, for example, in the section on expert evidence. Often the difficulty can arise when you are trying to agree the bundle with the other side and they insist on including application notices, court orders and Uncle Tom Cobley and all for fear of missing out something they perceive as crucial. If the court has ruled on an application notice, say for disclosure and there has been compliance then why include? Perhaps their relevance only applies if costs have been reserved.

The ideal is that both parties refer to the same paginated document. This can go awry where numerous duplicates appear in a bundle and the parties refer to different page references.

PD 39A, para 3 sets out the court's expectations regarding the contents of the bundle.

The suggested order is as follows:

- Case summary and chronology
- Pleadings

- Case Management order for directions
- Witness statements
- Expert reports
- Schedules of loss
- Medical records in a clinical negligence claim. Keep in a separate file.
- Miscellaneous/ correspondence

Each section should be separated with tab dividers and the pages numbered continuously throughout all the bundles rather than starting afresh for each bundle.

It is helpful if the witness box has a separate bundle containing witness statements where there are a considerable number. Likewise if the case has a large number of expert reports, they should be placed in a separate bundle.

On a strictly evidential basis, documents that are hearsay evidence should contain a Civil Evidence Act notice. But the parties should be encouraged to agree that the documents in the bundle may be treated as evidence of the facts stated in them. This applies particularly to medical records.

The trial bundles are usually prepared by the claimant's solicitors and must be lodged with the court between **3** and **7 days** before the start of the trial. A failure to do so could lead to a sanction with respect to costs.

If there is reliance on plans, photographs, sketches or models which are not annexed to a witness statement then under **rule 33.6** the party seeking to rely upon them must give notice to the opponent not later than the latest date for serving witness statements. They must also give notice at least **21 days** before the hearing indicating that such evidence will be produced.

8.3 Common approaches in all cases

8.3.1 The skeleton argument

There will be a certain amount of overlap with the opening speech (see below) although the skeleton should be briefer. It is the aperitif before the hor d'oeuvres (the opening speech). It must be precise and concise and be an outline of the main points in the trial. Tell the judge about the facts and why you should win. This is not story telling; it is more akin to a pleading but less formal. But it is advocacy; you are saying why you should win and why your opponent should not. The judge should have enough information so she knows the issues in the case. Set out the facts, the law and how they apply to it. You may, indeed you should, quote from your skeleton in your opening speech. Keep coming back to it whilst developing your arguments. That way you anchor it in the judge's mind. Continuous reinforcement. That does not mean reading your skeleton in your opening. That would be stultifying and lack spontaneity. If acting for the defendant, then you won't have the opportunity for an opening, in which case you should refer to your skeleton in your closing speech. At all costs, don't just prepare a skeleton and hope the judge will read it. They will, but it must become so familiar like meeting an old friend that you know the points you need to raise.

One of the main differences between the skeleton and opening speech is that your skeleton seeks to persuade. So analyse your opponent's position and state why your argument beats theirs.

The skeleton should be prepared early on in the claimant's claim. It focuses the mind on the issues and what needs to be proved and how you will do it. Of course it will be refined after issuing proceedings and on reviewing the defence. Further revision should take place on exchange of expert evidence.

Procedure

The Queen's Bench Guide, para 7.11.11 stipulates that skeletons are filed with the court not less than 2 days before the trial. However the model directions state 3 days so that should be observed. A sanction may apply if the skeleton is not filed in time, as the successful party may not receive the costs of preparing it on assessment.

The Guide at para 7.10.13 covers what is required:

(1) *concisely summarise the party's submissions in relation to each of the issues, (where appropriate by reference to the relevant paragraphs in the statement of case)*

(2) *cite the main authorities relied on, which may be attached,*

(3) *contain a reading list and an estimate of the time it will take the judge to read,*

(4) *be as brief as the issues allow and not normally be longer than 20 pages of double-spaced A4 paper,*

(5) *be divided into numbered paragraphs and paged consecutively,*

(6) *avoid formality and use understandable abbreviations, and*

(7) *identify any core documents which it would be helpful to read beforehand.*

PD52A, para 5.1(1) also covers the requirements about the contents of a skeleton when lodging an appeal. They apply equally to a trial.

8.3.2 Example. Let's look at a draft skeleton of a defendant in a personal injury claim involving a manual handling case. This actually went to trial and the claimant lost. Some of the facts, names of the parties, dates and court have been changed as will be clear.

IN THE COUNTY COURT AT LLANGEFNI Case No.

BETWEEN

MR JIM ROCKFORD <u>Claimant</u>

-and-

PICKWICK PAPERS LTD <u>Defendant</u>

DEFENDANT'S SKELETON ARGUMENT

---

1. Introduction

The claimant, a delivery driver sustained injury on 11 October 2016 whilst manually unloading boxes alone in the course of his employment. He seeks damages alleging that the defendant had not avoided the task causing the injury nor reduced the risks to the lowest level reasonably practicable. He maintains that the relevant box was overweight. The defendant puts the claimant to proof concerning the alleged accident and maintains that the job had been appropriately risk assessed. They assert that the claimant had received adequate manual handling training and supervision.

2. Issues

D submits that the following issues must be determined:

2.1 Did the accident happen as C alleges.

2.2 What was the weight of the box.

2.3 Did C's van have a sack barrow.

2.4 Was the weight of the box such as to exceed the Manual Handling Operations Guidelines.

2.5 Was C properly trained.

2.6 What should C have done whilst loading his van.

2.7 What should C have done whilst unloading his van.

3. <u>D's submissions on negligence and statutory duty</u>

3.1 C was employed as a delivery driver with D since June 2012 based in Pentraeth. In the course of a normal day C was required to load his van with boxes of maintenance manuals and drive to RAF Valley to unload them.

3.2 C's case is that he had to load his van by hand from pallets. D would not have had contact with the boxes as they arrived from the supplier on a pallet so D did not pack the contents. C did not report the accident when it was alleged to have happened so there was no opportunity to investigate at that time. There is no evidence of the weight of the load.

3.3 At RAF Valley, C started to unload the boxes. He alleges that he was aware that one of the boxes was especially heavy and weighed in excess of 15kg. The HSE guidance and the regulations suggest that a weight of 25kg is acceptable.

3.4 D will say that even on C's own case there is no breach of the regulations. The reference to the lack of scales is a red herring as C knew that the box was heavy and he does not say he would have acted any differently.

3.5 D will say that had C followed his own training then the accident would not have happened. C says in his statement at page 35 that he had not received any training since August 2013. D says that the documents and the training records (from page 55 to 78) will demonstrate that this patently is not true. The risk assessment and health and safety policies are available on the notice board at Pentraeth.

3.6 D will say that had C followed his training, he would not have been required to lift the load. The procedure is set out in the method statement at page 90. C was not required and was expressly informed that the unloading of heavy boxes by himself was forbidden. What he should have done was wait for another driver.

3.7 It is submitted on behalf of D that what C was doing at the time of his alleged accident was unusual and he ought not to have been doing it given his training. In those circumstances D relies on **BENNETTS V MINISTRY OF DEFENCE (2004)**. Any risk should be considered with a degree of realism in mind.

3.8 C's own witness, Frank Cannon (page 28), confirms the procedure that C should have followed. C had a number of options when he arrived at Valley; he could have asked for help, he could have used his sack barrow or he could have broken the load down. C simply failed to follow his training and any injury which he may have suffered was his own fault. C is under a statutory duty to comply with D's system pursuant to Reg 5 of the MHO Regulations 1992.

3.9 On causation, D disputes that any defect in the risk assessment was causative of the accident. D had in place a system to deal with manual handling procedures including risk assessments, training and provision of equipment and therefore is not in breach of the regulations. D's duty is restricted to that which is reasonably practicable. Under the Enterprise Act, it is not a strict duty whereas the duty owed by C is a strict one (regulation 5).

3.10 D denies liability but contends that if any breach applies and injury is proven, then C should bear significant contributory negligence to reflect his blameworthiness in failing to comply with D's guidelines and C's own training. It is submitted that C should be deemed 90% contributorily liable.

4. D's submissions on injury and quantum

4.1 C never reported or complained to D that he had an accident or suffered injury on the day of the alleged accident. A report was made 5 days later (see the Accident Book, page 92). In the intervening period C turned up for work and carried out his usual duties. D contends that no injury occurred as a result of the relevant accident.

4.2 In the event that the court finds C did have injuries to his shoulder and wrist, then D argues as below.

4.3 The court is referred to the contemporaneous medical records of Bangor General Infirmary. At page 70, an entry records C's attendance at the A&E department. Half way down that page is a note of the cause of the accident: '...*must have fallen.*' It is C's case that the cause of the injury was a strain by lifting a heavy box. He never alleged that he had fallen as a result.

4.4 In the circumstances, any injury is not attributable to the accident.

4.5 If the court finds factual causation of injuries by the relevant accident, D refers to its own medical report by Dr D Lewis-Jones at page 101. The expert states that the symptoms from which C suffered were intermittent and would on balance of probabilities have resolved within 3 weeks. It is significant that C did not seek any further medical attention and was discharged with a tubi-grip and painkillers.

4.6 The court is referred to D's counter-schedule of loss (page 120), wherein, subject to a finding of liability, the totality of the claim is assessed at £2500. There is no evidence in fact for C's claim in his schedule of loss (page 110) seeking £55,000.00. This is grossly inflated. Most elements of the claim relate to care and assistance. There are no statements or expert evidence to support such a claim.

8.3.3 Opening the case

8.3.3.1 The judge will have read the skeleton arguments for both parties and the pleadings so may dispense with an opening address (**PD29, para 10.2**). She may have read the witness statements and expert reports but this should not be assumed. In that situation, it would be beneficial for the claimant's advocate to suggest a short opening speech to set the scene and introduce the evidence and the principal issues. It allows one the opportunity to refer the court to the bundles and the documents contained within. Some judges will let the advocates do the work, others will be more interventionist by laying down the issues they consider are germane to the case, thus guiding the advocates on any areas of difficulty. This should act as a sounding board for the advocates and give them an early steer on particular areas of emphasis that may require especial attention.

The defendant does not normally make an opening speech but the judge may ask the defendant's advocate if there is anything they wish to add.

8.3.3.2 It is important to appreciate that the opening speech is not about being partial but explaining in objective terms what the case is about, significant facts that are agreed and those disputed and the extent of any admissions as well as areas of agreement and disagreement of the experts. Tell the judge in your first (or second sentence) the areas you will cover, for example, duty of care, breach, causation and the experts that will address them. Refer the court to any authorities that will feature in the claim. To coin a phrase you are providing a route map for the direction of travel.

You want to make it as easy as possible for the judge to understand the case and to assist her. You almost want to anticipate how she will write her judgment.

The opening should not be a repetition of the skeleton argument.

Beware the temptation to say a lot in an opening as the danger of labouring a point is to weaken it. The same applies to your written arguments. LESS really is more.

Do not treat the opening as an opportunity to make submissions and argue the merits. This is not an argument. However, be prepared to assist the judge on any questions they may have. This may frequently be about the course or timetabling of the trial.

Also, beware creating hostages to fortune by claiming what the witnesses will say. Whilst it is true that you know what the statements say, the witnesses may seek to refine what their evidence is at your client's expense under cross-examination. It might then appear that your case is underpinned with shaky foundations. Confidence in your case must not lead to exuberance. A cautious, forensic ability may suit you better. In other words, the opening should not represent the high point of your case – leave that to the closing.

You may feel happier drafting your opening speech or the main pointers but don't read it out. Use only as a reminder, so don't be afraid of pauses. Make one point, then if needs be glance at your draft and proceed to the next. You don't want to have long dramatic pauses otherwise the judge is liable to hurry you along and request your first witness.

8.3.3.3 The opening speech should cover:

1. An introduction of yourself and your opponent;
2. The nature of the case and the ISSUES;
3. A summary of the AREAS of DISPUTE;
4. A synopsis of the Statement of Case or the Defence;
5. The EVIDENCE that will be adduced;
6. The LEGAL PRINCIPLES.

The opening speech has another very important benefit, namely to settle yourself in to the case, almost as a 'warm up act' for the main part of the case – adducing the evidence.

8.3.3.4 By way of example here is an abridged version from the perspective of the claimant bringing a clinical negligence claim:

1. Set out the nature of the case

Your Honour, I appear for the claimant, my Learned Friend, Mr Kirk appears for the defendant. This is a claim for damages for clinical negligence arising from the repair of a ruptured left Achilles tendon performed by Mr Bones at the Anytown Hospital on 1st December 2008. Anytown hospital is part of the defendant NHS Trust. The operation involved surgical reconstruction of the tendon. A probe - which was a needle-like instrument broke whilst threading a polyester tape into a hole drilled into the calcaneal tunnel. In the course of the procedure the tape was fed through the eyelet of the probe and passed from the medial side of the foot to the lateral side. The purpose of the tape is to act like a giant suture to support the ligament.

The decision was made by the surgeon to leave the broken part of the probe in situ in the tunnel. Mr Spock, the claimant was not informed of this decision post operatively, nor was breakage of the instrument recorded in the operation notes. The claimant suffered from stabbing pains in his foot shortly following the operation and informed Mr Bones about his symptoms at a follow-up consultation. Despite the presence of swelling, he was reassured and discharged home. In total, Mr Spock made 4 visits to the hospital and on 4th April 2009, Mr Bones recommended an exploratory operation of the left heel with a view to achieving symptomatic relief. This was performed under general anaesthetic on 18th April at Anytown Hospital by Mr Bones. A foreign body, namely the broken probe was located and by releasing the tape, the probe fragment came out of the tunnel on the lateral side.

If I may, Your Honour, I refer you to page 88 which has some agreed photographs of a model ankle and also a diagram showing the anatomy of the calcaneal tunnel. You can see the site where the hole was drilled to accept the probe. There is also a photograph of a similar sized probe as used in the operation. A diagram drawn by Miss Uhura, the defendant's expert shows how the probe fragment may have looked, although it is clearly not to scale. Unfortunately the recovered fragment was not retained.

Mr Spock made a good recovery, achieving symptomatic relief. Mr Bones admitted that he had removed a probe fragment from the operation site when he next saw Mr Bones in a consultation on 1st May2009.

It is the claimant's case that the surgeon was negligent to have left a foreign body, namely part of the surgical probe in the calcaneal tunnel, and that this was causative of the claimant's symptoms. He has suffered loss as a result.

2. State the issues

The issues in this case fall within a narrow compass.
Should the surgeon have been able to and did he attempt to remove the probe fragment. Did any risk of leaving the fragment in situ pose a greater risk than attempting to remove it. If it was **Bolam** negligent to leave in situ, what damage has thereby been caused. What loss has been sustained.

3. Refer to the pleadings/trial bundle

Your Honour, you will see that there are two bundles in the form of lever arch files. They are agreed. File 1 contains the pleadings; witness statements; and expert reports. File 2 contains the claimant's medical records.

An agreed case summary is at the front of the first bundle from page 1. The particulars of claim appear at page 6. The defence is at page 12.

The factual evidence is found in the claimant's statement at page 25 whilst the defendant's statement from Mr Bones is at page 42.

The expert evidence encapsulates reports on breach of duty and causation from Mr Scott, consultant orthopaedic surgeon at page 60 and from Miss Uhura, consultant orthopaedic surgeon at page 72.

Expert evidence on condition and prognosis is from Mr Scott and his report is at page 85 whilst Miss Uhura's report is at page 99.

Their joint medical report and supplemental replies appears from page 111.

4. <u>Set out agreed facts and those to be established</u>

The parties are agreed about the procedure in introducing the tape through the eyelet of the probe into the calcaneal tunnel. There is no criticism about the decision to repair the tendon by this method. The surgeon accepts that a piece of the probe fractured and was left behind in the tunnel. It is agreed that the surgeon did not explore the tunnel to try and retrieve the fragment. He also accepts that the breakage of the instrument was not recorded in the operation notes. The parties agree, whether or not there was negligence, that a second operation was necessary to release the tape. During the second operation, Mr Bones retrieved the probe from the medial end of the tunnel. A short time later, Mr Spock's symptoms cleared up.

That is the extent of the consensus.

The facts to be determined are what risks existed or might exist on some future occasion by leaving the fragment in situ. In contrast, what risks were there by attempting to remove the fragment during the initial operation. Did the surgeon, make a clinical assessment not to explore the tunnel. Where was the probe fragment located on balance of probabilities at the time it fractured. Was it embedded in bone as suggested by Mr Bones. Could it have been removed and if so, would it have caused any damage to surrounding bone. Did the fragment subsequently migrate along the tunnel as alleged by D's expert but disputed by C's expert. What symptoms, if any, resulted from the retention of the probe fragment. If negligence is established, what, if any loss has been sustained.

5. Refer to the law of negligence and how the facts apply

• Breach of duty.

Did the surgeon make any attempt to locate and remove the foreign body. If not, is it shown that it was **Bolam** negligent to fail to do so. If negligent, what damage was thereby caused.

It is agreed between the two independent experts that in certain circumstances, it would be acceptable practice to leave a broken fragment in situ. Specifically, where the risks of attempted removal would exceed the risks of leaving the fragment in place. In the context of this case, if Mr Bones knew that the fragment was in an innocent site, embedded within the calcaneum and it could not be removed without surgical risk, then the claimant's expert would agree with the defendant's expert that it was appropriate to leave the foreign body in the tunnel.

However, it is the firm view of C's expert that it would have been straightforward to remove the tape entirely from the calcaneal tunnel, and in all probability there were no or minimal risks in removing the tape and re-passing it through the tunnel. On balance of probability, when removing the tape, the metal fragment would have come away too.

It is the claimant's case that Mr Bones failed to exercise the skill and care of a reasonably competent surgeon in not making a sufficient attempt to locate and remove the broken piece of probe. Mere removal of the tape, would have achieved the desired result.

Whilst D's expert suggests that there were risks of leaving the fragment in situ, namely that it could cause local irritation, the balance of risks militated against attempting to remove it. But nowhere does he identify what those risks were.

In any event, insofar as D's expert seeks to support the apparent decision-making process and judgment on the part of Mr Bones, when properly analysed, his position is untenable in accordance with the decision in **Bolitho v City and Hackney Heath Authority**. In short, the decision not to remove the tape in an attempt to locate/remove the fragment is not capable of withstanding logical analysis.

• Causation

Both experts agree that the broken piece of probe was capable of causing irritation. The claimant had unusual, unexpected and prolonged symptoms of pain, swelling as well as an inability to weight bear. Tightness of the tape alone is inherently unlikely to explain these significant symptoms. C's expert is of the view that it is more likely than not that the symptoms around the Achilles tendon insertion were due to the foreign body.

D's expert agrees that if the probe tip was protruding from the tunnel, this could have caused local symptoms at the level of the tunnel. However he does not accept that there was such a protrusion.

Of course it is possible that it was a mere coincidence that the claimant had severe symptoms of swelling and stabbing pain the cause of which was not understood by Mr Bones. It is also possible that the removal of the foreign material made no contribution to the claimant's symptomatic recovery thereafter. However, we say that the only sensible conclusion is that the very risk which leaving the fragment in situ posed did in fact materialise.

6. <u>Describe the claimant's condition – before and after negligence</u>

Turning to Mr Spock's condition. He sustained an injury to his left ankle whilst working out in the gym. He was diagnosed as having a complete rupture of his left Achilles tendon. He underwent surgery for reconstruction. The tendon was very oedematous with chronic changes. A tape was passed through the calcaneal tunnel and weaved through the gastrocnemius complex. The tendon was opposed and the tape tied in a reef knot.

Subsequent to the surgical procedure, the claimant suffered severe pain and swelling in and around the left ankle and foot. He made four follow-up appointments to Anytown Hospital and was seen by Mr

Bones on two of those occasions. On 20th March 2009, Mr Spock was noted to have ankle swelling and 10 days later he also had tightness and pain in the calf. On 4th April 2009, he was experiencing significant pain on walking which appeared to be along the line of the tendon. Mr Bones advised an exploratory operation.

At surgery on 18th April 2009, it was noted on the lateral side of the calcaneal tunnel that there was some oedematous tissue. On the medial side the tissue was stated as less oedematous but the tip of a probe slotted end was found as a foreign body. It was recorded in the operation notes (Your Honour, this is at page 205 in the second bundle should you wish to see it now), that the probe appeared to have come through the tunnel from the lateral side. It was removed but as I say, unfortunately it was not retained.

Thankfully Mr Spock made a very good uneventful recovery. He was able to weight bear fully within 1 week from the operation. Indeed a discharge summary recorded that a foreign body had been removed from the tunnel and it was said that this should help the clinical situation.

7. Refer to the expert reports

(Ascertain whether the judge has read the expert reports. If not, she may wish to retire to read them. Set out the arguments between the opposing experts. Use the joint statement as a template. Identify the issues that need resolving by the judge}.

Your Honour indicated earlier that she has read the expert reports and therefore I propose at this stage, if I may, to take Your Honour to the joint report of Mr Scott and Miss Uhura. This is at page 111. The experts have reached a measure of agreement. Mr Scott accepts that some of the claimant's symptoms after the first operation could be the result of the natural healing process and scarring and tightness of the tape causing irritation or infection. On balance, he says that this is attributed to the presence of the metal fragment irritating the tissues. Both agree that if the broken probe tip was embedded in the tunnel, it would be asymptomatic. If it was protruding from the medial side (which is not accepted by Miss Uhura), it could cause local symptoms at that side. Both agree that if it was known to the surgeon that the probe tip was in an innocent site, within the calcaneum, and there was no extra manoeuvre he could do without surgical risk, then it was reasonable to leave it in situ.

The major difference, Your Honour, between the experts is whether the surgeon made a reasonable attempt to locate and remove the broken probe tip. Miss Uhura does not accept Mr Scott's proposition that in order to comply with the duty of care owed, the surgeon should have pulled out the entire tape that he had just pulled through the tunnel. That, I might say is not Mr Scott's position. He does not argue that the tape had to be removed entirely, simply moved in a lateral direction to and from which would have dislodged the fragment and it would have dropped out as being at the medial end as indicated by Miss Uhura. There is a certain lack of clarity between the experts as to the exact likely position of the fragment at the time of fracture. It is of course highly relevant as Your Honour will need to adjudge whether it could have been dislodged and dropped out during that first operation, as opposed to when it was accessible at the time of the second operation. Miss Uhura maintains that in any event the fragment was likely to have been caught in the cancellous bone so wherever it was positioned, it was not going to come out.

In relation to the second operation, the experts do agree that having snipped the tape on the lateral side of the heel, it was perfectly possible that the tape then pulled back a little through the medial side, carrying the probe secondarily with it. In this way, it caused the probe to present and be prominent in the medial calcaneal tunnel.

In relation to causation, both experts are agreed that the likely cause of the discomfort in the calf which the claimant suffered post operatively was tightness or irritation from the tape. He would have needed a second operation in any event, to alleviate these symptoms. If the fragment was protruding, it could cause local pain. If there was such a protrusion it must have been on the medial side of the tunnel. They agree that at the time of the second operation there was in fact less local irritation on the medial than on he lateral side. The likely cause of the problem on the lateral side was mechanical irritation from the tape.

8. Address quantum/Schedules of loss

The claimant seeks General Damages for pain and suffering over a period of six months during which period he suffered (at times excruciating) pain. Because of his time off work, he suffered a significant loss of earnings. He was not able to obtain alternative employment following his redundancy. He lost out on bonus payments. The claim for past loss of earnings, Your Honour is set out in the schedule of loss at page 55. Mr Spock claims for past loss of services arising from reliance upon his partner for care and assistance which is set out on page 60.

It is hoped and anticipated that some agreement may be reached on quantum if the claimant is successful in his primary claim on liability.

9. Invite questions/ discuss running order with the judge

Your Honour that is the essence of the case. May I assist Your Honour further at this stage. If not, and subject to any issues that My learned friend, Mr Kirk may wish to raise, then I shall call Mr Spock. I see we have 2 days. We expect to deal with the factual witnesses today and make inroads into the cross-examination of the expert witnesses before close of today.

How long should an opening address last? This depends on the complexity of the case and number of statements, but typically if the case is listed for 2 days, then about 1 hour for the claimant would be apposite.

8.3.4 Examination–in-chief

Statements may be taken as read so there may be little opportunity to ask direct questions of your witnesses. If the judge so permits, such questions will be to amplify or to give evidence on new matters since exchange of witness statements (**rule 32.5(3)**).

It is more difficult than cross-examination because you cannot and should not go through the witness' statement. You need to know what **objective** you wish to achieve. And that is the evidence to put in your closing speech.

You may wish to mark the statements using coloured pens, highlighting single words, say red for the points that need to be elicited and blue for significant responses.

<u>Leading questions</u> (those which suggest the answer or putting words into the witness' mouth) may not be put on **matters in dispute.** But questions where the answer is not controversial such as date, time, location of accident and the details of the witness may be put to the witness.

Avoid questions starting with '*Did you..?*' or '*Were you...?*' as your question to the witness will be in the form of your own statement, inviting their agreement. This would be leading them.

Examples of phraseology of leading questions:

You said....?
You saw....?
Were you...?
You did...?
It was.....?
Was it...?

Leading questions that invite a denial from your witness about their actions are permissible. This may arise where an allegation has been made by the opponent's witness against your witness which does not form part of your witness' evidence. You need to elicit a denial so may put a leading question.

Of course, leading questions are essential in cross-examination.

Non-leading questions tend to invite an explanation rather than 'yes' or 'no' answers. They may be open or closed questions.

If in doubt, just ask <u>open questions</u> such as: Who, what, why, when, how, tell me. A neutral question such as describe your meeting with Mr Z or explain what happened, invites the witness to give full answers and if not careful, they may ramble.

Or ask <u>closed questions</u> where the witness has a limited defined selection of possible answers. It may either be a 'yes' or 'no' response or from a selection of words put to them by the advocate. The yes-no question can be very close to being a leading question but it will depend on how the evidence develops. The word choice question gives a variety to choose from. Frequently you will wish to ask open questions leading up to the closed question.

Example of a leading question

Did Mr Bevan explain to you the risk and alternatives in having an appendectomy via the keyhole approach.

Example of a permissible leading question

You had a fall, went to A&E and they diagnosed a fracture of your left tibia, that's right isn't it.

8.3.5 <u>Cross-examination</u>

The aim is to challenge the evidence in-chief where it differs from your client's own case and to elicit facts supportive of your own case. Are the witnesses dishonest, mistaken in their recollection or can't remember or exaggerating a point. Do they have the expertise and experience that they claim or are they simply unreliable. In cross-examination it is permissible and necessary to ask leading questions together with non-leading questions. If a witness is not cross-examined, then the opponent can rightly point out to the court that the evidence went unchallenged and the court may therefore accept it without further question.

Remember that the rules of evidence apply equally to cross-examination as to examination-in-chief.

How you proceed will depend obviously on the type of witness and case. Asking forensic questions of an expert paediatric neurologist will be very different to questions of a witness to a workplace accident. Whichever witness you question, the style should be the same, one of calm detachment and courtesy, not anger or unpleasantness or sarcasm. You are seeking concessions, admissions and a measure of agreement or consensus with your own witness evidence.

Clearly you must understand the expert report and identify within it where the issues that need resolving are stated. Some or much of the report may be irrelevant or conjecture based on the witness' experience, rather than accepted standards of practice.

It is about persuading the judge to accept your witness' version of events, not a full frontal attack on the opponent's witnesses. What must be achieved is to advance your client's case so that means undermining or casting doubt on your opponent's evidence. Remember this is not a criminal trial (not that a combative approach is appropriate there) so there is no playing to the jury or histrionics required.

Some basic principles

- Expert witness – qualifications and experience. Review CV and relevant publications. Taking the witness through them may reveal weaknesses. Has s/he undertaken the procedure. When were they last in clinical practice. Is their medico-legal practice exclusively or predominantly for claimants/defendants. Have they previously been criticised or censured in open court for partiality. Are they applying the standard technique of the procedure at the time or now. What evidence do they have to support/dispute Bolam negligence. Have they less experience in the area than your witness. How long did they examine the client. Get the other side's expert to comment on your expert's opinion and seek agreement where possible. Try to find areas of inconsistency or lacking logic. Be guided by your own expert on the issues and questions to be asked. Review them with your expert for their opinion. Find their strong points and attack them.

- Lay witnesses – Open questions are not appropriate, leading and closed questions are more pertinent. Elicit areas of agreement by putting your case to them. Beware the danger of giving the opponent's witness a platform to expound or clarify their evidence. Avoid giving an opinion or making a derogatory remark to their response. Don't argue with them! Don't fish not knowing what you will catch. Targeted questions work best.

Preparation

Don't go into cross-examination cold so have notes of the issues that need resolving after reviewing your side's witness statements. It is recommended that you prepare your opening questions but be alive to the inevitably that cross-examination can be unpredictable. You may need to deviate along a line of enquiry that was not anticipated. That is why notes rather than a full script is better as you need to be nimble of mind and not reliant on reading out your text.

Keep in mind how you prove your case or rebut the other side's evidence. Apply your case theory to eliciting favourable testimony or limiting damaging aspects to your own case. Discredit by showing that their evidence is mistaken or over stated or a wrong interpretation of the facts. Ultimately you want the judge to question the reliability of that witness. This may be because of lack of recall, bias, conduct or perception. Did they see or hear what happened.

Always ask what is the purpose or benefit of cross-examining the witness. May be it is necessary to put your case but if the witness does not damage your side, do they need to be cross-examined at all. Keep your questions relevant. Your structure may be to deal with the facts or assertions in a chronological manner or to deal with similar issues together.

8.3.6 Example of cross-examination of a defendant's witness

Let's go back to the clinical negligence opening speech earlier. This is an abridged and altered example from an actual case that went to trial.

The defendant's principal witness, the surgeon, is being examined as to the operation he performed to repair a ruptured Achilles tendon. The claimant must prove that it was negligent not to remove a foreign body, namely a broken piece of probe from the calcaneal tunnel. The technique employed by the surgeon therefore had to be examined. **Q** is the advocate and **R** is the surgeon. Not all responses are included for brevity and relevance. The areas of cross-examination are set out under headings for convenience and to demonstrate the topics that needed to be covered.

Broken probe

Q I see from your CV that you have been a Consultant Surgeon specialising in Orthopaedics for 10 years at the time of the operation on the claimant.

Q How many times has a surgical implement broken during surgery in your career?

R Once or twice, it's a rare event.

Q It's a significant event?

R It depends on your definition – don't want to leave unnecessary metalware in the patient, although it would be very rare to cause problems.

Q How many times have you performed this procedure using tape and a probe?

R Ten or twenty times.

Q Do you recall this incident and seeing the broken probe?

R I have no memory of the incident and the probe breaking.

Discussion with claimant

Q Do you remember your discussion with the claimant following discovery and removal of the probe fragment in the second operation?

R I have no recollection of the specifics of the discussion. There is a debate about what information should be told to the patient, but not on the day of the operation due to the effects of the anaesthesia.

Q The claimant came to see you on 5 occasions complaining of stabbing pain in his foot. Did you not think that this may have been caused by the metallic fragment?

R I was unsure what the problem was. I knew that there was a stabbing pain on the lateral side, caused by the tape held under tension on either side. (Explanation about procedure and demonstrated on a model foot).

Q You were requested by the Director of Clinical Governance to inform the claimant about discovery of the fragment?

R Yes. I told him that I had forgotten about it.

Q Did you not also say that it had delayed the rehabilitation?

R No., I did not say that. What I will have said was that I snipped the tape and found the probe but had forgotten to tell him. The piece of metallic probe will not have caused the tightness in the calf.

Q The claimant recalled the discussion and that you did mention the effect of the probe on his delayed recovery. If you cannot remember the facts of the discussion then you are not in a position to dispute the claimant's account.

Q Please refer to the statement of your colleague, Mr Smith at paragraph 15 at page 45. He witnessed the foreign body being removed. He takes the view that this caused the claimant's problems.

R It is not a view that I discussed with Mr Smith and disagree.

Q Did you attempt to remove the metallic fragment?

R No I did not but I cannot really recall the first operation at all.

Q If you cannot remember, how do you know what decisions had to be made?

Recording the incident

Q It was important to record the incident in the notes, in fact mandatory but you did not do so.

R I accept that.

Q Since you have no recollection, you cannot have known the probe remained in situ.

The second operation

Q What was your plan in the second operation where you actually removed the fragment?

R I intended to examine the heel and to cut the tape which was too tight. There might have been the possibility of an infection.

Q Referring to your statement at paragraph 8, page 30 why did you use a 2.5mm drill when the literature (page 70) refers to a recommended 3.5 mm drill?

R As smaller tape was being used, a smaller tunnel was appropriate.

Q The hole was too small wasn't it and as the probe was inserted and forced through the tunnel, the eyelet broke.

R I cannot recall but I know how it would have behaved and there would have been room. If the probe had indeed broken in the tunnel, then the assumption would be that the fragment had become embedded in the bone.

Q But you don't know. If, as we argue, the length of tape was protruding from the tunnel, then you would have seen it and felt it.

R No, I do not accept that the fragment migrated as it would have become embedded in the bone. Surgical probes become snagged easily on bone in the tunnel. I agree that the most likely place for the fragment to break was at the lateral end of the tunnel.

Q If it was loose, then it would be likely to migrate inside the tunnel. Why not remove it?

R The fragment was most likely stuck in the tunnel.

Q Why not pull the tape back and fore or simply remove it, thereby dislodging the fragment?

R It would have become frayed as it would have caught on the fragment.

Q If so, the frayed part could have been cut off or an alternative piece of tape used.

R A second piece of tape was not readily available as a scarce commodity in theatre.

Q It was indefensible not to remove the fragment wasn't it?

R No, the risk posed by an unsuccessful operation would have been greater than that leaving the fragment in situ.

Q You wanted to press on with the operation regardless of the risks.

R No, I was able to adjust the tape, indicating that the fragment was not snagged.

Q Would you look at page 105 in the bundle at your operation note 'tunnel widened at the lateral end'. What is the significance of that entry?

R The bone was worn away at the lateral end of the tunnel, and there was swelling of the tissue, but no evidence of infection. I noticed that the fragment was at the medial end of the tunnel lying in the soft tissue.

Q It had migrated as a consequence of the tape moving in the tunnel whilst moving the foot.

R The tape is under tension so does not move a great deal in the tunnel.

Q There was swelling to the oedematous tissue on the lateral side of the foot. That was caused by the fragment moving.

R The tape is designed to provoke a foreign body reaction and so was the more likely to cause irritation than metalwork.

Q If you turn to a research article at page 90 in the bundle, the expected median recovery time was 40 days, yet the claimant complained of excrutiating pain at 6 months from the date of the first operation.

R The pain was caused by tendon issues as the fragment could only cause pain to the lateral side of the foot if it had been protruding from that side.

Q I put it that the tight tape is capable of causing tightness in the calf, but not capable of causing a sharp, stabbing pain. The claimant had presented with far more serious symptoms than you have ever encountered.

8.3.7 Re-examination

Only to cover matters arising in cross-examination. Try to avoid as indicates weakness but used to clarify and repair any damage made by a concession or admission in cross-examination.

If something has arisen for the first time during cross-examination then it enables the party's own witness to emphasise some positive aspect arising out of that evidence. Also, if some inconsistency has arisen in their evidence, is there an explanation that is called for. It must be known because it is dangerous to ask a question in re-examination when you don't know the answer.

So in the situation above, the surgeon was re-examined on the number of times surgical implements broke, why the tape was considered to be a foreign body, confirmation that he must have known the probe had fractured and that using the probe to remove the fragment would have been difficult as the probe had jammed in the tunnel.

8.3.8 Closing speech

Defendants go first. Address the claimant's evidence first and then the defendant's. The order applies equally to the claimant's closing.

Have notes but don't read them. Refer the court to your skeleton submission. Make reference to pieces of evidence established in cross-examination helpful to your case. Deal with weak areas to explain why nevertheless your witness' account is to be preferred. Make concessions where appropriate.

This is where your case theory comes to the fore – why your case should succeed.

This is the opportunity to give a commentary but not to repeat the facts in the case or the issues.

Persuasion but not repetition.

Mention briefly the law and any cases referred in detail in your skeleton.

Invite the judge to look at the facts which are agreed and how they are consistent with your case. Where documentary evidence supports your client's witnesses, ask the judge to prefer their oral evidence.

Set out to the judge what findings of fact she needs to make

Apply the facts to the law.

Address the law but not in any detail. It will be in your skeleton. Remind the court of the burden and the standard of proof on the claimant.

Do not be tempted to repeat the evidence as that is not showing the court why you should win.

When inviting the court to prefer your expert witness evidence to that of the other side, were they more balanced and objective and more reliable. Were they consistent in their review of the facts and logical in their arguments. Did they make concessions when they should. Don't be afraid to say that the other side's evidence offends common sense if that is the case. Was a witness on the defensive.

Advise the court between any departures in the other side's statements and their oral evidence. Did they present new information that was not contained in their statements.

Invite the court to apply its own logic and analysis to find your client's account inherently more probable.

Know how to finish with your closing words. Don't ramble on.

Style.

Most advocates address the court by starting with '*May it please Your Honour…*'. In a clinical negligence claim for example, they will continue something like this:

> 'It is for the claimant to establish breach of duty. Here there are two principal allegations, whether the claimant has proved that the Trust was negligent by the surgeon (1) not pulling the woven tape in an effort to retrieve the probe fragment and secondly, (2) in the event that that procedure failed, to insert the probe through the drilled hole to push it out.

The nature of the breach of duty is the Bolam test, and whether those alleged failures would be recognised as omissions of reasonable practice by a responsible body of Orthopaedic surgeons and withstands logical analysis in accordance with Bolitho.

Be prepared for the judge to stop you and ask clarification questions. These will be significant and give an indication of the judge's thinking so require a careful response. Don't give the impression that you have been taken by surprise and hadn't thought of that point (even if it's a curve ball).

Key points

- Know your case theory to be developed in the opening speech

- Expand on your skeleton (do not read it)

- Do not give your personal opinion

- Know your law and how it is applied

- Be personable and concise but do not exaggerate the merits of the case, if anything understate it in a confident, relaxed manner

- Try to reach areas of agreement with your opponent so as to narrow the issues. This will endear both parties with the judge

- Identify weaknesses in your case and how they may be resolved with the judge. If they cannot be resolved, are they material

- Focus your questions on the witness, using open and closed techniques to elicit evidence for your closing.

- Make any concessions to appear reasonable but say why the court should accept your client's witness evidence.

- Comment on the other side's evidence and what has been revealed in cross-examination and refer to discrepancies.

- Be assured, confident and humble.

CHAPTER NINE
THE APPEAL

CPR 52

9.1 Losing one's appeal was bound to happen some time. But perhaps not. Perhaps you haven't yet gone to trial, let alone sought permission to appeal. It is tempting to avoid raising the prospect of failure with a client. But being prepared for all eventualities includes knowing whether an appeal should be pursued and the grounds for doing so. Clearly you can't just appeal to have another go. An appeal is a review and rarely a rehearing, except where the interests of justice require it.

You will need permission and that will require satisfying a judge that *there is a realistic, as opposed to a fanciful prospect of success* or that *there is some other compelling reason for the appeal to be heard.*

This chapter will concentrate on the venue for an appeal, the level of judge and the procedure entailed in appealing an interim order and the trial judgment, before considering the tests that need to be met firstly in obtaining permission and then how to prevail.

Changes were made to the procedure set out in **CPR 52** from 3rd October 2016 following *The Access to Justice Act 1999 (Destination of Appeals) Order 2016*. This has simplified the appeals process so that generally an appeal lies to the next level of judge who will decide the application without a hearing. Those refused permission to appeal may request an oral hearing provided there is some merit.

An appeal my be made as a result of a case management decision, following a small claims hearing, following a Part 8 Stage 3 portal assessment or a fast-track or multi-track trial. Such an appeal lies to the next tier of judge. Generally most cases save multi-track claims, will be heard by a District judge. Therefore a first appeal lies to a Circuit Judge. An appeal of a multi-track claim is then to a High Court judge. A second appeal against refusal of the first appeal is always to the Court of Appeal.

9.2 Avenues of appeal

Decision of:	Appeal to:	Court:
Deputy/District judge in County Court	Circuit judge	County Court
Circuit judge in County Court	High Court judge	High Court/DR
Master in High Court	High Court judge (single judge)	High Court
Deputy/High Court judge	Court of Appeal judge	Court of Appeal

Thus:

District judge → Circuit Judge/High Court judge → Court of Appeal

9.3 Appeals from Case management decisions

Such appeals are set out in **PD 52, para 4.6.** The appeal may concern a decision about disclosure, filing of witness statements or experts' reports, directions about the timetable of the claim, adding a party to a claim and security for costs.

The court hearing the request for permission to appeal may take into account whether –

(a) the issue is of sufficient significance to justify the costs of an appeal;

(b) the procedural consequences of an appeal (e.g. loss of trial date) outweigh the significance of the case management decision;

(c) it would be more convenient to determine the issue at or after trial.

The procedure regarding time limits, seeking permission and grounds for appeal are similar to that in an appeal against a final judgment, as considered below.

It is important to appreciate that an appeal is not an opportunity for a complete re-hearing. An appellate judge will only be able to interfere with the exercise of discretion of a District judge or Master in limited circumstances. This applies where there was an <u>error of law or the decision reached was outside the generous ambit within which a reasonable disagreement is possible</u>.

In relation to perhaps the most significant case management decision where relief from sanctions was refused and relief granted on appeal, the appeal judge should set out all relevant factors to be considered and then make his own assessment of the significance and weight so as to explain any error found, and the basis for the substituted exercise of discretion (see <u>Ryder plc v Beever</u> [2012] EWCA Civ 1737).

But in reflecting whether to appeal against a case management decision, think about the Court of Appeal dicta in <u>Mannion v Ginty</u> [2012] EWCA Civ 1667 where it was said that it is vital to uphold robust fair case management decisions.

9.4 Appeal from a stage 3 protocol low value claim

Permission to appeal against the assessment of quantum, whether made on the papers or at a hearing is initially made to a District judge. If permission is granted on paper then the appeal will be then heard by a Circuit judge. The procedure is the same as with other appeals as below.

9.5 Procedure for all appeals

CPR 52.3 – permission to appeal

(1) An appellant or respondent requires permission to appeal
  ....

(2) An application for permission to appeal may be made –

(a) to the lower court at the hearing at which the decision to be appealed was made; or

(b) to the appeal court in an appeal notice.

(1) Where the lower court refuses an application for permission to appeal –

(a) a further application for permission may be made to the appeal court; and

(b) the order refusing permission must specify –

(i) the court to which any further application for permission should be made; and
(ii) the level of judge who should hear the application.

Under **Part 52.4,** permission to appeal to the County Court and High Court is considered initially on paper without an oral hearing. However they do have the discretion to list for an oral hearing. Where the appeal judge refuses permission, then the appellant may request an oral hearing under **Part 52.4(2).**

If permission to appeal is considered as totally without merit by an appellate judge (A High Court or Designated Civil judge or a Specialist Circuit judge), then the judge may refuse an oral hearing (**Part 52.4(3)**).

An application for permission to appeal to the Court of Appeal is governed by **Part 52.5.** The application will be determined on paper by an appellate judge. They may wish to direct that an oral hearing is listed within 14 days of their direction to determine the issues. A first appeal to the Court of Appeal is now only possible on appeal from a decision of a High Court judge.

Whether permission to appeal has been rejected or has been granted, an appellant's notice, N161 must be filed with the same court that made the decision, alternatively to a higher court. The provisions for filing the Notice and accompanying documents are set out in **PD 52A** and **PD 52B**.

9.6 Documents for permission to appeal are:

- Form N161 plus 2 copies for the court and one for the respondent
- Court order dismissing claim or case management directions
- Transcript of judgment (if applicable)

9.7 Documents for appeal

- Form N161 (or N164 if small claims track) plus 2 copies for the court and one for the respondent, i.e. 4 in total
- Appeal bundle, indexed and paginated
- Permission to appeal
- Sealed order granting or refusing permission to appeal and a copy of the reasons for that decision (form EX52)
- Transcript and/or written judgment
- Skeleton argument
- Respondent's Notice (if filed)
- Respondent's skeleton argument (if filed)
- Court fee or fee remission application

9.8 Contents of the appellant's notice

If permission is being sought on paper, then the N161 notice will seek permission.

If permission is granted then a notice should state the following:

The grounds of appeal should state the reasons as to why **rule 52.21(3)** applies, namely why the lower court was <u>wrong or unjust through serious procedural or other irregularity</u> (**PD 52B, para 4.2(d)**).

The reasons must be set out in a skeleton argument. The specific incidents, directions or findings made by the court below must be identified so as to show why the decision was wrong or unjust.

PD 52A, para 5.1 covers the style and contents of a skeleton. When referring to an authority, it must state the proposition of law the authority demonstrates and identify the parts of the authority that supports the proposition. Importantly the skeleton must define the areas of controversy and cross-reference any relevant document in the appeal bundle.

So the appellant must <u>identify whether the appeal is on a point of law or findings of fact</u>. It should be noted that appeal courts are loath to interfere with decisions on the facts.

If the skeleton does not comply with the above requirements or is not filed within the time limits, the court may not allow the costs of preparation be recovered by the successful party.

Once the documents have been filed with the Appeal Centre court office, then the appeal judge may give directions which to be complied with.

9.9   Time limits for appellant

>   9.9.1 The application seeking <u>permission to appeal</u> should ideally be made orally immediately following the court judgment in the face of the court or no later than **21 days** to the appeal court, or such period as may be directed by the court (**52.12(2)(b)**). If time is needed following judgment to decide whether to appeal, an adjournment may be sought.

9.9.2 Where there is <u>refusal for permission</u> on paper, the appellant has 7 **days** following receipt of the notice refusing permission to request reconsideration at an oral hearing (**52.4(6)**).

9.9.3 The appellant's notice seeking permission must be served on each respondent no later than 7 **days** from filing the application (**52.12(3)(b)**).

9.9.4 The appellant's notice and bundle of documents must be filed with the court within **35 days** of filing the appellant's notice (**PD 52B, para 6.3**).

9.9.5 If it is not practicable for the appellant's skeleton argument to be filed at the same time as the appellant's notice then it may be lodged with the county court within **14 days** of filing the notice.

9.9.6 Once permission to appeal has been granted, the appeal bundle must be served on the respondent within **14 days** of receiving the order (**PD 52B, para 6.5(b)**).

9.10 The test

The test for permission to appeal on a first appeal is set out in **Part 52.6** whilst permission to appeal from a second appeal is set out in **Part 52.7**.

CPR 52.6(1) Permission to appeal is given only where –

(a) the court considers that the appeal would have a real prospect of success; or

(b) there is some other compelling reason for the appeal to be heard.

In contrast, a second appeal still requires the appellant to show a real prospect of success but also that there is an important point of principle or practice, or there is some other compelling reason for the Court of Appeal to hear it.

Lord Woolf MR said in *Swain v Hillman* [2001] 1 All ER 91 that a 'real' prospect of success must be realistic rather than fanciful. The court need not analyse whether the grounds of the proposed appeal will succeed, but whether there is a real prospect of success. In other words whether there is an arguable case, that the decision was *plainly wrong* or *unjust* through a serious irregularity. Examples may include an error of law or where there is considerable controversy, bias of the judge, where the lower court has failed to follow binding precedent or where a factual finding was perverse.

9.11 The grounds

Under **Rule 52.21(3)** the appeal court will allow an appeal where the decision of the lower court was –

(a) wrong; or

(b) unjust because of a serious procedural or other irregularity in the proceedings in the lower court.

'Wrong' means unsustainable (*Abrahams v Lenton* [2003] EWHC 1104. It is often the case that the lower court has a generous ambit in exercising its discretion, especially in fact finding, which makes it difficult to appeal. But it may be argued that furthering the overriding objective trumps the discretion as in *Law v St Margarets Insurance Ltd* [2001] EWCA Civ 30. Where there is a challenge to the interpretation of facts, an appeal is more likely where the judge has made inferences from the evidence rather than a finding based on eyewitness evidence. Where there is no evidence to support a finding of fact, or if the finding was against the weight of evidence then this may support a successful appeal.

Further evidence cannot be adduced on appeal unless the appeal court grants permission to do so.

9.12 Exercise of discretion

The role of the appellate court and its limited powers to interfere with the lower court's exercise of discretion was expounded by Lord Diplock in *Hadmor Productions Ltd v Hamilton* [1983] 1 AC 191 where he stated:

> "…..the function of an appellate court, whether it be the Court of Appeal or your lordship's house, is not to exercise an independent discretion of its own. It must defer to the judge's exercise of his discretion and must not interfere with it merely upon the ground that the members of the appellate court would have exercised the discretion differently. The function of the appellate court is initially one of review only. It may set aside the judge's exercise of his discretion on the ground that it was based upon a misunderstanding of the law or of the evidence before him or upon an inference that particular facts existed or did not exist, which, although it was one that might legitimately have been drawn upon the evidence that was before the judge, can be demonstrated to be wrong by further evidence that has become available by the time of appeal, or upon the ground that there has been a change of circumstances after the judge made his order that would have justified his acceding to an application to vary it."

Therefore, interference in a first instance decision may only be permitted by the appellate court where the initial judge has <u>exceeded the generous ambit within which a reasonable disagreement is possible.</u> This will be particularly pertinent in matters of fact-finding, costs assessment and orders given in case management conferences.

According to **Rule 52.21,**

> *(1) Every appeal will be limited to a review of the decision of the lower court unless –*

(a) a practice direction makes different provision for a particular category of appeal: or
(b) the court considers that in the circumstances of an individual appeal it would be in the interests of justice to hold a re-hearing.

9.13 Examples of possible grounds of appeal

- wrong decision
- failure to give reasons
- new point of law
- finding of fact not based on evidence or against the weight of evidence as a whole
- serious procedural irregularities
- fresh evidence

9.14 Respondent's appeal

If a respondent agrees with the decision of the lower court, then no notice is necessary but one may be filed if preferred, although permission is also necessary. Without permission, the respondent may take no part in the appellant's application.

The rules are set out in **rule 52.13**. The notice is in form N162 and is used where the respondent is seeking permission to appeal to have the order of the lower court set aside or varied (**52.13(2)(a)**) and secondly, where the respondent wishes the appeal court to uphold the lower court's order from reasons that are different from, or additional to those given by the lower court (**52.13(2)(b)**).

A respondent's notice seeking permission from the appeal court must be filed within **14 days** (or such other date as given by the lower court) of the date that they receive the appellant's notice concerning permission to appeal. The notice must also be served on the appellant within 7 **days** of filing.

9.15 Second appeal to the Court of Appeal

This is always to the Court of Appeal even if the first appeal was to a Circuit judge. The second appeal does not go to a High court judge. The Court of Appeal will only consider granting permission where the appeal would raise an important point of principle or practice or there is a compelling reason why the Court of Appeal must hear it (see **Part 52.7**).

Initially a court officer will consider the application on paper (**Rule 52.24(4)**). If refused, then the appellant may seek a review which will be considered by a single judge who will consider the application on paper, unless they direct an oral hearing (**rule 52.24(5)**). If the appellant does not want the review by a court officer, they may request that a single judge on paper deals with the application, although that same judge may direct a hearing (**rule 52.24(6)**).

9.16 Specimen Appellant's notice, N161

Let's consider a draft form of wording where it is submitted that the District Judge exercised his/her discretion wrongly so that as a matter of law, the decision is unsafe. There was a failure to take into account certain germane facts whilst other irrelevant ones were considered. The reasons why the decision is wrong may be set out in N161 but duplication should be avoided in the skeleton argument.

If the appeal is to the Court of Appeal, the reasons why the decision under appeal is wrong or unjust must be confined to the skeleton argument.

Section 7 **Grounds for appeal**

In dismissing the claimant's application for an extension of time for the exchange of witness statements and in striking out the claim, the District judge failed to take into account all the matters which he was under an obligation to take into account under CPR 3.9(1).

Section 8 **Arguments in support of grounds**

My skeleton argument is:-

☑ set out below   ☐ attached
☐ will follow within 14 days of filing this notice

I (the appellant) will rely on the following arguments at the hearing of the appeal:-

>   1. *The decision of the learned District Judge* [set out decision to be appealed] *was wrong as a matter of law because:*
>
>   *(a) in the exercise of [his/her] discretion the learned District Judge failed to take into account sufficiently the following facts or matters* [to specify]. *If [he/she] had taken into account those facts or matters then discretion would and should have been exercised so as to order* [specify order which should have been made].
>
>   *(b) In the exercise of [his/her] discretion, the learned District Judge took into account the following facts or matters which were* [irrelevant/not facts or matters which ought properly to be taken into account]. *If the learned District Judge had not taken into account those facts or matters then [he/she] would and should have exercised [his/her] discretion so as to order that* [briefly specify the order which should have been made].
>
>   *(c) The exercise by the learned District Judge of [his/her] discretion in deciding that* [briefly set out the decision] *will result in injustice* [set out the facts or matters in support of the contention that the decision will result in injustice] . *The learned District Judge should have exercised [his/her] discretion so as to order that* [briefly specify the order which should have been made].

Key points

- Ensure you have client's authority to appeal
- Seek permission following judgment. Know grounds for doing so – on fact (wrong or unjust or serious procedural error)
- An appeal against a case management decision will generally be to a Circuit judge whilst a trial heard by a Circuit judge or Recorder will be to High Court judge.
- Be aware of time limits of 21 days to seek permission. If refused orally, a further 7 days to seek permission on paper.
- No cost implications on seeking and obtaining permission as the appeal can always be abandoned.

CHAPTER TEN
CASE LAW TOOL KIT

CLINICAL NEGLIGENCE

10.1 Duty of care

• <u>Caparo Industries plc v Dickman</u> [1990] 2 AC 605

Redefined the neighbour principle in establishing duty of care in Donoghue v Stevenson. A three-part test of proximity, foreseeability of harm and it must be just, fair and reasonable for a duty of care to be imposed.

An auditor may be liable for financial losses suffered by investors where a financial report relied upon was negligent. The House of Lords held that a duty of care was not owed by the defendant to the claimant, an investor purchasing shares in a company audited by the defendant. The House held that it was necessary for a 'special relationship' to be created that the claimant had to prove that: the statement would be communicated to the claimant; that the statement was made in connection with the transaction; and that the claimant would be very likely to rely upon it in deciding whether or not to proceed with the transaction.

• <u>Darnley v Croydon Health Services NHS Trust</u> [2017] EWCA Civ 151

No duty on non-clinical receptionists in an A&E department giving incorrect advice about waiting time. The claimant left hospital and suffered serious injuries which would have been avoided had he been treated in hospital. This case was distinguished from that of *Kent v Griffiths* where liability was imposed on the basis that ambulance service receptionists pass on clinical information.

• <u>ABC v St George's Healthcare NHS Trust and ors</u> [2017] EWCA Civ 336

The Court of Appeal found that there was a duty imposed on clinicians treating a patient with a genetic disease to disclose the diagnosis to the claimant (daughter). The claimant found out that she had Huntingdon's disease and her daughter had a 50% risk of developing the disease. The claimant brought a claim for wrongful birth and breach of Article 8 HRA. The defendant accepted that under the *Caparo* test, foreseeability of injury and proximity were met but was it fair, just and reasonable to impose a duty of care. The CA found that it was.

10.2 Breach of duty

- Bolam v Friern Hospital Management Committee [1957] 2 All ER 118

Standard of care is a legal test, applying the conditions and practice employed at that time. This was a pure treatment case where the nature of the claimant's condition is known and the negligence concerned the decision to treat in a particular manner.

The claimant suffered depression and voluntarily attended a mental institution where on the second visit he received electro-convulsive therapy. This caused muscular spasms which through lack of protection caused dislocation of his femurs affecting future mobility. This was a jury verdict who found for the defendants based on the evidence that the doctor who prescribed the ECT in the manner that he did was following the practice that he had learnt. There was a body of reasonable medical opinion that would not restrain a patient.

Per McNair:

> '*A doctor is not guilty of negligence if he has acted in accordance with a practice accepted as proper by a responsible body of medical men skilled in that particular art.*
>
> *…Putting it the other way round, a doctor is not negligent, if he is acting in accordance with such a practice, merely because there is a body of opinion which takes a contrary view*'.

- *Bolitho v City and Hackney Health Authority* [1997] 4 All ER 771

Bolam was refined that responsible and reasonable opinion must have a logical basis, weighing of risks against benefits.

A 2 year-old boy suffered brain damage after suffering breathing problems but a doctor failed to examine him in hospital. Breach of duty was admitted but causation disputed. The House of Lords approved the authority of Bolam regarding the assessment of beach of duty and causation. But Lord Browne-Wilkinson went further stating that even if there was expert evidence for the defendant satisfying the Bolam standard, if it was not capable of withstanding logical analysis, then such opinion could not be reasonable or responsible.

Conclusion: Was the decision properly considered, rational and reasonable.

- *Penney v East Kent Health Authority* [2000] PNLR 323

In cases of diagnostic error where there is no weighing of risks or benefits or whether to treat or not, just a factual decision that was right or wrong, then the *Bolam* test does not apply. In this case the issue was one of interpreting objective data wrongly. Misreporting is either negligent or not, so both experts cannot both be right. Kerr J regarded *Penney* as authority permitting the court to choose between competing expert opinion on an issue for the court to decide.

The claimant developed cancer of the cervix. Her smear test results were reported falsely as negative at the pre-diagnostic stage. The screeners were negligent, Lord Woolf raising 3 questions: (1) what was to be seen in the slides (2) could a screener exercising reasonable care fail to see what was on the slides (3) could a reasonably competent screener treat the slide as negative? The initial trial judge correctly applied the *Bolitho* exception as D's expert evidence did not stand up to logical analysis.

10.3 Factual Causation

- <u>Barnett v Chelsea & Kensington Hospital Management Committee</u> [1969] 1 QB 428

Straightforward application of the 'but for' test in causation. The claimant failed as the outcome would have been the same absent breach of duty.

The claimant was not treated by a casualty officer when he attended hospital feeling ill. He subsequently died from arsenic poisoning and his estate brought a claim. There was a beach of duty in failing to examine and treat him but the claim was unsuccessful as it could not be shown that the breach caused the death.

- <u>Hotson v East Berkshire Area Health Authority</u> [1987] AC 750 (HL)

Loss of a chance claim was not permitted where the prospect of recovery absent negligence was less than probable so injury was inevitable. Causation could not be established on the balance of probabilities. The 'but for' test was applied despite there being a chance that the claimant might have avoided the additional damage but for the breach of duty but less than 50%.

A boy fell from a tree fracturing his hip. The injury went undiagnosed and as a result of the delay, he developed a deformity. Experts stated that the claimant would have had a 75% chance of deformity even if the diagnosis had been made correctly as a result of the injury. The House of Lords held that there was only a 25% chance that the negligence had caused the subsequent injuries and applying the balance of probabilities burden, the claimant was unable to recover damages.

10.4 Material contribution to the injury

- <u>McGhee v National Coal Board</u> [1973] 1 WLR 1 (HL)

Damages recoverable where material contribution causation. Where an injury is caused by two or more factors, one of which is a breach of

duty but cannot determine which, then actionable where claimant can prove that the breach of duty contributed substantially to causing the injury.

The claimant developed dermatitis after exposure to brick dust in the course of his employment. Employer found liable in negligence for materially increasing the risk.

- <u>Wilsher v Essex Area Health Authority</u> [1988] AC 1074 (HL)

Supports the traditional but-for test of factual causation so the claimant could not prove material increase in the risk of injury where it was not possible to prove causation or contribution where there were a number of alternative possible causes. The claimant had to show that the breach was the substantial vause of the damage. The House of Lords took a restrictive view of McGhee v National Coal Board.

The claimant was born prematurely and received too much oxygen given mistakenly by vein rather than an artery. The baby suffered from blindness due to one of the five possible causes. The claimant could not show which of the potential causes was more likely to have happened than any of the others so could not be proved on the balance of probabilities.

10.5 Material increase to the risk of injury

- <u>Fairchild v Glenhaven Funeral Services Limited</u> [2003] 1 AC 32

Followed the principle in McGhee v National Coal Board by allowing in limited circumstances liability for materially increasing the risk of injury, despite there being no causal connection established where multiple causes of potential breach.

Claimants exposed to asbestos by more than one employer resulting in development of mesothelioma. They could not prove which employer's exposure caused the injury. The House of Lords relaxed the burden of proof on the 'but for' test of causal connection, i.e. that the defendant's wrongful conduct caused the harm or loss. The grounds for doing so were to avoid an unjust result that would otherwise happen where damage flowed from one or other of two alternative causes.

• *Gregg v Scott* [2005] UKHL 2

Concerns a claim that the defendant's breach lowered the chance of a better outcome as traditional 'but-for' causation cannot be established. The Fairchild principle was not extended to clinical negligence cases.

There was a negligent delay following misdiagnosis of a malignant tumour. This resulted in the claimant's chance of surviving for 10 years was 42% at the time of misdiagnosis, reducing to 25% at the start of treatment. The House of Lords rejected loss of a chance as it must be shown as more probable than not that the injury would have been avoided if the negligence had not occurred.

• *Sanderson v Hull* [2008] EWCA Civ 1211

Significant case as reviewed the circumstances where the *Fairchild* exception may apply.

1. Where medical science was such that the cause of injury could not be established.

2. Defendant's wrongdoing must have materially increased the risk of the claimant suffering injury.

3. The defendant's conduct must have bee capable of causing the claimant's injury.

4. The injury must have been caused by the eventuation of the kind of risk created by the defendant's wrongdoing (distinguishing it from *McGhee* and *Wilsher*).

5. The claimant must prove that the injury was caused by the actual or similar agency from the defendant's wrongdoing.

6. The other possible source of injury was caused by the same defendant.

10.6 Legal causation or remoteness

• *The Wagon Mound (No 1)* [1961] AC 388 (PC)

The damage must have been caused by the breach of duty and not be too remote. The test for remoteness is reasonable foreseeability of the kind or type of damage in fact suffered by the claimant.

The claimant's two ships caught fire as a result of sparks from welding igniting oil on the water. The defendants had leaked the oil from a tanker and assured the claimants that it was safe to continue welding. The question was whether a reasonable person would anticipate, assuming a breach of duty, harm of the general type suffered would occur, then it was foreseeable. The Privy Council found that it was not reasonably foreseeable that bunkering oil with such a high flash-point would catch fire when spread on water.

• *Corr v IBC Vehicles Limited* [2006] EWCA Civ 1331

Recognised the overlap between duty of care, a novus actus and remoteness of damage. The issue of foreseeability is relevant.

The claimant brought a claim for damages for physical and psychological injuries causing the deceased to commit suicide. He had suffered serious injuries at work owing to the defendant's negligence and became depressed and killed himself. The House of Lords found the employers were liable as there was no novus actus (break in the chain of causation) as the suicide was due to depression resulting from the employer's tort.
1.7 Consent

• *Chester v Afshar* [2004] UKHL 41

A consent case which extended the causation principle developed in *Fairchild v Glenhaven Funeral Services Ltd*.

A neurosurgeon failed to warn the claimant of a small but unavoidable risk of nerve injury in having surgery, and therefore failed to obtain the claimant's informed consent to the procedure. This was despite the fact that had she postponed the operation the same risk would have presented itself on another date. The House of Lords recognised that the claimant's case would fail on conventional causation principles as the claimant had not been exposed to an increase in risk. But nevertheless the Law Lords held that causation was established as in all probability the risk would not have materialised on a future date, so the injury was causally linked to the defendant's non-disclosure of the risk.

- *Sidaway v Board of Governors of the Bethlem Royal Hospital* [1985] AC 871

Since overshadowed by *Montgomery*, though authority for it being the patient's decision to decide on treatment having been given sufficient information by the doctors.

- *Montgomery v Lanarkshire Health Board* [2015] UKSC 11

The law on consent has developed from *Sidaway v Bethlem Royal & Maudsley Hospital Governors* so as to remove any vestiges of medical paternalism. The doctors' duty is to discuss all material risks of the proposed treatment and any alternatives, including having no treatment. A two-fold test on duty. 1. What are the risks 2. The court should determine what information should have been given to the patient. Would a reasonable person think the risk was material.

The claimant gave birth to a baby boy with cerebral palsy following a vaginal delivery. She was not informed of the risk of shoulder dystocia occurring to the baby during vaginal delivery at 9-10%. The Supreme court considered the NICE (2011) guidelines that pregnant women should be offered evidence-based information to enable them to make informed decisions about their care and treatment. The risks to the mother as well as the baby had to be discussed with her to enable her to make an informed decision. The claimant argued that had she known of the risks she would have had a caesarean section and thus the baby would have been born unharmed which was accepted by the Supreme Court.

10.8 Burden of proof

• <u>Barnett v Medway NHS Foundation Trust</u> [2017] EWCA Civ 235

The court should try to make a finding of fact on expert evidence but in the last resort may rely on the burden of proof. In this case the claimant had not discharged the burden of proof in establishing the probability of infection.

PERSONAL INJURY

10.9 Duty

• <u>Edwards v London Borough of Sutton</u> [2016] EWCA Civ 1005

There is no duty under the Occupiers' Liability Act 1957 to warn of obvious risks. The relevant danger had to be assessed before deciding whether there was a serious risk of injury. The lack of previous accidents was relevant.

• <u>Tomlinson v Congleton B.C.</u> [2004] 1 AC 46

The scope of duty for occupiers' liability was examined in the light of the *Fairchild* elaboration between 'occupancy duties' and 'activity duties'. The former applies under the OLA 1957. 'The common duty of care is a duty to take such care as in all the circumstances of the case is reasonable to see that the visitor will be reasonably safe in using the premises for the purposes for which he is invited or permitted by the occupier to be there' (per Lord Hoffman).

- *Smith v Northamptonshire County Council* [2009] ICR 734

For work equipment to fall under PUWER (and possibly Defective Equipment Act), it must be under the employer's 'control' or adopted by them or incorporated into their undertaking.

10.10 Breach of duty

- *Paris v Stepney Borough Council* [1951] AC367

The duty of care is to each employee as an individual. The standard of care depends on the seriousness of possible injury, taking into account any special weakness or peculiarity of the worker, such as having one eye.

The claimant was a mechanic using a hammer when a chip of metal flew into his good eye, causing him to become blind. The defendant employers did not provide goggles which they would not normally do. However, they owed a higher standard of care to the claimant because of the much more serious consequences of injury.

- *Latimer v AEC Ltd* [1953] AC 643 (HL)

Examines the standard of care and cost and practicability of precautions.

This was a slipping case in the course of employment when the factory floor was flooded with rainwater which mixed with oil on the floor, creating a slippery surface. The cost of closing the factory to remove the risk was disproportionate to the relatively small risk of injury.

- *Brodie v British Railways Board* 1986 SLT 208

The duty on the employer is to take reasonable measures rather than to make premises safe in all the circumstances.

- *Wilsons and Clyde Coal Co v English* [1938] AC 57

The employer is responsible to the employee to ensure a safe system of work which cannot be delegated to someone else. The duty included safe premises, safe plant and equipment, safe working practices and the provision of competent staff.

- *McDermid v Nash Dredging and Reclamation Co Ltd* [1987] AC 906

The employer's duty is not just a safe system of work but a safe operation.

- *Knowles v Liverpool County Council* [1993] 1 WLR 1428 (HL)

Examination of 1(1)(b) of the Employers' Liability (Defective Equipment) Act 1969 only applies to defects that are not obvious or visible when caused by a third party. Equipment should be given a wide meaning, including a flagstone as here.

- *Pape v Cumbria County Council* [1992] ICR 132 (QBD)

Employers must ensure use of personal protective equipment and to warn against dangers of the work. Here, the risk was dermatitis and that gloves were to be worn to guard against the risk.

As an aside, strict liability still exists under this statute and is not affected by section 69 of *the Enterprise and Regulatory Reform Act 2013*.

- *Mitchell & ors v Co-operatives Ltd* [2012] EWCA Civ 348

Reviewed considerations in assessing breach of duty of care. The employer must weigh up the risk of the likelihood of injury occurring and the potential consequences if it does, balanced against the effectiveness of the precautions that can be taken and the expense and inconvenience involved.

The claimants were shop assistants in the defendant's store that was subjected to several robberies. They developed post-traumatic stress disorder. The defendant had introduced measures to reduce the risk of burglary but the claimants maintained that they should have gone further. The appellate court examined competing considerations of the effectiveness of the precaution set against the cost of taking it and ruled against the claimants, finding that the defendant had adopted standard risk management strategies for a store of that size.

- *Singh v City of Cardiff Council* [2017] EWHC 1499(QC)

Looked at various claims under the Occupiers' Liability Act 1957, the Highways Act 1980 and under the common law duty. S.41 HA is an absolute duty but the claimant's injury was not caused by a defect in the Highway when he fell off a footbridge landing in a brook below. There was no breach under s.2 OLA as there was no failure by the owner to keep his land reasonably safe for occupiers as the claimant had come off the designated footpath. There was no hazard or danger created.

10.11 Burden of proof

- Ward v Tesco Stores Limited [1976] 1 All ER 219

Application of res ipsa loquitur where there is a prima facie presumption of negligence. The Court of Appeal held that where someone slipped on a spillage on a supermarket floor, the burden is on the defendant to show on the balance of probabilities that the claimant would still have slipped even if there was a proper system of inspection and cleaning. The defendants tried to place the burden on the claimant to establish for how long the spillage was present which was not relevant according to Lawton LJ. The circumstances were such that an accident would not normally happen so it called for an explanation by the defendants to show why there was no breach of duty by them.

RELIEF FROM SANCTIONS' CASES

• *Mitchell v News Group Newspapers Ltd* [2013] EWCA Civ 1537

Compliance with CPR 3.9 must be observed to avoid sanctions. Obligation is to conduct litigation efficiently and at proportionate expense. In considering an application for relief, the court will examine the nature of the non-compliance. If trivial, the court would usually grant relief provided the application is made promptly. If not trivial, the court would ascertain why the default occurred. If there was good reason, the court would likely grant relief. In this case the defaults by the claimant were not minor trivial and there was no good excuse for them so relief was not granted.

The claimant failed to file his costs budget until the day before the case management and costs budget hearing. The reason given was pressure of work elsewhere in the law firm representing the claimant. The mandatory sanction applied restricting the budget to court fees under rule 3.14. This was by analogy as it had not yet come into force as PD 51D applied, requiring costs budgets to be exchanged in advance of the case management conference. An application for relief from sanction was made where the court considered all the circumstances, including (a) the interests of the administration of justice; (b) whether the application for relief has been made promptly; (c) whether the failure to comply was intentional; (d) whether there is a good explanation for the failure; (e) the extent to which the party in default has complied with other rules, practice directions, court orders and any relevant pre-action protocol; (f) whether the failure to comply was caused by the party or his legal representative; (g) whether the trial date can still be met if relief is granted; (h) the effect which the failure to comply had on each party; and (i) the effect which the granting of relief would have on each party. At first instance the court dismissed the application for relief and the appeal also failed. The overriding objective and the strict wording in CPR 3.9 highlighted the emphasis on rule compliance.

- *Denton v TH White Ltd* [2014] EWCA Civ 906

Considered in the light of the *Mitchell* decision, the criteria to be applied in considering relief from sanction. Viewed as a more lenient test for the defaulting party to meet than in *Mitchell*. That case was criticised as the 'triviality' test amounted to an 'exceptionality' test. Also the factors (a) and (b) were described as 'paramount considerations' when they should all be given equal weight. Thirdly, all the circumstances of the case should be considered so as to enable the court to deal justly with the application. The *Denton* test is in 3 stages. (1) Identify the seriousness or significance of the failure to comply with the rule, practice direction or court order, which engages rule 3.9(1). Other failures should not be considered at this stage. If the breach is not serious or significant then relief will usually be granted and that is an end to the enquiry but otherwise proceeds to the second stage. (2) Identify why the failure or default occurred. (3) Under rule 3.9(1), the court shall consider all the circumstances of the case, so as to enable it to deal justly with the application. Factors (a) and (b) may not be of 'paramount importance' but they are of particular importance, and should be given particular weight when all the circumstances of the case are considered. The promptness of the application is a relevant circumstance to be weighed in the balance.

Whilst this case was heard with two others before the Court of Appeal, we shall only recite the brief facts for *Denton*. The claimant served an additional six witness statements one month before trial. The sanction under CPR 32.10 applied so that the witness could not be called to give oral evidence unless the court granted permission. The first instance judge granted the claimant relief by adjourning the trial. The defendant appealed which was allowed. The initial judge had applied the wrong test. Had he applied the correct test, then it was very likely that relief would not be granted at stages 1 and 2 because late service was a significant breach as it caused the trial date to be vacated and so disrupted the conduct of litigation. There was no good reason for the breach. Had the third stage been considered taking all the circumstances into account, particularly to factors (a) and (b) then this would have weighed against the claimant in favour of holding the trial date.

STATUTE LAW TOOL KIT

Law Reform (Contributory Negligence) Act 1945

Apportionment of liability in case of contributory negligence

(1) Where any person suffers damage as the result partly of his own fault and partly of the fault of any other person or persons, a claim in respect of that damage shall not be defeated by reason of the fault of the person suffering the damage, but the damages recoverable in respect thereof shall be reduced to such extent as the court thinks just and equitable having regard to the claimant's share in the responsibility for the damage:

Provided that –

(a) this subsection shall not operate to defeat any defence arising under a contract;

(b) where any contract or enactment providing for the limitation of liability is applicable to the claim, the amount of damages recoverable by the claimant by virtue of this subsection shall not exceed the maximum limit so applicable.

Consumer Protection Act 1987

Liability for defective products

2 – (1) Subject to the following provisions of this Part, where any damage is caused wholly or partly by a defect in a product, every person to whom subsection (2) below applies shall be liable for the damage.

(1) This subsection applies to –

(a) the producer of the product;

(b) any person who, by putting his name on the product or using a trade mark or other distinguishing mark in relation to the product, has held himself out to be the producer of the product;

(c) any person who has imported the product into a member State from a place outside the member States in order, in the course of any business of his, to supply it to another.

Highways Act 1980

Duty to maintain highways maintainable at public expense

4 1 – (1) The authority who are for the time being the highway authority for a highway maintainable ay the public expense are under a duty, subject to subsections (2) and (4) below, to maintain the highway.

Special defence in action against a highway authority for damages for non-repair of highway

58 – (1) In an action against a highway authority in respect of damage resulting from their failure to maintain a highway maintainable at the public expense it is a defence (without prejudice to any other defence or the application of the law relating to contributory negligence) to prove that the authority had taken such care as in all the circumstances was reasonably required to secure that the part of the highway to which the action relates was not dangerous for traffic.

(2) For the purposes of a defence under subsection (1) above, the court shall in particular have regard to the following matters:

(a) the character of the highway, and the traffic which was reasonably to be expected to use it;

(b) the standard of maintenance appropriate for a highway of that character and used by such traffic;

(c) the state of repair in which a reasonable person would have expected to find the highway;

(d) whether the highway authority knew, or could reasonably have been expected to know, that the condition of the part of the highway to which the action relates was likely to cause danger to users of the highway;

(e) where the highway authority could not reasonably have been expected to repair that part of the highway before the cause of action arose, what warning notices of its condition had been displayed;

but for the purposes of such a defence it is not relevant to prove that the highway authority had arranged for a competent person to carry out or supervise the maintenance of the part of the highway to which the action relates unless it is also proved that the authority had given him proper instructions with regard to the maintenance of the highway and that he had carried out the instructions.

Occupiers' Liability Act 1957

Extent of occupier's ordinary duty

2 – (1) An occupier of premises owes the same duty, the 'common duty of care', to all his visitors, except in so far as he is free to and does extend, restrict, modify or exclude his duty to any visitor or visitors by agreement or otherwise.

(2) The common duty of care is a duty to take such reasonable care as in all the circumstances of the case is reasonable to see that the visitor will be reasonably safe in using the premises for the purposes for which he is invited or permitted by the occupier to be there.

(3) The circumstances relevant for the present purpose include the degree of care, and of want of care, which would ordinarily be looked for in such a visitor, so that (for example) in proper cases –

(a) an occupier must be prepared for children to be less careful than adults; and

(b) an occupier may expect that a person, in the exercise of his calling, will appreciate and guard against any special risks ordinarily incident to it, so far as the occupier leaves him free to do so.

(4) In determining whether the occupier of premises had discharged the common duty of care to visitor, regard is to be had to all the circumstances, so that (for example) –

(a) where damage is caused to a visitor by a danger of which he had been warned by the occupier, the warning is not to be treated without more as absolving the occupier from liability, unless in all the circumstances it was enough to enable the visitor to be reasonably safe; and

(b) where damage is caused to a visitor by a danger due to the faulty execution of any work of construction, maintenance or repair by an independent contractor employed by the occupier, the occupier is not to be treated without more as answerable for the danger if in all the circumstances he had acted reasonably in entrusting the work to an independent contractor and had taken such steps (if any) as he reasonably ought in order to satisfy himself that the contractor was competent and that the work had been properly done.

(5) The common duty of care does not impose on an occupier any obligation to a visitor in respect of risks willingly accepted as his by the visitor (the question whether a risk was so accepted to be decided on the same principles as in other cases in which one person owes a duty of care to another).

(6) For the purposes of this section, persons who enter premises for any purpose in the exercise of a right conferred by law are to be treated as permitted by the occupier to be there for that purpose, whether they in fact have his permission or not.

Occupier's Liability Act 1984

Duty of occupier to persons other than his visitors

(1)

(3) An occupier of premises owes a duty to another (not being his visitor) in respect of any such risk as is referred to in subsection (1) above if -

(a) he is aware of the danger or has reasonable grounds to believe that it exists;

(b) he knows or has reasonable grounds to believe that the other is in the vicinity of the danger concerned or that he may come into the vicinity of the danger (in either case, whether the other has lawful authority for being in that vicinity or not);and

(c) the risk is one against which, in all the circumstances of the case, he may reasonably be expected to offer the other some protection.

(4) Where, by virtue of this section, an occupier of premises owes a duty to another in respect of such a risk, the duty is to take such care as is reasonable in all the circumstances of the case to see that he does not suffer injury on the premises by reason of the danger concerned.

(5) Any duty owed by virtue of this section in respect of a risk may, in an appropriate case, be discharged by taking such steps as are reasonable in all the circumstances of the case to give warning of the danger concerned or to discourage persons from incurring the risk.

(6) No duty is owed by virtue of this section to any person in respect of risks willingly accepted as his by that person (the question whether a risk was so accepted to be decided on the same principles as in other cases in which one person owes a duty of care to another).

(7) No duty is owed by virtue of this section to persons using the highway, and this section does not affect any duty owed to such persons.

(8) Where a person owes a duty by virtue of this section, he does not, by reason of any breach of the duty, incur any liability in respect of any loss of or damage to property.

(9) In this section –

'highway' means any part of a highway other than a ferry or waterway;

'injury' means anything resulting in death or personal injury, including any disease and any impairment of physical or mental condition; and

'movable structure' includes any vessel, vehicle or aircraft.

SIX-PACK REGULATIONS

The Workplace (Health, Safety and Welfare) Regulations 1992

Maintenance of workplace, and of equipment, devices and systems

5 – (1) The workplace and the equipment, devices and systems to which this regulation applies shall be maintained (including cleaned as appropriate) in an efficient state, in efficient working work and in good repair.

(2) Where appropriate, the equipment, devices and systems to which this regulation applies shall be subject to a suitable system of maintenance.

(3) The equipment, devices and systems to which this regulation applies are -

(a) equipment and devices a fault in which is liable to result in a failure to comply with any of these Regulations;

(b) mechanical ventilation systems provided pursuant to regulation 6 (whether or not they include equipment or devices within sub-paragraph (a) of this paragraph); and

(c) equipment and devices intended to prevent or reduce hazards.

Condition of floors and traffic routes

12– (1) Every floor in a workplace and the surface of every traffic route in a workplace shall be of a construction such that the floor or surface of the traffic route is suitable for the purpose for which it is used.

(2) Without prejudice to the generality of paragraph (1), the requirements in that paragraph shall include requirements that –

(a) the floor, or surface of the traffic route, shall have no hole or slope, or be uneven or slippery so as, in each case, to expose any person to a risk to his health or safety; and

(b) every such floor shall have effective means of drainage where necessary.

(3) So far as is reasonably practicable, every floor in a workplace and the surface of every traffic route in a workplace shall be kept free from obstructions and from any article or substance which may cause a person to slip, trip or fall.

(4) In considering whether for the purposes of paragraph (2)(a) a hole or slope exposes any person to a risk to his health or safety -

(a) no account shall be taken of a hole where adequate measures have been taken to prevent a person falling; and

(b) account shall be taken of any handrail provided in connection with any slope.

(5) Suitable and sufficient handrails and, if appropriate, guards shall be provided on all traffic routes which are staircases except in circumstances in which a handrail cannot be provided without obstructing the traffic route.

The Provision and Use of Work Equipment Regulations 1998

Suitability of work equipment

4 – (1) Every employer shall ensure that work equipment is so constructed or adopted as to be suitable for the purpose for which it is used or provided.

(2) In selecting work equipment, every employer shall have regard to the working conditions and to the risks to the health and safety of persons which exist in the premises or undertaking in which that work equipment is to be used and any additional risk posed by the use of that work equipment.

(3) Every employer shall ensure that work equipment is used only for operations for which, and under conditions for which, it is suitable.

Maintenance

5 – (1) Every employer shall ensure that work equipment is maintained in an efficient state, in efficient working order and in good repair.

(2) Every employer shall ensure that where any machinery has a maintenance log, the log is kept up to date.

Inspection

*6 – (1) Every employer shall ensure that, where the safety of work equipment depends
on the installation conditions, it is inspected -*

    (a) after installation and before being put into service for the first time; or

    (b) after assembly at a new site or in a new location, to ensure that it has been installed correctly and is safe to operate

(2) Every employer shall ensure that work equipment exposed to conditions causing deterioration which is liable to result in dangerous situations is inspected -

    (a) at suitable intervals: and

    (b) each time that exceptional circumstances which are liable to jeopardise the safety of the work equipment have occurred, to ensure that health and safety conditions are maintained and that any deterioration can be detected and remedied in good time.

(3) Every employer shall ensure that the result of an inspection made under this regulation is recorded and kept until the next inspection under this regulation is recorded.

The Manual Handling Operations Regulations 1992

Duties of employers

4– (1) Each employer shall –

(a) so far as is reasonably practicable, avoid the need for his employers to undertake any manual handling operations at work which involve a risk of their being injured: or

(b) where it is not reasonably practicable to avoid the need for his employees to undertake any manual handling operations at work which involve a risk of their being injured -

(i) make a suitable and sufficient assessment of all such manual handling operations to be undertaken by them, having regard to the factors which are specified in column 1 of Schedule 1 to these Regulations and considering the questions which are specified in the corresponding entry in column 2 of that Schedule.

(ii) take appropriate steps to reduce the risk of injury to those employees arising out of their undertaking any such manual handling operations to the lowest level reasonably practicable, and

(i) take appropriate steps to provide any of those employees who are undertaking any such manual handling operations with general indications and, where it is reasonably practicable to do so, precise information on -

(aa) the weight of each load, and

(bb) the heaviest side of any load whose centre of gravity is not positioned centrally

(2) ....

(3) In determining for the purposes of this regulation whether manual handling operations at work involve a risk of injury and in determining the appropriate steps to reduce that risk regard shall be had in particular to -

(a) the physical suitability of the employee to carry out the operations;

(b) the clothing, footwear or other personal effects he is wearing;

(c) his knowledge and training;

(d) the results of any relevant risk assessment carried out pursuant to regulation 3 of the Management of Health and Safety at Work Regulations 1999:

(e) whether the employee is within a group of employees identified by that assessment as being especially at risk; and

(f) the results of any health surveillance provided pursuant to regulation 6 of the Management of Health and Safety Regulations 1999.

The Personal Protective Equipment at Work Regulations 1992

Provision of personal protective equipment

4 – (1) Subject to paragraph (1A) every employer shall ensure that suitable personal protective equipment is provided to his employees who may be exposed to a risk to their health or safety while at work except where and to the extent that such risk has been adequately controlled by other means which are equally or more effective

(1A)...

(2) ....

(3) Without prejudice to the generality of paragraphs (1) and (2), personal protective equipment shall not be suitable unless -

(a) it is appropriate for the risk or risks involved, the conditions at the place where exposure to the risk may occur, and the period for which it is worn;

(b) it takes account of ergonomic requirements and the state of health of the person or persons who may wear it, and of the characteristics of the workstation of each such person;

(c) it is capable of fitting the wearer correctly, if necessary, after adjustments within the range for which it is designed;

(d) so far as is practicable, it is effective to prevent or adequately control the risk or risks involved without increasing overall risk;

(e) it complies with any enactment (whether in an Act or instrument) which implements in Great Britain any provision on design or manufacture with respect to health or safety in any relevant Community directive listed in Schedule 1 which is applicable to that item of personal protective equipment

Assessment of personal protective equipment

6 – (1) Before choosing any personal protective equipment which by virtue of regulation 4 he is required to ensure is provided, an employer or self-employed person shall ensure that an assessment is made to determine whether the personal protective equipment he intends will be provided is suitable.

Information, instruction and training

9 – (1) Where an employer is required to ensure that personal protective equipment is provided to an employee, the employer shall also ensure that the employee is provided with such information, instruction and training as is adequate and appropriate to enable the employee to know –

(a) the risk or risks which the personal protective equipment will avoid or limit;

(b) the purpose for which and the manner in which personal protective equipment is to be used; and

(c) any action to be taken by the employee to ensure that the personal protective equipment remains in an efficient state, in efficient working order and in good repair as required by regulation 7(1) and shall ensure that such information is kept available to employees.

Use of personal protective equipment

***10** – (1) Every employer shall take all reasonable steps to ensure that any personal protective equipment provided to his employees by virtue of regulation 4(1) is properly used.*

APPENDIX I

I-1 Where sanctions apply

They arise by operation of various rules prescribed by the CPR as tabulated below but also are imposed by court order in case management directions.

Some less serious defaults such as a failure to file a budget or a hearing fee or a directions questionnaire (where the court has made an unless order requiring compliance within 7 days), will result in the statement of case (or defence, as appropriate) being struck out.

Step in litigation	CPR provision	Prescribed sanction for default
Pre-action protocols	PD Pre-action conduct, Para 4.6	Range of sanctions, including stay of proceedings until compliance, adverse costs and interest orders
Serve claim form	CPR 7.6	No extension, claim struck out
Serve particulars of claim	CPR 7.4	None unless outside 4 months from issue of claim form, then stuck out
Request for further Information	CPR 18	None, but if unless order obtained then struck out
Directions questionnaire	CPR 26.3(7A)	Statement of case/defence struck out if unless order ignored after 7 days
Disclosure	CPR 31.21	Defaulting party cannot rely on undisclosed document unless the court gives permission. Also note sanctions for non-compliance with protocol, or if unless order obtained failing request for specific disclosure. Contempt of court for false disclosure statement.

Costs budgets	CPR 3.14	Automatic sanction limiting costs to court fees only
Witness statements	CPR 32.10	If not served in time, witness may not be called to give oral evidence unless the court gives permission
Experts' reports	CPR 35.13	Report may not be used or expert may not be called to give oral evidence unless the court gives permission
Non-payment of Court fee	CPR 3.7	Automatically struck out. This may apply where a fee is required on filing a directions questionnaire or pre-trial check list or hearing fee. A fee notice is sent to the claimant with the notice of trial. Strike out also applies for failure to pay the issue fee on a counterclaim
Undervaluing claim on issue	CPR 3.4/24	The court may strike out the case or order summary judgment for the defendant on application. The grounds would represent an abuse of process

I-2 Knowing your CPR

PART 1	Overriding Objective
PART 2	Application and Interpretation of the Rules
PART 3	The Court's Case and Costs Management Powers
PART 4	Forms
PART 5	Court Documents
PART 6	Service of Documents
PART 7	How to Start Proceedings – the Claim Form
PART 8	Alternative Procedure for Claims
PART 9	Responding to Particulars of Claim – General
PART 10	Acknowledgment of Service
PART 11	Disputing the Court's Jurisdiction
PART 12	Default Judgment
PART 13	Setting Aside or Varying Default Judgment
PART 14	Admissions
PART 15	Defence and Reply
PART 16	Statements of Case
PART 17	Amendments to Statements of Case

PART 18	Further Information
PART 19	Parties and Group Litigation
PART 20	Counterclaims and other Additional Claims
PART 21	Children and Protected Parties
PART 22	Statements of Truth
PART 23	General Rules about Applications for Court Orders
PART 24	Summary Judgment
PART 25	Interim Remedies and Security for Costs
PART 26	Case management – Preliminary Stage
PART 27	The Small Claims Track
PART 28	The Fast Track
PART 29	The Multi-Track
PART 30	Transfer
PART 31	Disclosure and Inspection of Documents
PART 32	Evidence
PART 33	Miscellaneous Rules about Evidence
PART 34	Witnesses, Depositions and Evidence for Foreign Courts
PART 35	Experts and Assessors

PART 36	Offers to Settle
PART 37	Miscellaneous Provisions about Payments into Court
PART 38	Discontinuance
PART 39	Miscellaneous Provisions Relating to Hearings
PART 40	Judgments, Orders, Sale of Land etc
PART 41	Damages
PART 42	Change of Solicitor
PART 43	(abandoned)
PART 44	General Rules about Costs
PART 45	Fixed Costs
PART 46	Costs – Special Cases
PART 47	Procedure for Detailed Assessment of Costs and Default Provisions
PART 48	Part 2 of The Legal Aid, Sentencing And Punishment Of Offenders Act 2012 Relating to Civil Litigation Funding And Costs: Transitional Provision In Relation To Pre-Commencement Funding Arrangements
PART 49	Specialist Proceedings
PART 50	Application of the Schedules
PART 51	Transitional Arrangements and Pilot Schemes

PART 52	Appeals
PART 53	Defamation Claims
PART 54	Judicial Review and Statutory Review
PART 55	Possession Claims
PART 56	Landlord and Tenant Claims and Miscellaneous Provisions about Land
PART 57	Probate, inheritance and presumption of death
PART 58	Commercial Court

APPENDIX II

II-1 HEARSAY NOTICE

TAKE NOTICE that at the trial of this action the claimant wishes to put in evidence the witness statement of Mr Dafydd Lewis-Jones dated 4th December 2016.

A copy of the statement is attached hereto.

AND FURTHER TAKE NOTICE that Mr Dafydd Lewis-Jones cannot be called as a witness at the trial because he is beyond the seas, namely in Outer Mongolia and that it will not be practicable for him to return for the trial.

II-2 MEDIATION AGREEMENT

[Name of Mediator}

1. **Parties**

2. **Date of mediation**

3. **Venue**

4. **The conditions of the mediation**

The parties have agreed to settle their dispute by mediation and accept the following:

(i) that the procedure adopted at the mediation will be determined by the mediator;

(ii) that the process is voluntary with the result that either party may withdraw from the mediation at any time;

(iii) that the mediator may withdraw from the mediation if, for any reason, he considers it impossible or impracticable for him to continue;

(iv) that the process is confidential and 'without prejudice' and that, in consequence, each party will be bound by the provisions of Clause 5 below;

(v) that the mediator will not give legal advice in connection with the dispute or the terms of any settlement reached and that the parties will be responsible for drawing up a suitable form of written settlement agreement being achieved;

(vi) that no agreement reached during the mediation will be binding on the parties until incorporated in a written agreement signed by or on behalf of the parties;

(vii) that they will make no claim of any kind against the mediator arising from or in connection with (whether directly or indirectly) the mediation and/or any settlement achieved and will indemnify the mediator against any legal action that might be brought by any third party for any act or omission in connection with the mediation;

(viii) that either before or at the commencement of the mediation they will each nominate one participant at the mediation who will have full authority to agree to a settlement at the mediation.

5. The confidentiality clause

In consequence of the agreement, acknowledgment and acceptance by the parties that the process is confidential and 'without prejudice' it is agreed (without prejudice to the requirements of the general law and save as may be required to secure the implementation or enforcement of any agreement reached during the mediation):

(i) that no record or other form of continuous transcript or record of the mediation will be made;

(ii)　that all material produced in whatever form for the purposes of the mediation, and any note or other record made during the mediation by any participant, is to be treated as privileged and neither disclosable nor admissible in evidence in any subsequent proceedings of any kind save where it would otherwise have been disclosable or admissible;

(iii)　that all participants in the mediation will maintain confidentiality in respect of all information given and all material produced for the purposes of and during the mediation save as may be (a) required by a court of competent jurisdiction or other competent public authority and (b), so far as the mediator is concerned, reasonably required in his opinion to prevent significant damage to the health or safety of any person or where the failure to disclose information might lead to him becoming the subject of criminal proceedings;

(iv)　that neither party will ask the mediator to provide a witness statement relating to the dispute or the mediation or call him as a witness in any proceedings arising from or in connection with the dispute or the mediation.

6. Costs and expenses

(i)　The parties will, subject to any alternative agreement between them or subject to any order of the court, bear their own costs in relation to the mediation.

(ii)　The parties will, subject to any alternative agreement between them or subject to any order of the court, bear equally:
   (a) the costs of providing the mediation venue and any ancillary costs and expenses associated therewith, and
   (b) the mediator's fees and expenses – and the parties' solicitors will remain jointly and severally liable for all such costs, fees and expenses.

(iii)　The mediator's fees and expenses will be calculated in accordance with the Schedule to this agreement and will be payable within 14 days of the receipt of any fee note or expenses claim.

SIGNED by ……………………… (Name + Firm)
on behalf of ………………………

DATE:

SIGNED by ……………………… (Name + Firm)
on behalf of ………………………

DATE:

II-3 MODEL DIRECTIONS ORDER IN CLINICAL NEGLIGENCE

On [date]

Before District Judge Z sitting at the County Court at Darlington, Consicliffe Road, Darlington, County Durham

The District Judge heard the solicitor for the claimant and the solicitor for the defendant and made the following order

1) The claim is allocated to the Multi-Track and is assigned to District Judge Z for case management.

2) At all stages the parties must consider settling this litigation by any means of Alternative Dispute Resolution (including round table conferences, early neutral evaluation, mediation and arbitration); any party not engaging in any such means proposed by another is to serve a witness statement giving reasons within **21 days** of receipt of that proposal. That witness statement must not be shown to the trial judge until questions of costs arise.

3) Documents are to be retained as follows:

   a) The parties must retain all electronically stored documents relating to the issues in this claim.

b) The defendant must retain the original clinical notes relating to the issues in this claim. The defendant must give facilities for inspection by the claimant, the claimant's legal advisers and experts of these original notes on 7 days written notice.

c) Legible copies of the medical and educational records of the claimant/deceased are to be placed in a separate paginated bundle by the claimant's solicitors and kept up to date. All references to medical notes are to be made by reference to the pages in that bundle.

4) Disclosure of documents relevant to the issues of breach of duty and causation and quantification of damages will be dealt with as follows:

a) **By 4pm on** [date] both parties must give to each other standard disclosure of documents by list and category.

b) **By 4pm on** [date] any request must be made to inspect the original of, or to provide a copy of, a disclosable document.

c) Any such request unless objected to must be complied with within 14 days of the request.

d) **By 4pm on** [date] each party must serve and file with the court a list of issues relevant to the search for and disclosure of electronically stored documents in accordance with Practice Direction 31B.

5) Evidence of fact will be dealt with as follows:

a) **By 4pm on** [date] both parties must serve on each other copies of the signed statements of themselves and of all witnesses on whom they intend to rely in respect of breach of duty and causation and all notices relating to evidence, including Civil Evidence Act notices.

b) For the avoidance of doubt statements of all concerned with the relevant treatment and care of the claimant must be included.

c) **By 4pm on [date]** both parties must serve on each other copies of the signed statements of themselves and of all witnesses on whom they intend to rely in respect of condition, prognosis and loss and all notices relating to evidence, including Civil Evidence Act notices.

d) Oral evidence will not be permitted at trial from a witness whose statement has not been served in accordance with this order or has been served late, except with permission from the court.

e) Evidence of fact is limited to x witnesses on behalf of each party.

f) Witness statements must not exceed x pages of A4 in length.

6) Expert evidence is directed as follows.

7) In respect of breach of duty and causation the parties each have permission to rely on the following written expert evidence:

a) The claimant:

i) an expert in [specialism], whose report must be served by [date].

b) The defendant:

i) an expert in [specialism], whose report must be served by [date].

8) In respect of condition, prognosis and quantification of damages the parties each have permission to rely on the following written expert evidence:

a) The claimant:

i) an expert in [specialism], whose report must be served by [date].
ii) an expert in [specialism], whose report must be served by [date].

b) The defendant:

   i)   an expert in [specialism], whose report must be served by [date].
   ii) an expert in [specialism], whose report must be served by [date].

9) Unless the reports are agreed, there must be a without prejudice discussion between the experts of like discipline by 4pm on [date] in which the experts will identify the issues between them and reach agreement if possible. The experts will prepare for the court and sign a statement of issues on which they agree and on which they disagree with a summary of their reasons in accordance with rule 35.12 Civil Procedure Rules, and each statement must be sent to the parties to be received by 4 pm on [date] and in any event no later than 7 days after the discussion.

10) Unless otherwise agreed by all parties' solicitors, after consulting with the experts, a draft Agenda which directs the experts to the remaining issues relevant to the experts' discipline, as identified in the statements of case shall be prepared jointly by the claimant's solicitors and experts and sent to the defendant's solicitors for comment at least 35 days before the agreed date for the experts' discussions.

11) The defendants shall within 21 days of receipt agree the Agenda, or propose amendments.

12) 7 days thereafter all solicitors shall use their best endeavours to agree the Agenda. Points of disagreement should be on matters of real substance and not semantics or on matters the experts could resolve of their own accord at the discussion. In default of agreement, both versions shall be considered at the discussions. Agendas, when used, shall be provided to the experts not less than 7 days before the date fixed for discussions.

13) A copy of this order must be served on each expert.

14) The parties have permission to call oral evidence of the experts of like discipline limited to issues that are in dispute.

15) Any unpublished literature upon which any expert witness proposes to rely must be served at the same time as service of his report together with a list of published literature. Any supplementary literature upon which any expert witness relies must be notified to all parties at least one month before trial. No expert witness may rely upon any publications that have not been disclosed in accordance with this order without the permission of the trial judge subject to costs as appropriate.

16) Experts will, at the time of producing their reports, incorporate details of any employment or activity which raises a possible conflict of interest.

17) For the avoidance of doubt, experts do not require the authorisation of solicitor or counsel before signing a joint statement.

18) If an expert radically alters an opinion previously recorded, the joint statement should include a note or addendum by that expert explaining the change of opinion.

19) Schedules of Loss must be updated to the date of trial as follows:

   a) **By 4pm on** [date] the claimant must send a schedule of loss to the defendant.

   b) **By 4pm on** [date] the defendant, in the event of challenge, must send
   a counter-schedule of loss to the claimant.

   c) The schedule and counter-schedule must contain a statement setting out that party's case on the issue of periodical payments pursuant to Rule 41.5 Civil Procedure Rules.

20) The trial will be listed as follows.

   a) The trial window is between [date] and [date] inclusive.

b) Category: B

c) Time estimate: x days

d) **By 4pm on** [date] Pre-Trial Check Lists must be sent to the court.

21) Pre-trial directions are as follows:

a) There will be a review case management conference on [date] at [time] with a time estimate of [ ]

c) The case management conference will/may be conducted by telephone if the parties so agree, unless the court orders otherwise. The claimant must make the relevant arrangements in accordance with Practice Direction 23A Civil Procedure Rules.

d) At least 3 clear days before the case management conference the claimant must file and send to the court preferably agreed and by email:

i) draft directions
ii) a chronology
iii) a case summary.

22) Not more than **7 nor less than 3 clear days** before the trial, the claimant must file at court and serve an indexed and paginated bundle of documents which complies with the requirements of Rule 39.5 Civil Procedure Rules and Practice Direction 39A. The parties must endeavour to agree the contents of the bundle before it is filed. The bundle will include a case summary and a chronology.

23) The parties must file with the court and exchange skeleton arguments at least three days before the trial, by email.

24) Costs in the case.

II-4 MODEL DIRECTIONS ORDER IN PERSONAL INJURY CLAIM

Warning: you must comply with the terms imposed upon you by this order otherwise your case is liable to be struck out or some other sanction imposed. If you cannot comply you are expected to make a formal application to the court before any deadline imposed upon you expires.

On [date[

District Judge Z sitting at Y the County Court at Bishop Auckland heard the solicitor for the Claimant and the solicitor for the Defendant and

Ordered that:

1) The Claim is allocated to the Multi-Track and is assigned to District Judge Z for case management.

2) The case has been costs budgeted and the amended front sheets of the parties' respective budgets are appended to the Order.

3) At all stages the parties must consider settling this litigation by any means of Alternative Dispute Resolution (including round table conferences, early neutral evaluation, mediation and arbitration); any party not engaging in any such means proposed by another is to serve a witness statement giving reasons within 21 days of receipt of that proposal. That witness statement must not be shown to the trial judge until questions of costs arise.

4) Documents are to be retained as follows:

   a) the parties must retain all electronically stored documents relating to the issues in this claim.

5) Disclosure of documents will be dealt with as follows:

a) by 4pm on [date] the parties must give to each other standard disclosure of documents by list and category.

b) By 4pm on [date] any request must be made to inspect the original of, or to provide a copy of, a disclosable document.

c) any such request unless objected to must be complied with within 14 days of the request.

6) Evidence of fact will be dealt with as follows:

a) by 4pm on [date] all parties must serve on each other copies of the signed statements of themselves and of all witnesses on whom they intend to rely and all notices relating to evidence, including Civil Evidence Act notices.

b) Oral evidence will not be permitted at trial from a witness whose statement has not been served in accordance with this order or has been served late, except with permission from the Court,

c) Evidence of fact is limited to X witnesses on behalf of each party.

d) Witness statements must not exceed x pages of A4 in length.

7) Expert evidence is directed as follows.

8) The parties each have permission to rely on the following written expert evidence:

a) The Claimant:

i) an expert Orthopaedic Surgeon, namely Miss A, whose report must be served by [date].
ii) an expert Neurologist, namely Dr B, whose report must be served by [date].

b) The Defendant:

i) an expert Orthopaedic Surgeon, namely Mr C, whose report must be served by [date].

   ii) an expert Neurologist, namely Dr D, whose report must be served by [date].

9) Unless the reports are agreed, there must be a without prejudice discussion between the experts of like discipline by 4 pm on [date] in which the experts will identify the issues between them and reach agreement if possible. The experts will prepare for the court and sign a statement of the issues on which they agree and on which they disagree with a summary of their reasons in accordance with Rule 35.12 Civil Procedure Rules, and each statement must be sent to the parties to be received by 4pm on [date].

10) A copy of this order must be served on the expert by the Claimant with the expert's instructions.

11) A party seeking to call oral expert evidence at trial must apply for permission to do so before pre-trial check lists are filed.

12) Schedules of loss must be updated as follows:

   a) by 4pm on [date] the Claimant must send an up to date schedule of loss to the Defendant.

   b) By 4pm on [date] the Defendant, in the event of challenge, must send as up to date counter-schedule of loss to the Claimant.

   c) The schedule and counter-schedule must contain a statement setting out that party's case on the issue of periodical payments pursuant to Rule 41.5 Civil Procedure Rules.

13) The trial will be listed as follows:

   a) The trial window is between [date] and [date] inclusive.

   b) The estimated length of trial is x days.

c) By 4pm on [date] the parties must file with the court their availability for trial, preferably agreed and with a nominated single point of contact. They will be notified of the time and place of trial.

14) The trial directions are as follows:

a) Not more than 7 nor less than 3 clear days before the trial, the Claimant must file at court and serve an indexed and paginated bundle of documents, which complies with the requirements of Rule 39.5 Civil Procedure Rules and Practice Direction 39A. The parties must endeavour to agree the contents of the bundle before it is filed. The bundle will include a case summary and a chronology.

b) The parties must file with the court and exchange skeleton arguments at least 3 days before the trial, by email.

c) Parties may by agreement in writing, extend the time for direction in this Order, by up to [days] without the need to apply to Court. If further time is required beyond 28 days, the parties shall agree a Consent Order which will be filed at Court with an email explaining the reason for the extension and the Court will confirm whether a formal application is required.

15) The Claimant's costs budget is agreed in the figure of £ and the Defendant's costs budget is agreed in the sum of £. Front sheets of the agreed Costs Budgets are to be filed with the court by [date].

16) Costs in the case.

MORE BOOKS BY LAW BRIEF PUBLISHING

A selection of our other titles available now:

'Practical Mediation: A Guide for Mediators, Advocates, Advisers, Lawyers, and Students in Civil, Commercial, Business, Property, Workplace, and Employment Cases' by Jonathan Dingle with John Sephton
'A Comparative Guide to Standard Form Construction and Engineering Contracts' by Jon Close
'A Practical Guide to Compliance for Personal Injury Firms Working With Claims Management Companies' by Paul Bennett
'A Practical Guide to the Landlord and Tenant Act 1954: Commercial Tenancies' by Richard Hayes & David Sawtell
'A Practical Guide to Personal Injury Claims Involving Animals' by Jonathan Hand
'A Practical Guide to Psychiatric Claims in Personal Injury' by Liam Ryan
'Introduction to the Law of Community Care in England and Wales' by Alan Robinson
'A Practical Guide to Dog Law for Owners and Others' by Andrea Pitt
'Ellis and Kevan on Credit Hire, 5th Edition' by Aidan Ellis & Tim Kevan
'RTA Allegations of Fraud in a Post-Jackson Era: The Handbook, 2nd Edition' by Andrew Mckie
'A Practical Guide to Holiday Sickness Claims' by Andrew Mckie & Ian Skeate
'RTA Personal Injury Claims: A Practical Guide Post-Jackson' by Andrew Mckie
'On Experts: CPR35 for Lawyers and Experts' by David Boyle
'An Introduction to Personal Injury Law' by David Boyle
'A Practical Guide to Running Housing Disrepair and Cavity Wall Claims' by Andrew Mckie, Ian Skeate, Simon Redfearn

'A Practical Guide to Claims Arising From Accidents Abroad and Travel Claims' by Andrew Mckie & Ian Skeate
'A Practical Guide to Cosmetic Surgery Claims' by Dr Victoria Handley
'A Practical Guide to Chronic Pain Claims' by Pankaj Madan
'A Practical Guide to Claims Arising from Fatal Accidents' by James Patience
'A Practical Approach to Clinical Negligence Post-Jackson' by Geoffrey Simpson-Scott
'A Practical Guide to Personal Injury Trusts' by Alan Robinson
'Occupiers, Highways and Defective Premises Claims: A Practical Guide Post-Jackson' by Andrew Mckie
'Employers' Liability Claims: A Practical Guide Post-Jackson' by Andrew Mckie
'A Practical Guide to Subtle Brain Injury Claims' by Pankaj Madan
'The Law of Driverless Cars: An Introduction' by Alex Glassbrook
'A Practical Guide to Costs in Personal Injury Cases' by Matthew Hoe
'A Practical Guide to Alternative Dispute Resolution in Personal Injury Claims – Getting the Most Out of ADR Post-Jackson' by Peter Causton, Nichola Evans, James Arrowsmith
'A Practical Guide to Personal Injuries in Sport' by Adam Walker & Patricia Leonard
'A Practical Guide to Marketing for Lawyers' by Catherine Bailey & Jennet Ingram
'The No Nonsense Solicitors' Practice: A Guide To Running Your Firm' by Bettina Brueggemann
'Baby Steps: A Guide to Maternity Leave and Maternity Pay' by Leah Waller
'The Queen's Counsel Lawyer's Omnibus: 20 Years of Cartoons from the Times 1993-2013' by Alex Steuart Williams

These books and more are available to order online direct from the publisher at www.lawbriefpublishing.com, where you can also read free sample chapters. For any queries, contact us on 0844 587 2383 or mail@lawbriefpublishing.com.

Our books are also usually in stock at www.amazon.co.uk with free next day delivery for Prime members, and at good legal bookshops such as Hammicks and Wildy & Sons.

We are regularly launching new books in our series of practical day-to-day practitioners' guides. Visit our website and join our free newsletter to be kept informed and to receive special offers, free chapters, etc.

You can also follow us on Twitter at www.twitter.com/lawbriefpub.

Printed in Great Britain
by Amazon